8/10

Hispanic American Biographies

Volume 6

Montoya, Carlos Garcia—Ponce, Mary Helen

GROLIER

an imprint of

www.scholastic.com/librarypublishing

First published 2006 by Grolier,
an imprint of Scholastic Library Publishing,
Old Sherman Turnpike,
Danbury, Connecticut 06816

© 2006 The Brown Reference Group plc

Set ISBN-13: 978-0-7172-6124-6
Set ISBN-10: 0-7172-6124-7
Volume ISBN-13: 978-0-7172-6130-7
Volume ISBN-10: 0-7172-6130-1

Library of Congress Cataloging-in-Publication Data
Hispanic American biographies.
    v. cm.
  Includes bibliographical references and index.
  Contents: v. 1. Acevedo-Vilá, Aníbal - Bocanegra, Carlos -- v. 2. Bonilla,
Tony - Corretjer, Juan Antonio -- v. 3. Cortés, Carlos - Gálvez, Bernardo
de -- v. 4. Gamboa, Harry, Jr. - Julia, Raul -- v. 5. Juncos, Manuel
Fernández - Montez, Maria -- v. 6. Montoya, Carlos Garcia - Ponce, Mary
Helen -- v. 7. Ponce de León, Juan - Seguín, Juan N. -- v. 8. Selena -
Zúñiga, Martha.
  ISBN-13: 978-0-7172-6124-6 (set : alk. paper) -- ISBN-10: 0-7172-6124-7
(set : alk. paper) -- ISBN-13: 978-0-7172-6125-3 (v. 1 : alk. paper) -- ISBN-
10: 0-7172-6125-5 (v. 1 : alk. paper) -- ISBN-13: 978-0-7172-6126-0 (v. 2 :
alk. paper) -- ISBN-10: 0-7172-6126-3 (v. 2 : alk. paper) -- ISBN-13: 978-0-
7172-6127-7 (v. 3 : alk. paper) -- ISBN-10: 0-7172-6127-1 (v. 3 : alk. paper)
-- ISBN-13: 978-0-7172-6128-4 (v. 4 : alk. paper) -- ISBN-10: 0-7172-6128-
X (v. 4 : alk. paper) -- ISBN-13: 978-0-7172-6129-1 (v. 5 : alk. paper) --
ISBN-10: 0-7172-6129-8 (v. 5 : alk. paper) -- ISBN-13: 978-0-7172-6130-7
(v. 6 : alk. paper) -- ISBN-10: 0-7172-6130-1 (v. 6 : alk. paper) -- ISBN-13:
978-0-7172-6131-4 (v. 7 : alk. paper) -- ISBN-10: 0-7172-6131-X (v. 7 : alk.
paper) -- ISBN-13: 978-0-7172-6132-1 (v. 8 : alk. paper) -- ISBN-10: 0-7172-
6132-8 (v. 8 : alk. paper)
  1. Hispanic Americans--Biography--Encyclopedias--Juvenile literature. I.
Grolier Publishing Company.
E184.S75H5573 2006
973'.046800922--dc22
[B]
                                        2006012294

For information address the publisher:
Grolier, Scholastic Library Publishing,
Old Sherman Turnpike,
Danbury, Connecticut 06816

FOR THE BROWN REFERENCE GROUP PLC

Project Editor: Chris King
Editors: Henry Russell, Aruna Vasudevan,
                           Tom Jackson, Simon Hall
Design: Q2A Solutions, Seth Grimbly,
                           Lynne Ross
Picture Researcher: Sharon Southren
Index: Kay Ollerenshaw
Design Manager: Sarah Williams
Production Director: Alastair Gourlay
Senior Managing Editor: Tim Cooke
Editorial Director: Lindsey Lowe

ACADEMIC CONSULTANTS:

Ellen Riojas Clark,   Arnoldo de Leon,
Division of Bicultural Bilingual   Department of History,
   Studies,   Angelo State University
University of Texas at San Antonio

Printed and bound in Singapore

ABOUT THIS SET

This is one of a set of eight books chronicling the lives of Hispanic Americans who have helped shape the history of the United States. The set contains biographies of more than 750 people of Hispanic origin. They range from 16th-century explorers to 21st-century musicians and movie stars. Some were born in the United States, while others immigrated there from countries such as Mexico, Cuba, or Puerto Rico. The subjects therefore come from a wide range of cultural backgrounds, historical eras, and areas of achievement.

In addition to the biographical entries, the set includes a number of guidepost articles that provide an overview of a particular aspect of the Hispanic American experience. These guidepost articles cover general areas such as civil rights and religion as well as specific historical topics such as the Treaty of Guadalupe Hidalgo. These articles serve to help place the lives of the subjects of the biographies in a wider context.

Each biographical entry contains a box listing key dates in the subject's life as well as a further reading section that gives details of books and Web sites that the reader may wish to explore. Longer biographies also include a box about the people who inspired the subject, people the subject has influenced in turn, or the legacy that the subject has left behind. Where relevant, entries also contain a "See also" section that directs the reader to related articles elsewhere in the set. A comprehensive set index is included at the end of each volume.

The entries are arranged alphabetically, mostly by surname but also by stage name. In cases where the subject has more than one surname, he or she is alphabetized under the name that is most commonly used. For example, Héctor Pérez García is usually known simply as Hector P. Garcia and is therefore alphabetized under "G." Pedro Albizu Campos, meanwhile, is generally known by his full name and is alphabetized under "A." Both variants are included in the index. Where names are commonly spelled in a variety of ways, the most widespread version is used. Similarly, the use of accents is dictated in each individual case by general usage.

Contributors: David Arbesu; Robert Anderson; Frank Argote-Freyre; Faisal Azam; Berta Bermúdez; Kelvin Bias; Erica Brodman; P. Scott Brown; Bec Chalkley; Eda Correa; Anita Dalal; Zilah Deckker; George T. Diaz; Conrado Gomez; Leon Gray; Susan Green; José Angel Gutiérrez; Héctor Fernández L'Hoeste; Luz Angelica Kirschner; Nashieli Marcano; Louis McFarland; Rashaan Meneses; Luisa Moncada; Carmen Nava; Carlos Ortega; Roy Perez; Melissa Segura; Chris Wiegand; Emma Young.

CONTENTS

MONTOYA, Carlos Garcia
Musician

Carlos Garcia Montoya was a Spanish flamenco guitarist who settled in the United States in the late 1930s. He established the flamenco guitar as a solo instrument, as opposed to its traditional role as an accompaniment for singers and dancers. By settling in the United States, Montoya helped bring flamenco music to a wider audience, and influenced several Hispanic American musical styles.

Gypsy musician

Montoya came from a musical gypsy family. He was the nephew of renowned flamenco guitarist Ramón Montoya (1880–1949). While the young Montoya was inspired by his uncle, he did not consider Ramón to be his main mentor. Montoya learned to play the guitar from his mother and Pepe el Barbero, a Madrid guitarist who was also a local barber.

By age 14, Montoya was playing with groups that accompanied dancers in Spain. After a few years, Montoya toured Europe and the Americas with various flamenco singers and dancers.

American life

In 1934, Montoya toured the United States for the first time. He returned there in 1938 as part of the company of the Argentine dancer Encarnación López Juvez (1897–1945). He remained in the United States to avoid the Spanish Civil War (1936–1939). He settled in New York, married an American, and later became a U.S. citizen.

In New York, Montoya gave his first solo performance in 1948. His light style of playing was readily accessible to a wide audience, and he soon became one of the most popular flamenco guitarists in the United States.

He followed a busy career as a soloist, but also played in recitals and with orchestras. He recorded extensively, and appeared on television. His composition "Suite Flamenca" was recorded with the St. Louis Symphony

▲ *Carlos Montoya was a pioneer in solo flamenco guitar performances and developed flamenco jazz.*

Orchestra in 1966. Montoya also reinvigorated the flamenco guitar repertoire with influences from jazz and other Latin musical styles such as the Argentine tango and the Cuban rumba.

Legacy

While Montoya was successful with audiences, critics did not accept his innovative style, and he was dismissed by scholars of flamenco music. However, to later generations of flamenco musicians, such as Spanish star Paco de Lucia (1947–), Montoya had a reputation as a serious musician. He is considered the pioneer of the flamenco jazz that is now an accepted part of world music.

Further reading: Pohren, D. E. *Lives and Legends of Flamenco: A Biographical History.* Madrid, Spain: Society of Spanish Studies, 1988.
http://www.deflamenco.com/articulos/carlosmontoya/indexi.jsp (essay on Montoya).

KEY DATES	
1903	Born in Madrid, Spain, on December 13.
1948	Gives first solo flamenco guitar concert.
1966	Records "Suite Flamenca."
1993	Dies in Wainscott, New York, on December 13.

MONTOYA, Delilah
Artist

Delilah Montoya is part of the second wave of Chicana artists that developed during the 1980s, when Chicano art had become a topic studied in art schools. She explores issues of identity through her work as a printmaker and photographer.

Education and influences

Montoya was born in Fort Worth, Texas, in 1955 and grew up in Nebraska. She studied photography and art at the Metropolitan Technical College in Omaha, Nebraska, and then moved to Albuquerque, New Mexico, to study art at the University of New Mexico. She completed her bachelor's degree in studio art in 1984. A master's degree in printmaking followed in 1990, and finally a master of fine art degree in 1994.

Montoya discovered a love for photography, but soon became dissatisfied with straight photography. She developed a composite style that involved her various skills as a printmaker, painter, and photographer.

▼ *Delilah Montoya produced* **La Guadalupana** *in 1998. The original work is a 7-foot- (2.1m-) high montage of photographs.*

KEY DATES

1955 Born in Fort Worth, Texas, on December 10.

1991 Included in *Chicano Art: Resistance and Affirmation (CARA) 1965-1985*, a major Hispanic American exhibition in Los Angeles, California.

1992 Produces Codex Delilah: A Journey from México to Chicana for the Chicano Codices exhibition in San Francisco, California.

2000 Becomes photography instructor at Santa Fe Community College in New Mexico.

Recognized artist

Montoya's rise as a recognized Hispanic American artist started with her inclusion in the exhibition of Chicano artists in the Southwest named *Sin Fronteras: Crossing Borders* at the Gallery of Contemporary Art, in Colorado Springs, Colorado, in 1989. She subsequently showed work in the *Chicano Art: Resistance and Affirmation (CARA) 1965–1985* exhibition at UCLA's Wight Art Gallery in 1991. Her work there, *Se Abre el Mundo/The World Opens* (from 1981), is a photocollage that explores the topography of Aztlán—the mythical Aztec homeland purported to be in what is now the Southwest United States.

For the *Chicano Codices* exhibition at the Mexican Museum in San Francisco, California, in 1992, Montoya produced the *Codex Delilah: A Journey from México to Chicana*, with a poem by Cecilio García-Camarillo. It depicts a journey both in space, north toward Aztlán, and in time, encountering notable Mexican Americans in history. Recently her work has been characterized by a central figure surrounded by motifs, such as in *Sacred Heart* (1994) and *La Guadalupana* (1998). Some of her work is held by the Smithsonian Institution, Washington, D.C.

Montoya has held several teaching positions in art and photography, including as an instructor at the Institute of American and Indian Arts, Santa Fe, New Mexico, in 1994 and as a visiting professor at Hampshire College, Amherst, Massachusetts, from 1997 to 1999.

Further reading: Gaspar de Alba, Alicia. *Chicano Art Inside/Outside the Master's House: Cultural Politics and the CARA Exhibition.* Austin, TX: University of Texas Press, 1998. http://www.delilahmontoya.com (Montoya's Web site).

MONTOYA, José
Poet, Artist

José Montoya is one of the most enduring writers and artists of the Chicano civil rights and art movements. He is well known as a painter and as a poet. Montoya combines art with activism and education to shed light on the history of Chicanos and Chicanas and how it informs their cultural identity.

Early life

José Montoya was born in 1932 in El Gallego, New Mexico. In the 1940s, Montoya's family moved to California, where he grew up in the San Jaoquin Valley. One of seven children, Montoya joined the rest of his family working as a farmhand in order to survive. His experiences in the fields made him an early supporter of labor leader César Chávez, and he later supported the United Farm Workers with his poetry, song lyrics, and painted art for posters and murals. In 1952, Montoya's parents divorced.

Art collective

While his older brothers and sisters did not attend school beyond the seventh grade, Montoya was able to go to San Diego City College. He later transferred to California College of Arts and Crafts in Oakland, receiving a bachelor of arts degree in 1962. He then became a high-school teacher while completing his master's degree in his spare time. While in Oakland, Montoya became involved with Mexican American artist collectives, eventually founding his own with Esteban Villa (1930–) and his brother Malaquías (1938–) in 1970. They called their enterprise

the RCAF, initials that were variously taken to stand for Royal Chicano Art/Air Force or Rebel Chicano Art Front.

In 1971, Montoya received his master of arts degree from California State University at Sacramento (CSUS). He went on to become a teacher at CSUS for 27 years. Owing to Montoya's influence, a fountain of the United Farm Workers' eagle stands outside the student union on the CSUS campus dedicated to Sacramento mayor Joe Serna (1939–1999).

Poetry style

In school, teachers told Montoya to leave his Chicano identity and politics out of his poetry and art. Those subjects were ultimately the source of his creativity, however, and gave his work its strength.

Montoya uses his work as a way of educating people, and as a means to organize for social change. A frequent topic of his poetry and visual art is the *pachuco*, or urban Chicano youth of the 1930s and 1940s. Montoya continues to be discouraged by some contemporary artists who see their work as a means of making money, rather than as an end in itself.

Montoya's early writings were self-published, and his early art took the form of posters and murals because Chicano writers and artists were excluded from mainstream publishing houses and art galleries. In 1985 Montoya helped curate the largest national touring exhibit of Chicano art, entitled *Chicano Art Resistance and Affirmation (CARA) 1965–1985.*

Poet laureate

In 2002, Montoya was appointed the poet laureate of Sacramento, California, a position he held until 2004. He was only the third poet laureate in the city's history. The honor validated Montoya's multilingual poetic style, which mixes English, Spanish, and barrio vernacular, and aims to legitimize the histories and identities of the Mexican American people.

KEY DATES

1932 Born in El Gallego, New Mexico.

1962 Receives bachelor of arts degree from California College of Arts and Crafts. Becomes high-school teacher.

1970 Cofounds the Royal Chicano Art/Air Force (RCAF) or Rebel Chicano Art Front.

1971 Receives master of arts degree from California State University, Sacramento (CSUS). Takes job teaching in the CSUS Department of Art Education.

1974 Founds Art in the Barrios program in Sacramento, California.

2002 Becomes poet laureate for Sacramento.

See also: Chávez, César

Further reading: Montoya, José. *In Formation: 20 Years of Joda.* San Jose, CA: Chusma House Publications: 1992. http://cemaweb.library.ucsb.edu/montoya_bio.html (biography).

MONTOYA, Joseph
Politician

Joseph Manuel Montoya had an impressive political career. A Democrat, he was the youngest person to be elected to the New Mexico House of Representatives and the youngest to gain a seat in the state's Senate. Later becoming a respected national politician, Montoya was known as a moderate who supported civil rights, health and safety, education, and environmental legislation.

Early life
Born in Peña Blanca, New Mexico, in 1915, Montoya was the son of Thomas and Frances Montoya. He was educated in local public schools and in 1931 carried on his studies at Regis College, Denver, Colorado. In 1934 he decided to study law at Georgetown University in Washington, D.C.

Interest in politics
In 1936, while still a student, Montoya ran for and won a seat in the New Mexico House of Representatives. Two years later Montoya's graduation from Georgetown coincided with his reelection to office. In 1940 Montoya was elected to the New Mexico State Senate, where he

▼ *Joseph Montoya entered both houses of the U.S. Congress by replacing incumbent congressmen who had died in office.*

KEY DATES	
1915	Born in Peña Blanca, New Mexico, on September 24.
1936	Elected to the New Mexico House of Representatives.
1940	Elected to the New Mexico State Senate.
1947	Becomes lieutenant governor of New Mexico.
1957	Elected to U.S House of Representatives.
1964	Wins U.S. Senate election.
1978	Dies in Washington, D.C., on June 8.

remained for six years. During this time he was also appointed chairman of the Judiciary Committee. In 1947 Montoya became lieutenant governor of New Mexico, a position to which he was reelected three more times.

In 1957, following the death of New Mexico congressman Antonio Manuel Fernández (1902–1956) who had recently been reelected to office, Montoya won his seat in a special election. Over the next few years he sponsored several education and environmental acts. In 1964 he was elected to finish New Mexico senator Dennis Chavez's term of office, following the politician's death.

Entering the upper house
As a senator Montoya served on several committees, including the Senate Agriculture Committee, where he became interested in consumer health and safety issues and introduced several acts to help improve working conditions. He also sponsored the Bilingual Education acts of 1968 and 1974. Montoya attracted public attention when he served on the Watergate Committee established to investigate the conduct of President Richard M. Nixon.

Montoya held the New Mexico seat until 1976, when he was defeated by former astronaut Harrison Schmitt (1935–). Following his defeat, Montoya joined Senator Pete Domenici (1932–), working to keep federal installations open in New Mexico. He died in Washington, D.C., in 1978.

See also: Chavez, Dennis

Further reading: http://bioguide.congress.gov/scripts/ biodisplay.pl?index=M000876 (biography).

MONTOYA, Nestor
Journalist, Politician

As an editor and politician, Nestor Montoya spent the greater part of his career campaigning for New Mexican statehood and working tirelessly for the inclusion of Spanish-speaking people in U.S. society.

Land disputes

Montoya was born in Old Albuquerque in what is now the state of New Mexico in 1862. He attended public schools, and graduated from St. Michael's College in Santa Fe, New Mexico, in 1881. Montoya began working as a U.S. Post Office clerk and then worked in the U.S. Treasury office in Santa Fe.

During this time, New Mexico Territory was plagued by boundary disagreements instigated by bogus surveying techniques and racial discrimination. After decades of disenfranchisement, some Hispanos (people of Spanish-Mexican descent) protested these injustices by ignoring questionable boundaries and damaging the property of unscrupulous landowners. Hoping to clarify the protestors' motives and encourage political discussion among Hispanos, Montoya founded a weekly Spanish-language newspaper called *La Voz del Pueblo* (The Voice of the People) in 1889.

▼ *Nestor Montoya sought to preserve Hispano (Spanish-Mexican) culture in New Mexico.*

KEY DATES

1862   Born in Old Albuquerque, New Mexico, on April 14.

1889   Founds weekly Spanish-language newspaper, *La Voz del Pueblo* (The Voice of the People).

1901   Purchases *La Bandera Americana* (The American Flag) newspaper, which espouses New Mexico statehood.

1921   Elected to U.S. Congress.

1923   Dies in Washington, D.C., on January 13.

Public servant

In the 1890s, Montoya worked as an interpreter for the Second Judicial District Court. There he developed impressive oratorical skills. In 1901, Montoya purchased another newspaper, *La Bandera Americana* (The American Flag), which he used to advocate New Mexican statehood.

In order to deter further eruptions of violent protest, Montoya began working with the judicial system to address the concerns of his people. In 1892 he was elected to the lower house of the territorial legislature, where he served until 1903, and then to the upper house until 1906. He was an elected delegate to the New Mexico Constitutional Convention in 1910, where he helped draft provisions that ensured the protection of Hispano rights in the future state of New Mexico. In 1912, after many years of conflict and debate, New Mexico was finally admitted into the Union.

Though he had now realized his chief political ambition, Montoya spent the next 10 years in various appointed positions: regent of the University of New Mexico at Albuquerque, chairman of the Bernalillo County draft board during World War I (1914–1918), and member of the Council of National Defense. He gained a seat in the U.S. House of Representatives in 1921. While in Congress, Montoya was a member of both the Indian Affairs Committee and the Committee on Public Lands. After a lifetime of public service, Montoya died in office in 1923.

Further reading: Vigil, Maurilio E. *Hispanics in Congress: A Historical and Political Survey.* Lanham, MD: University Press of America, 1996.
http://www.loc.gov/rr/hispanic/congress/montoyan.html (biography).

MORA, Magdalena
Activist

Mexican-born Magdalena Mora was one of the leading figures of the Chicano movement of the 1970s and was closely associated with the militant Chicano organization CASA. A rising academic, Mora used her scholarly work to reflect, and contribute to, the struggle for rights of the United States's Hispanic American workers.

Without borders
Mora was born in Mexico in 1952, but spent most of her childhood in San Jose, California, where her parents were based as migrant workers. While still at high school in the 1960s, Mora became involved in radical student politics, and in particular with the burgeoning Chicano (Mexican American) civil rights movement.

After high school, she went to study at the University of California, Berkeley, from which she graduated with a bachelor's degree in history in 1974. Mora subsequently took up postgraduate research work at the University of California, Los Angeles (UCLA), where, since 1969, there had been a flourishing multidisciplinary research center for Chicano studies.

CASA
One of the ideas behind the Chicano student movement was to return to work with the Hispanic American community after graduation. Mora took this ideal one step further, and became active in the civil rights struggle while still studying.

While at UCLA, Mora became deeply involved with CASA (Centro de Acción Social Autónoma—Hermandad General de Trabajadores; Center of Independent Social Action—General Brotherhood of Workers). Founded in 1968, CASA had begun as a help and advice center for undocumented migrant workers arriving from Mexico.

By the mid-1970s, CASA had evolved into a Marxist organization that sought to mobilize and educate poorly paid Mexican American workers who were being unfairly treated by employers and were not supported by labor laws. Mora worked on CASA's bilingual newspaper, *Sin Fronteras* (Without Borders).

Mora also became involved at the grassroots level with the movement's other activists. Most notably, in 1975, Mora helped organize a strike among Hispanic American women cannery workers at Tolteca Foods in Richmond, California.

KEY DATES	
1952	Born in Mexico.
1974	Graduates from the University of California, Berkeley.
1980	Publishes *Mexican Women in the United States: Struggles Past and Present*.
1981	Dies in Los Angeles, California.

She made history
In her academic work, Mora focused on the plight of Mexican migrant workers like her parents. She attempted to set these people in the context of the long history of exploitation of migrant Mexican labor in the Southwest United States.

A committed feminist, Mora took a special interest in women workers, who at the time were an even more poorly paid group than their male counterparts. With Adelaida R. del Castillo (1950–; now a professor at San Diego State University in the Chicano studies department), Mora edited a groundbreaking collection of essays in 1980 about the experience of Hispanic American women in the United States. Her combination of scholarly reflection with grassroots activism led Juan Gómez-Quiñones, director of the UCLA Chicano Studies Research Center, to say of her: "She made history."

Sudden death
Mora died at the age of just 29 from a brain tumor. Her loss was widely mourned in the Chicano movement. Her life and death inspired an elegy, "Canción de invierno" (Winter Song) by the poet Lucha Corpi. Mora is also remembered by the University of California at Berkeley's Casa Magdalena Mora, a residential program devoted to Mexican and Chicano studies.

See also: Corpi, Lucha; Goméz-Quiñones, Juan

Further reading: Mora, Magdalena, and Adelaida R. Del Castillo. *Mexican Women in the United States: Struggles Past and Present*. Los Angeles, CA: Chicano Studies Research Center Publications, University of California, 1980.
uniondelbarrio.org/lvp/newspapers/97/janmay97/pg01.html
(tribute to Mora by Carlos Vasquéz).

MORAGA, Cherríe
Writer, Academic

Cherríe Moraga is best known for her groundbreaking work as a Chicana feminist. She was one of the first Chicana writers to deal openly with lesbianism and sexuality. She coedited the anthology *This Bridge Called My Back: Writings by Radical Women of Color* with the well-respected Chicana author Gloria Anzaldúa. The collection paved the way for other Latino and Latina writers to publish their work and share their views and experiences. Moraga also cofounded Kitchen Table: Women of Color Press.

Early life
Born in Whittier, California, on September 25, 1952, Moraga was the daughter of a Chicana mother, Elvira Moraga, and an Irish American father, Joseph Lawrence. Her father left the family when Moraga was very young, and Elvira Moraga worked hard to support her children by herself. As a child, Moraga listened to her mother and aunts tell stories while sitting at the kitchen table. These gatherings were crucial in shaping Moraga's identity as a writer. She often cites her mother as one of her greatest influences (*see box on page 11*). Moraga's mother discouraged her children from speaking Spanish, in the hope that they would successfully assimilate in the United States. Moraga was light-skinned, and she was aware from a young age of the significance of skin color in U.S. society. As a young adult, Moraga struggled to learn Spanish and to come to terms with her Mexican heritage.

In 1974, Moraga received a BA in English from Immaculate Heart College in Los Angeles. In the same year, she openly admitted her homosexuality. By recognizing and accepting her own sexuality, Moraga was able to address and challenge issues of race and gender in her writing. Her subsequent work helped create a forum for public discussion of matters that had previously been shrouded in secrecy. After teaching for three years in Los Angeles, in 1977 Moraga moved to San Francisco, and enrolled at California State University. She studied for an MA in literature with a special major in feminist studies, and graduated in 1980.

Bridge work
In 1981, Moraga coedited with friend and colleague Gloria Anzaldúa *This Bridge Called My Back: Writings by Radical Women of Color*. The anthology was a response to the racism both women had encountered

▲ **Cherríe Moraga has a distinct style, mixing Spanish and English and traditional narrative and poetic forms in her writing.**

within mainstream feminism. Anzaldúa and Moraga wanted to create what they called "bridge work" through their own literature and the writings of other women of color. Believing that women of color were revolutionary forces who straddled or bridged the divisions within society, Anzaldúa and Moraga wanted to foster empathy and dialogue among oppressed and disenfranchised communities. The anthology inspired a widespread movement of Third World feminism, which gave voice to women of color who came from economically poor backgrounds. *This Bridge Called My Back* was critically acclaimed; it also won the American Book Award (1986).

Dealing with sexuality and race
In 1983, Moraga published an autobiographical anthology of poems and prose, *Loving in the War Years* (*Lo Que Nunca Pasó Por Sus Labios*). The first book to deal openly with lesbianism in Chicana culture, *Loving in the War Years* examines sexual and gender identities through the lens of a Chicana. Moraga uses both Spanish and English in the text to embrace her mixed Mexican and American background.

INFLUENCES

Cherríe Moraga has often said that her mother, Elvira, was one of the most important influences on her life. Elvira Moraga grew up in the Central Valley of California, a predominately agricultural area. From a young age, Elvira worked in the fields; she eventually left school at age 14 to support her brothers and sisters.

When Elvira was bringing up Moraga, she stressed the importance of education to her. Her mother's illiteracy fueled Moraga's own ambition to teach and to write. Elvira also passed on to Moraga her own love of storytelling and showed her the importance of nurturing female relationships.

Moraga was also influenced by the playwright Maria Irene Fornes, who encouraged her to write plays. Moraga loved the sensuality of the Spanish writer Federico García Lorca, and was inspired by the technique of other playwrights, such as black American Suzan Lori Parks and Puerto Rican Migdalia Cruz.

Playwright

In 1985, Moraga studied at the Hispanic Playwright's Lab at New York's International Arts Relations (INTAR) theater. Under the guidance of Cuban American playwright María Irene Fornes, Moraga developed the play *Shadow of a Man*, which won the Ford Fund for New American Plays Award. Fornes encouraged Moraga to use her strengths as a poet to develop stories and characters in playwriting. Fornes is herself a highly acclaimed playwright, and has received six Obie Awards. She is recognized as the only Latina playwright to appeal successfully to larger audiences outside the Latina and Latino community.

KEY DATES

1952 Born in Whittier, California, on September 25.

1974 Graduates from Immaculate Heart College in Los Angeles, with a BA in English.

1980 Receives an MA from California State University, San Francisco, in literature.

1981 Coedits with Gloria Anzaldúa *This Bridge Called My Back: Writings by Radical Women of Color*.

1983 Publishes *Loving in the War Years* (*Lo Que Nunca Pasó Por Sus Labios*).

1991 Appointed playwright in residence at the Theater Center of San Francisco; remains in post until 1997.

1993 Awarded the National Endowment for the Arts Theatre Playwrights Fellowship.

1994 Becomes artist in residence and instructor for Latino theater, playwriting, creative writing, and U.S. Latino/a literature at the department of drama and the department of Spanish and Portuguese, Stanford University.

2001 Receives the National Association for Chicana and Chicano Studies Scholars award.

Moraga's plays were widely respected. She was later commissioned by the Brava Theater in San Francisco to write several more plays. Brava produces work solely from women of color. Moraga has written several influential plays, including *Hungry Women: A Mexican Medea*, based on the Mexican folklore of La Llorona, and *Heroes and Saints*, a work that deals with environmental racism, the Catholic church, and women's body issues. The play *Watsonville* addresses the rights of Mexican migrant workers in California and the controversial issue of illegal immigration. Moraga's nonfiction work includes *The Last Generation* (1993), a memoir, and *Waiting in the Wings: A Portrait of Queer Motherhood* (1997).

An important voice

Moraga has built a reputation as a strong writer who handles traditionally taboo subjects with unflinching honesty and openness. Her work addresses themes that are historically marginalized in mainstream literature and political movements. Moraga confronts and challenges sexism, homophobia, racism, and what she sees as weaknesses in the women's movement. Her work also appears in many collections.

Moraga has received many honors, including the 2001 National Association for Chicana and Chicano Studies Scholars award. In 1994, she took up an appointment as artist in residence at the department of drama at Stanford University. She also teaches drama, Spanish, and Portuguese at the university.

See also: Anzaldúa, Gloria; Fornes, Maria Irene

Further reading: Yebro-Bejerano, Yvonne. *The Wounded Heart: Writing on Cherríe Moraga.* Austin, TX: University of Texas Press, 2001.
www.cherriemoraga.com (Moraga's official site).

MORALES, Alejandro
Writer

The academic Alejandro Morales is one of the country's leading Chicano writers. His novels express a deep understanding of Chicano culture, convincingly portraying a group of people cut adrift from mainstream U.S. society.

Early life

Alejandro Morales was born in the Simons barrio (Hispanic American neighborhood) of Montebello, California. His parents, Delfino Morales Martínez and Juana Contreras Ramírez, were first-generation immigrants from Guanajuato, Mexico. Morales, the youngest of five children, spent most of his childhood in the Chicano stronghold of East Los Angeles, where he attended school. He graduated from California State University at Los Angeles with a bachelor of arts degree, and went on to Rutgers University in New Jersey. There, he gained a master's degree in 1973 and a PhD two years later.

In 1975 Morales became associate professor in the Department of Spanish and Portuguese at the University of California at Irvine. He was promoted, eventually becoming a full professor of Latin American and Chicano literature in 1987, a position he continues to hold at the university.

Fact and fiction

In 1975 Morales published his first novel, *Caras Viejas y Vino Nuevo*, in Mexico City, Mexico, because he was unable to find a publisher in the United States. The work was not translated into English until 1981, when it was published as *Old Faces and New Wine*. The novel is about two teenagers, Mateo and Julian. The pair live in the barrio, and the plot explores the different pressures the boys face. The world of the Anglos is the "otro lado," or other place. Morales portrays many of the Anglo characters, particularly a policeman, in a negative light.

Morales's subsequent novels continued to explore the Chicano world, specifically life in the barrio and the rural problems common to both Mexico and the Southwest United States. *La Verdad Sin Voz* (1979; published as *Death of an Anglo* in 1988) focuses on the negative aspects of life for many young Hispanic Americans in the United States. Set in Mathis, Texas, the story is based on an actual event, the murder by a white policeman of Michael Logan, an Anglo physician who helped Chicanos. The novel is narrated by a university professor, himself a victim of racism.

KEY DATES

1944 Born in Montebello, California, on October 14.

1973 Receives PhD from Rutgers University, New Jersey; publishes *Caras Viejas y Vino Nuevo* (*Old Faces and New Wine*) in Mexico City, Mexico.

1975 Publishes *La Verdad Sin Voz* (*Death of an Anglo*).

1981 First novel translated into English.

1988 Publishes *The Brick House,* his first English-language novel.

2001 Publishes *Waiting to Happen*.

Morales's third novel, *Reto en el Paraíso* (1982; Challenge to Paradise), has a complicated structure and was notable for its stylistic innovations. Covering more than 100 years of Chicano history, it charts the decline of a native California family and the rise of an Irish immigrant family. Morales uses the book to explore the effects of the Land Law of 1851 on Native American and Hispanic American families.

Morales published his next two novels, *The Brick People* (1988) and *The Rag Doll Plagues* (1992), in English. As with his earlier novels, he combined factual events with fictionalized characters. *The Rag Doll Plagues* has as its protagonist a Hispanic American doctor who fights the plague in three different locations and at three different times—old Mexico, modern South California, and a future place where Mexico and California have merged. In *The Brick People*, Morales describes the interaction between Chicano employees and Anglo factory owners.

Into the future

Morales's novel *Waiting to Happen* appeared in 2001. Its structure is complicated, as the plotlines weave backward and forward to present a double view of Mexico and the United States both in the past and in the future. In addition to his writing, Morales is an active member of a number of Chicano societies, including the Yale Project of Chicano Writers and the Association of Mexican American Educators.

Further reading: Morales, Alejandro. *Fiction Past, Present, Future Perfect.* Tempe, AZ: Bilingual Review/Press, 1996.

MORALES, David
DJ, Producer, Musician

David Morales is widely credited as one of the first disc jockeys (DJs) to introduce Chicago house music to New York City. A fashionable underground DJ for many years, Morales became an internationally known "superstar DJ" when house music became popular with mainstream audiences. His early work established a style common in dance music today, and Morales has enjoyed considerable success from his own releases as well as from his production work and remixes for pop stars including Madonna, Michael Jackson, U2, and Mariah Carey. Twice previously nominated for a Grammy award, Morales was awarded the Grammy for Remixer of the Year in 1998.

David Morales was born in Brooklyn, New York City, on August 21, 1961, to Puerto Rican immigrant parents. Regularly DJing at house parties as a teenager, Morales dropped out of high school by the age of 14 to work as a cook by day and a DJ by night. He DJed at every major nightclub in the city and effortlessly weathered New York's transition from disco to house music, playing a pivotal role in introducing Chicago house music to the city. With Chep Nuñez and Clivilles & Cole, Morales created one of the first underground house hits, "Do It Properly" (1987), using the moniker 2 Puerto Ricans, A Black Man, and A Dominican.

▲ **Prolific DJ, remixer, and producer David Morales performs to the crowds at the MTV Ibiza 99 festival.**

Mainstream success
Morales started remixing songs in 1986, and founded Def Mix Productions in 1987. In 1993, Morales released his debut album, *The Program,* which included "In De Ghetto," a track that became a "clubland" hit the following year. Mainstream success came after his remix of Mariah Carey's "Dreamlover" (1993), and his skills became sought after by the world's most successful recording artists. Some of Morales's best-known remixes include Madonna's "Deeper and Deeper" (1992), Jamiroquai's "Return of the Space Cowboy" (1995), and "Scream" by Michael and Janet Jackson (1995).

Morales launched Definity Records in 1997. The label's first release was "Needin' U," which reached number one on the *Billboard* dance chart. The success of the track was repeated in 2001 when it was re-released as "Needin' U II."

Recent work
Morales has a regular show on New York's dance station WKTU Radio, he guest-DJs on MTV's *The Grind,* and DJs throughout the world, with residencies at clubs including Pacha in Ibiza, Spain, and Discotheque in New York. In 2004 Morales released his first studio album for a decade, entitled *2 Worlds Collide.*

Further reading: Brewster, Bill, and Frank Broughton. *Last Night a DJ Saved My Life: The History of the Disc Jockey.* New York, NY: Grove Press, 2000.
http://www.defmix.com (Morales's Web site).

KEY DATES	
1961	Born in New York City on August 21.
1993	Releases debut album, *The Program.*
1997	"Needin' U" reaches number one on dance chart.
1998	Wins Grammy award for Remixer of the Year.

MORALES, Esai
Actor, Activist

A cofounder of the National Hispanic Foundation for the Arts, Esai Morales is an established film and television actor. Aside from his interest in the greater public relevance of Hispanics in the media and entertainment industries, Morales is actively involved in environmental and social causes.

A native New Yorker, Morales was born in Brooklyn on October 1, 1962, to parents of Puerto Rican descent who divorced when he was still a baby. Until age five, he spoke only Spanish. As a child, Morales lived with his mother, an organizer for the International Ladies' Garment Workers' Union. At age 12, Morales expressed his first interest in becoming an actor, but promptly received his mother's disapproval. Determined in his ambitions, he ran away from home. Against the odds, Morales managed to enroll at New York's prestigious High School for the Performing Arts, living in a group home as a voluntary ward of the state.

Acting career

After graduating, Morales made his acting debut in *El Hermano,* at the Ensemble Studio Theater, and then appeared in Joseph Papp's production of *The Tempest* for New York's Shakespeare in the Park festival. Other stage credits followed, including the Los Angeles Theater Center's production of *Tamer of Horses,* for which he won the Los Angeles Drama Critics Circle Award, and Oscar Wilde's *Salome* at New York's Circle in the Square.

Morales's views on social issues had an impact on his choice of work. His film debut came in 1983, opposite Sean Penn, in *Bad Boys,* a drama about youth violence. In 1987, he played the part of Bob, the half-brother of Latino rock legend Ritchie Valens, in *La Bamba.* Other credits include *Rapa Nui* (1994), HBO's *The Burning Season—The Chico Mendes Story* (1994), and *The Disappearance of Federico Garcia Lorca* (1997).

Morales has worked extensively in television, acting in *Miami Vice, Fame, The Outer Limits, The Twilight Zone,* and, later, as Lt. Tony Rodríguez in *NYPD Blue* and Esteban Gonzales in PBS's *American Family.*

Esai Morales is involved in a number of social causes, working for the Wildlife Preservation Fund, Health Education AIDS Liaison, and El Rescate, a refugee service agency. In 1997 he cofounded the National Hispanic Foundation for the Arts.

KEY DATES

1962   Born on October 1, in Brooklyn, New York.

1974   Becomes interested in an acting career after seeing Al Pacino in *Dog Day Afternoon.*

1983   Makes screen debut acting alongside Sean Penn in *Bad Boys.*

1997   Cofounds the National Hispanic Foundation for the Arts to advance the presence of Latinos in media.

▲ **Esai Morales plays Chucho in the epic drama My Family (1995). The actor is well known for playing tough and rebellious screen characters.**

See also: Valens, Ritchie

Further reading: http://www.hispanicarts.org/esaibio.htm (official biography at the National Hispanic Foundation for the Arts).

MORALES, Felix H.
Entrepreneur

Felix H. Morales was a civic-minded Mexican American entrepreneur who dignified impoverished Hispanic communities by honoring the dead and uplifting the living.

Born on May 27, 1907, in New Braunfels, Texas, Felix Hessbrook Morales was one of 10 children born to Felix and Hillary (Hessbrook) Morales. He attended racially segregated schools during most of his childhood and, after the death of his father, worked to help support his family by shining shoes, selling newspapers, and doing construction work. As a young man, he moved to San Antonio, Texas, where he owned a small taxicab business and worked at his brother Andrew's funeral home. On March 12, 1928, he married Angeline Vera, with whom he had one son.

An entrepreneurial and civic spirit

Prompted by San Antonio's refusal to allow Mexicans to be buried in cemeteries within city limits, Morales moved to Houston, Texas, with his wife in 1930, and established his own funeral home. With limited resources, Morales built caskets while Angeline sewed garments to clothe the dead. During the Great Depression, the Morales Funeral Home donated services to the destitute and provided "death benefits" to make services more affordable. In addition, Morales established a notary public service to help the Hispanic community translate official documents, and began sponsoring English and citizenship classes. By simultaneously fulfilling the Hispanic community's need for funeral services and civic programs, which the local government failed to deliver, Morales emerged from the Depression with a reputation as a resourceful entrepreneur who had come to the aid of Mexican Americans in the face of poverty and discrimination.

Financially secure by the 1940s, Morales decided to invest in a new venture that would serve the Hispanic community in a different way: He purchased time from a radio station and produced a Spanish-language program.

▲ *Felix Morales (center) broadcasts from Spanish-language KLVL radio station, which he established.*

After being granted a broadcasting license in 1950, radio station KLVL, La Voz Latina (The Latin Voice), became the first Spanish-language radio station to cover news in the Gulf Coast area. By airing daily peace prayers, musical and dramatic diversions, and shows such as *Yo necesito trabajo* (I Need a Job), during which unemployed persons called in and received job referrals, the station became a source of charity and support. Affectionately known as "la madre de los Mexicanos" (the mother of the Mexicans), KLVL once collected more than $10,000 and eight carloads of food and clothing to help local flood victims. Twenty-four years later, Morales opened an FM station in San Antonio, KFHM (for Felix H. Morales), which became the first bilingual radio station in the city.

Lasting reputation

One of the nation's most successful Hispanic businessmen, Felix H. Morales died on June 8, 1988. In memory of a man committed to the advancement of Latino and Latina people, several scholarships and a school have since been named in his honor.

Further reading: http://www.tsha.utexas.edu/handbook/online/articles/MM/fmobk.html (a brief biography of Felix H. Morales). http://www.lacadenadelavida.org/Portal/ (link to the KLVL 1480 AM radio website).

KEY DATES	
1907	Born in New Braunfels, Texas, on May 27.
1930	Establishes funeral home in Houston.
1950	Establishes Spanish-language radio station, KLVL.
1988	Dies on June 8.

MORALES, Pablo
Swimmer

Pablo Morales is one of the greatest butterfly swimmers of all time. His career was marked by three Olympic gold medals, a world championship title, and 11 national swimming titles.

Early life
Morales was born on December 5, 1964, in Chicago, Illinois. His parents, who were Cuban immigrants, moved to California shortly after the birth of their son. Pablo grew up in the suburbs and took swim training at the Santa Clara Swim Club. Morales was an exceptional butterfly swimmer with a relentless training regimen. He broke the high school 100-yard butterfly record and, by the age of 20, had secured a place on the 1984 U.S. Olympic team, setting a new world record for the 100-meter butterfly.

Swim success
Morales's medal tally at the 1984 Los Angeles Olympics was impressive. With teammates Rick Carey, Steve Lundquist, and Rowdy Gaines, Morales won the gold medal in the 4 x 100-meter medley relay, setting a new world record in the process. He also took silver in the 100-meter butterfly and silver in the 200-meter individual medley. Morales was the 1984 World Swimmer of the Year.

In the years that followed, Morales scored a series of further gold medal wins. In the Pan-American games of 1985, he took gold in the 100-meter butterfly and the 200-meter individual medley. A year later, he qualified for the World Championships in Madrid by setting a new world record in the 100-meter butterfly of 52.84 seconds (a record

▲ *Pablo Morales swims the 100-meter butterfly to take gold during the 1992 Olympic Games in Barcelona.*

that stood for nearly 10 years). Morales went on to win gold in the 100-meter butterfly and 4 x 100-meter medley relay.

In 1987, Morales scored his 11th National Collegiate Athletic Association (NCAA) individual title—a record that still stands. As team captain, Morales also led his Stanford University team to a third consecutive NCAA title.

Trials and tribulations
With such an impressive record, Morales expected to breeze through national trials for the 1988 Olympics in Seoul. He finished third in both races, however, and failed to make the team. Deeply disappointed, Morales retired and took up law studies at Cornell University.

Three years later, however, Morales returned to the pool in an attempt to win an individual Olympic gold medal. He not only qualified for the 1992 Olympics, but also represented the swim team as captain. Morales then astounded the critics by winning Olympic gold in the 100-meter butterfly. He also helped the 4 x 100-meter medley relay team to gold in another world record time. Morales was the oldest person ever to win an Olympic swimming gold medal. In recognition of his achievement, the United States Olympic Committee chose Morales as the 1992 Sportsman of the Year.

KEY DATES
1964 Born in Chicago, Illinois, on December 5.
1984 Wins two silver medals and one gold at the Los Angeles Olympics.
1986 Sets new world record for the 100-meter butterfly and wins two gold medals at the World Championships in Madrid.
1987 Wins his 11th NCAA title.
1992 Wins two gold medals at Olympics in Barcelona. Named Sportsman of the Year by the U.S. Olympic Committee.
2001 Becomes head coach for the University of Nebraska women's swimming and diving team.

Further reading: Migdol, Gary. *Stanford: Home of Champions.* Champaign, IL: Sports Publishing LLC, 1997.
http://www.ishof.org/98pmorales.html (biography).

MORALES CARRIÓN, Arturo
Politician, Writer

Arturo Morales Carrión was an important figure in Puerto Rican political life. Morales Carrión was the first Puerto Rican to achieve a high position within the U.S. administration. He was also a historian, educator, and essayist. In 1989 Puerto Rico's future governor, Pedro Rosselló González, acknowledged Morales Carrión's great contribution to the country's development.

Early life
Arturo Morales Carrión was born in Havana, Cuba, in November 1913 to Puerto Rican parents. His family moved from Cuba back to their native country when Morales Carrión was a young boy. He was educated at the Escuela Vila Mayo de Río Piedras, and then at the Escuela Superior de la Universidad de Puerto Rico. Morales Carrión went to study at the University of Puerto Rico, from which he graduated in 1935 with a BA. A year later, he received an MA from the University of Texas.

Academic career
In the late 1930s, Morales Carrión returned to Puerto Rico, where he taught history at the University of Puerto Rico. By 1946, he was chair of the department. Between 1947 and 1949, Morales Carrión was a visiting lecturer at Columbia University in the United States. While teaching, Morales Carrión studied for his PhD, which he received in 1950. He then returned to Puerto Rico, where he became involved in politics.

A man of many talents
After a period working in Puerto Rico's External Affairs Department, and as undersecretary of Puerto Rico's State Department, Morales Carrión returned to the United States in 1953. He lived in Washington, D.C., and worked for George Washington University's Center for International Studies. He was also a member of the U.S. delegation at inter-American conferences. One of the key responsibilities of the group was to report on possible communist threats in Latin America.

In 1961, Morales Carrión was invited to join President John F. Kennedy's task force on U.S. policy toward Latin America. The committee of experts agreed that the United States should support Latin American development, promote democracy, and help internal institutional reform. Following Kennedy's assassination in 1963, Morales

Carrión became a special adviser to the secretary general of the Organization of American States (OAS), a position he held until 1969.

In the 1970s, Morales Carrión returned to Puerto Rico, where he served as president of the University of Puerto Rico between 1973 and 1979. He then worked as the executive director of the Puerto Rico Endowment for the Humanities.

Contribution
In addition to his political work and his university career, Morales Carrión was a noted author. He wrote a number of books on the history of Puerto Rico in both Spanish and English. He also published a large number of articles, speeches, and addresses. Morales Carrión argued that, in the postwar period, the family, above all other elements, had bound Puerto Ricans together.

Arturo Morales Carrión died of cancer on June 28, 1989, in San Juan, Puerto Rico. He was survived by a wife and three children. Morales Carrión is viewed by many commentators as one of the most important political and intellectual figures in 20th-century Puerto Rico.

KEY DATES	
1913	Born in Havana, Cuba, in November.
1935	Receives a BA from the University of Puerto Rico.
1936	Awarded an MA from the University of Texas.
1950	Receives a PhD from Columbia University, where he is also a visiting lecturer.
1953	Appointed undersecretary of the State Department of Puerto Rico.
1961	Serves on President John F. Kennedy's task force on Latin America.
1973	Becomes president of the University of Puerto Rico.
1989	Dies of cancer in San Jose, Puerto Rico, on June 28.

See also: Rosselló, Pedro

Further reading: Morales Carrión, Arturo. *Puerto Rico: A Political and Cultural History*. New York, NY: W.W. Norton & Co., 1983.

MORENO, Antonio
Actor

Antonio Moreno was a celebrated actor of the silent movie era. Spanish born, he was one of the first Hispanic actors to rise to starring roles in Hollywood. He was instrumental in the creation of the Hollywood "Latin lover"—the sensuous and romantic stereotype that has endured in the film industry to the present day.

Antonio Garrido Monteagudo Moreno was born in Madrid, Spain, in 1887. His father was in the Spanish army but died when Moreno was still young, and the family moved to Algeciras in southern Spain. Much of Moreno's early life is surrounded by myths, but it is known that in his teens he sailed to the United States to try life there. Moreno was supported in New York by a family friend, but was later adopted by Charlotte Morgan, a widow who took him to Northampton, Massachusetts, where he attended the Williston Seminary. Moreno continued to live in Northampton until 1908, when he returned to Spain to visit his mother. During this time, he undertook a variety of jobs and developed an interest in theater.

A talent for acting

On his return to the United States in 1910, Moreno had his first acting opportunity in the play *Two Women* at the Lyric Theater, New York. He went on to perform in several other Broadway plays, including *Thais* (by Paul Willstach, Criterion Theater, 1911), *C.O.D.* (by Frederic Chapin, Gaiety Theater, 1912), *Gypsy Passion* (a dance play, Plymouth Theater, 1912–1913), and *The Old Firm* (Harris Theatre, 1913).

Moreno abandoned stage performances soon after he debuted in the silent movie *The Voice of Millions* (Rex–Universal, 1912). His striking and photogenic features were well suited to the genre, and he rose rapidly to leading roles. Following his success in this first film, he signed with Biograph and worked with D. W. Griffith on 15 films between 1912 and 1914, when he was signed by Albert E. Smith to Vitagraph. Moreno starred in 40 films at

▼ *Antonio Moreno pleads his love for Marion Davies in a scene from the film* **Beverly of Graustark** *(1926).*

INFLUENCES AND INSPIRATION

Antonio Moreno represented the finer ideals of the gentleman in Hollywood and was widely acknowledged in movie circles for not having succumbed to many of the extravagances of stardom. It is known that Moreno believed that an actor should always strive to serve his audience and be respectful of his public. Moreno was an inspiration to many aspiring actors of his day, and helped and advised other Spanish-speaking newcomers to Hollywood. Recently, Moreno's popularity has risen again, as Spanish-speaking Americans are establishing their own distinct identity within the worlds of stage and screen. Moreno's career has come to be regarded as an early example of Latino success, and is providing inspiration to a whole new generation.

Vitagraph between 1914 and 1917, playing leading roles and costarring with the great actresses of the studio, such as Edith Storey, in *The Island of Regeneration* (1915), *Dust of Egypt* (1915), and *A Price for Folly* (1915). In 1917, Moreno worked with Pathé, allegedly requested by the actress Helene Chadwick, for *The Angel Factory* (1917). At Pathé, Moreno did his first serial, *The House of Hate* (1918, in 20 weekly episodes). Serials were very popular during the early years of cinema, since they were short and easy to produce and encouraged a return audience. Moreno became such a success in serials that he was taken up again by Vitagraph for four serials between 1918 and 1920: *The Iron Test* (1918), *The Perils of Thunder* (1919), *The Invisible Hand* (1920), and *The Veil Mystery* (1920).

Hollywood stardom

By the 1920s, serials had fallen in popularity and serious actors moved into feature films. Moreno moved to Paramount and established himself as a major feature film actor in *The Trail of the Lonesome Pine* (1923), starring with Mary Miles Minter. In 1923, Moreno married the wealthy socialite Dorothy Canfield Danzinger (divorced in 1931, died 1933) and further enhanced his status in Hollywood. Moreno's success continued during the 1920s, when he starred with major actresses of the time including Gloria Swanson, Clara Bow, and Greta Garbo in a variety of

genres. His most notable performance was as costar to Garbo in her second film in the United States, *The Temptress* (MGM, 1926).

Sounds of change

With the advent of sound in film in the late 1920s, actors had to adapt to the new demands of speaking roles. Although Moreno adapted well, his acting appeal was restricted by his poor English. Talking films from Hollywood were immediately restricted to English-speaking countries.

Initially, some films were made in different versions for other countries, which prompted Moreno to star in *El Cuerpo del Delito* (Paramount, 1929; Spanish version of *The Benson Murder*) and *El Hombre Malo* (First National, 1930; Spanish version of *The Bad Man*). Sound movies also prompted national industries to make films in their own languages, and Moreno became involved in filmmaking in Mexico and directed the first Mexican sound film, *Santa* (Companhia Nacional Produtora de Peliculas, 1932). The production of multiple versions of sound films proved an expensive solution, however, and dubbing or subtitling became the norm.

In the late 1930s, Moreno's market was restricted to character roles. He was taken up by Hollywood for a wave of Latin-themed films brought about by the Good Neighbor Policy in the United States during World War II, including *Two Latins from Manhattan* (Columbia, 1941). In the late 1940s and the 1950s, Moreno appeared in minor roles in films such as *Notorious* (RKO, 1946) and *The Creature from the Black Lagoon* (Universal, 1954). His last American film role was in *The Searchers* (Warner Bros., 1956).

KEY DATES

1887	Born in Madrid, Spain.
1912	Acts in his first film: *The Voice of the Millions.*
1923	Marries Dorothy Canfield Danzinger.
1926	Costars with Greta Garbo in *The Temptress.*
1956	Acts in his last Hollywood movie.
1967	Dies in Beverly Hills, California, on February 15.

Further reading: Katchner, George A. *Eighty Silent Film Stars: Biographies and Filmographies of the Obscure to the Well Known.* Jefferson, NC: McFarland & Company, Inc., 1991. http://www.goldensilents.com/stars/antoniomoreno.html (brief biography).

MORENO, Arturo
Businessman

A well-respected Mexican American businessman, Arturo ("Arte") Moreno was the first Hispanic to own the largest stake in a major professional United States sports franchise. In May 2003 Moreno purchased the Los Angeles Angels of Anaheim (then known as the Anaheim Angels) from the Walt Disney Company for more than $183.5 million.

Early life

The eldest of 11 children, Moreno was born and raised in Tucson, Arizona, where his parents owned and operated a print shop and published a Spanish-language newspaper. Moreno played baseball at Rincon High School and developed a love of the game. In 1966 he was drafted into the U.S. Army and served in Vietnam. Upon completion of his tour of duty, Moreno returned to Tucson and enrolled at the University of Arizona. He graduated in 1973 with a degree in marketing.

The road to success

Moreno began working for an outdoor (billboard) advertising business, where he worked his way up to senior management. In 1984 Moreno entered into a

▼ **Arte Moreno has said that all he wants in the world is for the Angels to win the World Series.**

KEY DATES	
1946	Born in Tucson, Arizona.
1966	Drafted into the U.S. Army and serves in Vietnam.
1973	Graduates from the University of Arizona and goes to work for an outdoor advertising business.
1999	Outdoor Systems is sold to Infinity/CBS and merges with Viacom a year later.
2003	Becomes owner of the Los Angeles Angels of Anaheim on May 21.

partnership with Outdoor Systems, which he built into the largest outdoor advertising company in North America. The company became the first of its kind to go public on the stock market. In 1999 Infinity Broadcasting/CBS purchased Moreno's business for a reported $8.3 billion.

Baseball

From 1986 to 1993 Moreno was a co-owner/partner of the minor league Salt Lake City Trappers, and after selling his business he purchased the largest share of the Angels.

Moreno's ownership style pleased Angels fans: One of Moreno's first acts was to lower the price of family-ticket packages and cut the cost of premium draft beer from $8.50 to $6.75. Moreno also increased the team's payroll by signing some of MLB's top free agents the following winter, including frontline starting righthanded pitchers Bartolo Colón (four-years, $51 million) and Kelvim Escobar (three-years, $18.75 million). Those signings were a precursor to Moreno's biggest coup, however, the free-agent signing on January 12, 2004, of Vladimir Guerrero to a five-year, $70 million contract. The prominent signings of top Latino players helped increase the Spanish-speaking fan base. Both Anaheim and nearby Santa Ana, the Orange County seat, have large Hispanic populations. Some MLB owners were upset because they felt Moreno was inflating the market with his lavish free-agent signings. However, Moreno stood by his actions.

Further reading: Reed, Vita. Arturo "'Arte'" Moreno." *Orange County Business Journal*. Volume 28, Issue 1. www.time.com/time/nation/article/0,8599,1093635,00.html (short article on Moreno).

MORENO, Luisa
Activist, Unionist

One of the first Latinas to be a leading member of a major U.S. trade union, the Guatemalan-born activist Luisa Moreno fought racial prejudice and helped protect Hispanic American workers from exploitation.

Early life

Born in Guatemala City, Guatemala, on August 30, 1907, and christened Blanca Rosa López Rodríguez by her upper-class parents, Ernesto and Alice López Rodríguez, she became known as Alicia or Luisa. Moreno later changed her surname to prevent her family, who disagreed with her political views, from suffering any embarrassment.

Educated first in Guatemala, Moreno moved with her parents to Oakland, California, in 1916, where she attended school. While still a teenager, Moreno helped persuade Guatemalan universities to accept female students, yet chose not to study for a degree herself. Instead, she moved to Mexico, where she became a journalist and produced a volume of poetry.

"An injury to one is an injury to all"

In 1927, Moreno married the Guatemalan artist Miguel Angel de León. The couple moved to New York City in 1928. In the early 1930s, Moreno was forced to work as a sewing machine operator in a Spanish Harlem sweatshop in order to support her young daughter and unemployed husband. She was shocked at the way in which ethnic minorities were treated in the workplace, and became actively involved in labor activism. She also joined the Communist Party, and was kept under surveillance by the FBI for many years.

In 1934, Moreno joined the Congress of Industrial Organizations (CIO), an alliance of unions for unskilled workers. Her efforts brought her to the attention of the American Delegation of Labor, who employed her in 1935. She became the first female and the first Latina member of the California CIO Council. By 1938, Moreno also held a key role in the major union, the United Cannery Agricultural Packing and Allied Workers of America (UCAPAWA). She helped thousands of women gain equal pay and access to free legal advice. She also set up unions for Mexican workers throughout the Southwest.

After divorcing de León in 1937, Moreno moved to San Diego, California. She helped organize strike action in the tuna industry there. Major employers of Latinos, the industry owners exploited their workers, often making them work in sweatshop conditions.

In 1938, Moreno helped found a major Hispanic civil rights assembly called El Congreso de Pueblos que Hablan Español (The National Spanish-Speaking Congress) to promote dialogue between Mexican American organizations and develop a civil rights agenda.

From 1940, Moreno was the chief organizer of UCAPAWA in Los Angeles and San Diego. She secured nondiscriminatory pledges from the Royal packing plant and the California Walnut Growers Association. She also supported the Anti-Nazi League, and campaigned against racism in the local media.

After remarrying in 1947, Moreno retired from activism. Despite that, in 1950 the U.S. government deported Moreno. She settled in Mexico City, and ran a poultry farm with her second husband. She returned to Guatemala in 1992, and died in the same year at age 85.

KEY DATES	
1907	Born in Guatemala City, Guatemala, on August 30.
1928	Moves to New York City with her husband.
1934	Joins the Congress of Industrial Organizations.
1935	Joins staff of the American Delegation of Labor.
1938	Appointed to senior role at the United Cannery Agricultural Packing and Allied Workers of America.
1938	Helps found El Congreso de Pueblos que Hablan Español.
1940	Chief organizer of UCAPAWA in Los Angeles and San Diego.
1950	Deported from United States; settles in Mexico City, Mexico.
1992	Dies in Guatemala on November 4.

Further reading: Ruiz, Vicki L. *Cannery Women, Cannery Lives: Mexican Women, Unionization, and the California Food Processing Industry, 1930–1950.* Albuquerque, NM: University of New Mexico Press, 1987.
http://college.hmco.com/history/readerscomp/rcah/html/ah_061100_morenoluisa.htm (biography).

MORENO, Rita
Actor, Singer, Dancer

Actor, singer, and dancer Rita Moreno is widely regarded as one of the most successful Puerto Rican performers of the last century. Her best-known roles include Anita in *West Side Story* and Sister Peter Marie Reimondo in the HBO prison drama *Oz*. With a career that has spanned seven decades, Moreno has won numerous prestigious awards. The first Hispanic actor to win a Tony award, Moreno was also the first Hispanic actor—and the first female—to win all four of the major entertainment awards. In addition to her Tony, she has won an Oscar, a Grammy, and two Emmy awards. She remains one of only a small group to achieve this feat.

Early life
Rita Moreno was born Rosa Dolores Alverio in Humacao, Puerto Rico, on December 11, 1931. Nicknamed "Rosita," Rosa Dolores was born into a family of small independent farmers who lost their livelihood during the Great Depression and subsequent industrialization of Puerto Rico. Her mother, Rosa María, immigrated to New York City in order to find work in the garment industry and a year later was joined in her tenement apartment by Rosita, then aged only five. Rosita left her father and brother behind in Puerto Rico and would never see them again.

Although on a small wage, Rosita's mother recognized her daughter's talents and secured dancing lessons with Rita Hayworth's uncle Paco Cansino, who encouraged Rosita to perform with the children's theater at Macy's department store. By the age of just 11, Rosita was beginning to find success, getting work providing

▲ *Rita Moreno's glittering acting career has covered both stage and screen.*

KEY DATES

1931 Born in Humacao, Puerto Rico, on December 11.

1961 Wins Best Supporting Actress Oscar and Golden Globe awards for *West Side Story*.

1972 Wins Best Recording for Children Grammy award for *The Electric Company*.

1975 Wins Best Featured Actress Tony award for *The Ritz*.

1977 Wins Outstanding Supporting Actress Emmy award for *The Muppet Show*.

2004 Awarded the Presidential Medal of Freedom by George W. Bush.

INFLUENCES AND INSPIRATION

Rita Moreno has influenced generations of Hispanic actors by demonstrating that it is possible to escape the narrow limits set by Hollywood's ethnic typecasting. Although this stereotyping has slowly begun to diminish, some critics point out that there are still relatively few lead roles available to Hispanics in Hollywood or the world of television. As the fastest-growing ethnic group in North America, the Hispanic community is underrepresented in both areas. For example, Moreno remains one of only a small group of nonwhite actors to win an Oscar. However, by consistently playing roles that are not tied to her ethnic identity, such as that of Norma Desmond in *Sunset Boulevard*, while also portraying well-developed Latina parts, such as Sister Peter Marie Reimondo in *Oz*, Moreno continues to push the boundaries for other Hispanic actors.

voice-overs for Spanish-language versions of popular U.S. films. At the age of 13, she landed her first Broadway role in the musical *Skydrift*.

Rita Moreno's first Hollywood role was a minor part in *A Medal for Benny* (1945). Rosita Alverio had already adopted the surname of her mother's third husband to become Rosita Moreno, and, at the urging of MGM studio chief Louis B. Mayer, shortened her name to Rita. Moreno was to wait five years for her next film role, in *So Young, So Bad* (1950). Unhappy that many of her film roles required her to play stereotypical fiery Latinas, Moreno was in contrast able to undertake roles in several distinguished theater productions during the same period, including Arthur Miller's *A View from the Bridge*.

Breaking the mold

Moreno's developing movie career continued to be characterized by stereotypical roles that she thought exploited her ethnic heritage. A number of higher profile roles began to arrive, though, including Zelda Zanders in *Singin' in the Rain* (1952) and Tuptim in *The King and I* (1956). It was the role of Anita in *West Side Story* (1961), however, that brought Moreno wider recognition. Many successful Hollywood films followed, including *The Night of the Following Day* in 1968, *Marlowe* and comedy-drama *Popi* in 1969, *Carnal Knowledge* (1971), *The Four Seasons* (1981), *Age Isn't Everything* (1991), *I Like It Like That* (1994), and *Angus* (1995).

Moreno was finally able to break free from Hollywood typecasting when she became the first Latina to play silent screen star Norma Desmond in *Sunset Boulevard* in 1996. Her endeavors to break the mold in film and television set an important precedent for Hispanic actors who followed, although typecasting remained difficult for Moreno to avoid. Her later movie credits included *The Slums of Beverly Hill* (1998), *Pinero* (2001), *Casa de Los Babys* (2003), *King of the Corner* (2004), and *Play It by Ear* (2005).

Moreno's television career has been equally successful, covering many of the most popular series of the last four decades of the 20th century, including *The Rockford Files, The Muppet Show, The Cosby Show, Miami Vice, The Golden Girls,* and, later, *Oz.* Moreno also provided the voice of Carmen Sandiago for the animated series *Where in the World Is Carmen Sandiago.*

Moreno has won numerous prestigious awards, including both an Oscar and a Golden Globe for Best Supporting Actress in *West Side Story* (1961) and the Joseph Jefferson Award for Best Chicago Theater Actress in 1968. Moreno won a Grammy award for *The Electric Company* in 1972, and in 1975 won the Best Featured Actress Tony award for her role in the Broadway show *The Ritz.* In the subsequent film version a year later, Moreno re-created her role of Googie Gómez, a portrayal that made fun of her early typecast Latina roles. She also won Emmy awards for *The Muppet Show* in 1977 and *The Rockford Files* in 1978.

In 1985, Moreno won the Sarah Siddons Award for her Broadway role in *The Odd Couple*, and a decade later was given a star on the Hollywood Walk of Fame. She was also nominated for or won the American Latin Media Arts (ALMA) award for outstanding actress every year from 1998 to 2002 for her role in *Oz.*

In 2004 Moreno was honored with a lifetime achievement award by the Los Angeles Latino International Film Festival for her work, and in the same year she was awarded the Presidential Medal of Freedom by George W. Bush for her "meritorious contribution" to cultural endeavors. Moreno is married to her manager, Lenny Gordon. They have one child and live in Berkeley, California.

See also: Hayworth, Rita

Further reading: Suntree, Susan. *Rita Moreno (Hispanics of Achievement).* New York, NY: Chelsea Press, 1992.
http://www.thegoldenyears.org/moreno.html (film Web site).

MORÍN, Raúl
Soldier, Author

War veteran and author Raúl Morín documented the military experiences of many of his Latino comrades.

Upbringing

Morín was born in Lockhart, central Texas, in 1913 to parents Petra and Evaristo. Morín's father died when he was only three years old, and by the age of six, despite being a wiry, thin child, Morín was in the cotton field picking like an adult alongside his stepfather. Morín and his stepfather never got along, however, so the teenage Morín dropped out of school and worked his way to western Texas, doing odd jobs and seasonal agricultural work. Morín was interested in art and taught himself to draw, eventually becoming a sign painter. When the Depression hit, he joined the Civilian Conservation Corps and worked clearing brush and making roads in Arizona. Rather than return to Texas, Morín kept heading west, eventually settling in Santa Barbara, California, where a brother lived. Morín made a living doing odd jobs and sign painting, and took up drawing caricatures of people, especially during the annual Old Mission Days Festival.

While painting scenery and backdrops for a community play, Morín met his future wife, Ramona Tijerina. They married in 1937, and moved to Los Angeles. There they started a family. Olivia was born in 1938, David in 1941, and Eddie in 1942 (they later had two further children, Tom and Samuel). The family lived in the Ramona Gardens Housing Project in Los Angeles until Morín was drafted into the U.S. Army during World War II (1939–1945).

As for so many of his generation, World War II had a tremendous impact on Raúl Morín and his young family.

▲ **Raúl Morín chronicled the important but largely untold stories of American Hispanic soldiers.**

He was assigned to the 79th Infantry Regiment in France and was seriously wounded during the Battle of the Bulge (December 16, 1944–January 25, 1945) when a grenade blew off part of his leg. Morín was sent back to the United States to recover.

Raúl Morín returned from the war determined to chronicle the largely unrecognized heroic deeds of Mexican–American soldiers, particularly the recipients of the Medal of Honor. He began to write columns for community newspapers about Mexican-American war heroes, and eventually had enough material to write a book. The book, *Among the Valiant: Mexican-Americans in World War II and Korea,* was published in 1961 and was soon in great demand because it was the single source on Mexican American heroes from World War II and the Korean War (1950–1953). Morín died in 1967; his son, Eddie, continues to publish later editions of the book.

Further reading: Morín, Raúl. *Among the Valiant: Mexican–Americans in World War II and Korea.* Los Angeles, CA: Valiant Press, 1961.

KEY DATES

1913 Born in Lockhart, Texas.

1937 Marries on November 27, in Santa Barbara, California, and moves to Los Angeles.

1961 Publishes *Among the Valiant: Mexican–Americans in World War II and Korea.* There have been 8 reprintings by various publishers.

1967 Dies in Los Angeles, California, on May 4.

2004 A commemorative plaque is placed in his honor at the base of the war monument located at Five Points in East Los Angeles.

MUNIZ, Frankie
Actor

A gifted actor with a wide fan base, Frankie Muniz first found fame in Fox's hit sitcom *Malcolm in the Middle*. Muniz has also successfully tackled a range of cinematic material. He moved into an executive producer role before his 20th birthday.

Early life

Francisco James Muniz IV was born in 1985 in New Jersey, and raised in Knightdale, North Carolina. His father was of Puerto Rican descent, and his mother was of Italian and Irish heritage. He made his stage debut in a local theater as the unfortunate Tiny Tim in *A Christmas Carol*. After his parents' divorce, he moved with his mother to California, where he won small roles on television, and was praised for his work in the TV film *What the Deaf Man Heard* (1997). Three years later, the wacky family comedy *Malcolm in the Middle* gave him his first lead role. As bright spark Malcolm, Muniz showcased his considerable comedic ability to an audience of more than 20 million for the series' first episode.

▼ *Frankie Muniz plays teenage spy Cody Banks in the movie* **Agent Cody Banks: Destination London.**

KEY DATES

1985   Born in Hackensack, New Jersey, on December 5.

2000   Plays the title role in the hit television series *Malcolm in the Middle*.

2001   Nominated for an Emmy award for his performances in *Malcolm in the Middle*.

2003   Appears in the movie *Agent Cody Banks*.

In 2001, the 15-year-old Muniz was nominated for an Emmy award for Outstanding Actor in a Comedy Series. The other nominees in his category were considerably older, such as Kelsey Grammar *(Frasier)* and Eric McCormack *(Will & Grace)*, who actually won the award. Muniz's portrayal of Malcolm also earned him two Golden Globe nominations, in 2001 and 2002.

Muniz at the movies

Between appearing in several seasons of *Malcolm in the Middle*, Muniz acted in a number of movies. One of his first pictures, *My Dog Skip* (2000), remains one of his best. His other credits include the comedy *Big Fat Liar* (2002) and the tough adult drama *Deuces Wild* (2002). The action adventure *Agent Cody Banks* (2003) cast Muniz as a super spy, and provided him with a $2 million paycheck. It was followed by a 2004 sequel, *Agent Cody Banks 2: Destination London*.

Muniz has also emerged as a talented voice artist, bringing animal characters to life in *Dr. Dolittle 2* (2001) and *Racing Stripes* (2005). He provided the voice for one of the heroes in *Choose Your Own Adventure: The Abominable Snowman* (2005), a groundbreaking interactive DVD movie that gave audiences the ability to determine the fate of the characters. Muniz also had an executive producer credit on the project. Eager to avoid being pigeonholed, Muniz has concentrated on how to best mature into an adult star. He continued to select intriguing projects, including *Stay Alive* (2006), his first foray into horror.

Further reading: Krulik, Nancy E. *Frankie Muniz: Boy Genius*. New York, NY: Pocket Books, 2000.
http://www.fox.com/malcolm (official Web site for *Malcolm in the Middle*).

MUÑIZ, Ramsey
Activist, Felon

Ramsey Muniz was a 1970s' Texas politician who was imprisoned for drug trafficking.

Early life
Born in 1942 in Texas, Muñiz was raised with four siblings in the barrio of Corpus Christi by his Chicano parents, Rodolfo and Hilda. Later, when Muñiz became involved in politics, he adopted the forename "Ramiro" to emphasize his Latino heritage.

In his youth, Muñiz developed into a powerful athlete. He also did well in school, despite a stammer. He lettered in high school football, and was awarded a full scholarship to Baylor University in Waco, Texas. At Baylor, Muñiz continued to excel as a football player and made the Little All-America team. After graduating with a degree in science, he pursued a law degree at Baylor.

Candidate for governor
In 1970, Muñiz became interested in La Raza Unida, the political party formed by the Mexican American Youth Organization (MAYO). When José Angel Gutiérrez, the lead organizer for La Raza Unida, visited Waco, Muñiz signed on as a candidate for the 1972 election to the State Board of Education. He then changed to become a gubernatorial candidate. Muñiz ran for governor of Texas in 1972, and again in 1974. His energetic candidacy won him a significant number of votes—nearly 7 percent of the total cast in 1972, and just under 6 percent in 1974. Voters of Mexican ancestry identified with the energetic young law graduate, his beautiful wife, Abbie, and their daughter, Delinda.

Life behind bars
In 1976, the federal government brought drug conspiracy charges against Ramsey Muñiz and his brother, Roberto. Supporters rallied to his defense, and began fund-raising

▲ **Twice candidate for governor of Texas, Muñiz fell afoul of the law and is serving a life sentence.**

to exonerate him, but Muñiz jumped bail and fled to Mexico. Months later he was captured. He pleaded guilty, and was sentenced to five years with ten years' probation.

After release from prison in the mid-1980s, Muñiz began a career as a legal assistant, but was soon caught on a parole violation for unauthorized travel. He was again incarcerated, and then released on probation. Muñiz remarried, and once again began a legal career, but freedom was short-lived. In 1994, he was charged with a drug offense involving 88 pounds (40kg) of cocaine. He was tried, found guilty, and sentenced to life in prison for a third felony conviction. His family and friends believe he is a political prisoner, the victim of a government witch hunt. To others, he simply crossed the line into the fast lane of drugs and quick dollars. Muñiz has adopted the México (Aztec) name "Tezcatlipoca" while serving his sentence in Leavenworth, Kansas.

See also: Gutierrez, José Angel

Further reading: http://www.freeramsey.com/historyof.html (biography from Ramsey Muñiz defense organization).

> **KEY DATES**
>
> **1942** Born in Corpus Christi, Texas, on December 13.
>
> **1972** First becomes a candidate for governor of Texas for La Raza Unida Party.
>
> **1994** Convicted of a second drug offense; sentenced to life without parole for his third violation of federal laws. Adopts the Mexica name "Tezcatlipoca."

MUÑOZ, Anthony
Football Player

With his imposing frame of 6 feet 6 inches (1.98m) and 278 pounds (126kg), Anthony Muñoz was one of the best offensive linemen in National Football League (NFL) history. A model of consistency, Muñoz played all 13 of his NFL seasons with the Cincinnati Bengals and helped take the team to two Super Bowls. Muñoz, who rarely missed a game, was a popular fixture on the Bengals' offensive line.

Early life

A Mexican American, Muñoz was born on August 19, 1958, in Ontario, California, a suburb 46 miles (74km) east of downtown Los Angeles. As a youth, Muñoz wanted to play Pop Warner football, but was not allowed because he was too big. Instead, Muñoz played baseball. Talented in the classroom as well as on the sports field, Muñoz went to the University of Southern California (USC), and joined their baseball program. In 1978, he pitched for USC's baseball national title team. It soon became clear, however, that Muñoz was much more suited to playing football.

▼ *Cincinnati Bengals' Anthony Munoz grits his teeth as he goes through weight lifting exercises in 1982.*

Career in football

Muñoz was named an All-America lineman in 1978 and 1979, but he missed almost all of his 1980 senior football season at USC with a knee injury. At the end of the season, however, he returned to put on an impressive display in USC's 17–16 win over Ohio State in the Rose Bowl. The Cincinnati Bengals' general manager Paul Brown was impressed and, despite injury concerns, took a chance on Muñoz. Brown's gamble paid off. Muñoz was elected to the Pro Bowl 11 consecutive times from 1981 to 1991.

During his first six years in the NFL, Muñoz protected quarterback Ken Anderson's blind side. When Boomer Esiason, a lefthander, became starting quarterback, Muñoz was the lead blocker on Esiason's rollout plays to the left. Muñoz went to the 1982 and 1989 Super Bowls with the Bengals, who lost to the San Francisco 49ers on both occasions (26–21 and 20–16). Muñoz was named the NFL Offensive Lineman of the Year three times (1981, 1987, and 1988), and the NFL Players Association Lineman of the Year four times (1981, 1985, 1988, and 1989). He even caught seven passes, scoring four touchdowns, on tackle-eligible plays. Muñoz attributed his long, healthy career to his dedicated workout regimen. He installed a complete set of weights in his basement and worked out year round.

Muñoz retired in 1992. Today, he passes on his strong work ethic through the Anthony Muñoz Foundation, which he launched in April 2002 to promote social and racial harmony among the underprivileged youth of Cincinnati and surrounding areas of Ohio, Indiana, and Kentucky.

Further reading: Ludwig, Chick. *The Legends: Cincinnati Bengals: The Men, The Deeds, The Consequences.* Wilmington, OH: Orange Frazer Press, 2004.
http://www.munozfoundation.org (Muñoz Foundation Web site).

MUÑOZ, Elías Miguel
Novelist, Poet

Cuban-born Elías Miguel Muñoz is one of the United States's leading contemporary Latino writers. Like many other Cuban Americans of his generation, Muñoz has used his works to explore the difficulties faced by first- and second-generation Cuban Americans coexisting between two strong cultures—Cuban Spanish and American. Muñoz is also homosexual, and he has written movingly about the discrimination and persecution faced by homosexuals both within Castro's Cuba and in the U.S. Cuban community.

KEY DATES	
1954	Born in Ciego de Ávila, Cuba.
1969	Settles with his family in California.
1984	Publishes first novel, *Los Viajes de Orlando Cachumbambé*.
1991	Publishes the novel *The Greatest Performance*.
1998	Publishes the novel *Brand New Memory*.

Between cultures and languages
Born in Ciego de Ávila, Cuba, in 1954, Muñoz moved with his family first to Spain and then to the United States in the late 1960s. By 1969 the family had settled permanently in Southern California.

Muñoz completed his high-school education and went on to study at the State University of California, Dominguez Hills, on the outskirts of Los Angeles; he

▼ *Elías Miguel Muñoz challenges stereotypical perceptions of Cubans and Cuban Americans in his work; he also explores how homosexuality is treated by both communities.*

received a bachelor's degree in French and Spanish in 1976. He continued his studies at the University of California, Irvine (UCI), earning a master's before researching his doctoral thesis on Spanish and Latin American literature in 1984.

Muñoz initially embarked on a career in academia, teaching at UCI, Wichita State University, and in California high schools. During this time he published works of literary criticism as well as his first novel, *Los Viajes de Orlando Cachumbambé* (The Travels of Orlando Cachumbambé, 1984), all of which were written in Spanish. In 1988 he gave up teaching in order to concentrate on his writing; in that same year he published his second novel, *Crazy Love* (1988), in English. Two more English-language novels followed: *The Greatest Performance* (1991) and *Brand New Memory* (1998). He also published short stories and collections of Spanish-language or bilingual poetry.

Challenging perceptions of identity
In his writing, Muñoz has challenged many one-dimensional notions about both Cuban American and Cuban, or *cubanidad*, identity. In the 1991 book *The Greatest Performance*, Muñoz depicts two Cuban exiles who, after experiencing persecution as homosexuals in their homeland, also struggle to find acceptance in the United States. Muñoz is a versatile writer, as seen in the later novel *Brand New Memory*, in which he depicts a wealthy Cuban American husband and wife who have completely assimilated to the U.S. way of life, while their daughter struggles to find out more about her Cuban heritage after she meets her Cuban grandmother.

Further reading: Muñoz, Elías Miguel. *The Greatest Performance*. Houston, TX: Arte Público Press, 1991.

MUÑOZ, Luis
Musician, Composer

Luis Muñoz is an important figure in the contemporary Latin music scene. Muñoz, who trained as a classical musician and played in pop and rock bands when he was a young man, is best known for his contribution as a percussionist, composer, and arranger of Latin jazz.

Born in San José, Costa Rica, on August 19, 1953, Muñoz grew up in a musical family. From an early age he was familiar with many of the different types of Latin music, from the Argentine tango and Brazilian samba to the norteña and ranchera music of Mexico, the bomba and plena from Puerto Rico, and the varied music of Cuba. Muñoz also fell in love with American jazz through listening to the records of such stars as Miles Davis, Ornette Coleman, John Coltrane, and Thelonious Monk. As a teenager, Muñoz also began listening to the Beatles and other British bands. Muñoz showed an early talent as a musician; he began playing pop and rock when he was a teenager.

Muñoz went on to study architecture at the University of Costa Rica; he also studied music privately at the National Music Conservatory. He said, "I was in awe of the vast emotional spectrum of classical music. The passion and depth, the rapture and relevance, the sheer magic that can only be found in some of the greatest works ever written."

Making a career in music

In 1974 Muñoz moved to the United States. He studied music at the University of California, Santa Barbara, graduating with a degree in music composition, after which he embarked on a professional music career as a composer, arranger, and percussionist. Although living in the United States, Muñoz first became known in Latin America. As a percussionist he played with some of the great names in Latin Jazz, including Brazilians Airto Moreira and Flora Purim. In 1980 he composed and recorded *Costa Rica-Costa Rica*, commissioned by the Costa Rica government. In 1988 he recorded *La Verdad* (*The Truth*).

In 1996 Muñoz recorded the critically acclaimed album *The Fruit of Eden*. Following the success of this recording, Muñoz developed a distinctive style: In 1998 he released *Compassion*, an album that incorporated a range of music styles and instruments, including the chromatic harmonica, vibes, cello, accordion, and acoustic guitar.

▲ *Luis Muñoz grew up listening to a wealth of different music styles in his native Costa Rica.*

The 2005 recording *Vida* (*Life*) is considered by many critics to be Muñoz's best work. He composed, arranged, and produced the album; he also collaborated with the Panamanian songwriter Rómulo Castro and the musician Linda Ronstadt, among others. The album represents a whole spectrum of Latin music influences—from Afro–Latin Jazz in "Mad Bop" to Costa Rican folk in "Los Ojos De La Ausencia," and merengue in "Carmesí."

KEY DATES	
1953	Born in San José, Costa Rica, on August 19.
1972	Studies architecture at the University of Costa Rica; studies music privately at the National Music Conservatory.
1974	Moves to the United States.
1980	Composes *Costa Rica–Costa Rica*.
1996	Releases *The Fruit of Eden*.
2005	Releases *Vida* (*Life*).

See also: Airto; Ronstadt, Linda

Further reading: http://www.luismunoz.net (official Web site).

MUÑOZ MARÍN, Luis

Politician, Writer

Luis Muñoz Marín is known as the "Father of Modern Puerto Rico." After serving in the Senate of Puerto Rico, he became the first democratically elected governor of the island in 1949, a post he stayed in for 16 years. Muñoz Marín worked with the U.S. government to draft the Puerto Rican Constitution, by which the country became a commonwealth of the United States. During his time in office, Muñoz Marín worked tirelessly for agricultural reform, increased industrialization, and the general improvement of socioeconomic conditions in Puerto Rico. Muñoz Marín's political vision for Puerto Rico moved progressively from independence to the concept of a free but associated state (*see box on page 31*). Although nationalists criticized Muñoz Marín for compromising, he is generally perceived as one of the most influential Puerto Rican politicians of the 20th century.

Early life

Born on February 18, 1898, in San Juan, Puerto Rico, José Luis Alberto Muñoz Marín was the only son of the writer and politician Luis Muñoz Rivera and Amalia Marín Castilla. Muñoz Marín spent a considerable part of his childhood and youth in the United States. He began studying at Georgetown Preparatory School in 1911, and in the following year became a law student at Georgetown University in Washington, D.C. He cut his studies short, however, when his father's illness in 1916 forced him to return to Puerto Rico.

From the United States to Puerto Rico

After his father's death, Muñoz Marín returned to New York, where he lived with his first wife Muna Lee, a poet from the South, with whom he had two children. For some time Muñoz Marín debated whether to pursue a career in politics or in letters. He worked as a writer and translator. The articles he wrote, which dealt with social and political issues, brought together his love of writing and his interest in politics. He also published the books *Borrones* and *Madre Haraposa*. During his time in the United States, he was also secretary to the representative of Puerto Rico in the United States Congress. In 1926 he returned to Puerto Rico to become editor of *La Democracia*, a newspaper founded by his father.

In the 1930s Muñoz Marín dedicated himself completely to politics. He joined the Partido Liberal

▲ *In 1963 Luis Muñoz Marín (right) was awarded the presidential medal of freedom by President John F. Kennedy (left).*

founded by Antonio R. Barceló, and in 1932 both men won seats in the Puerto Rican Senate. Following disagreements with Barceló, however, Muñoz Marín was expelled from the Partido Liberal.

A political man

In 1937 Muñoz Marín founded the group Accíon Social Independista (Social Independence Action). A year later he created the Partido Democrático Popular (Popular Democratic Party), which supported a closer relationship with the United States. Muñoz Marín ran for the Senate under the PDP, and in 1940 became president of the Senate. During this time, Muñoz Marín worked with Governor Rexford G. Tugwell to improve the living conditions of *jíbaros* ("farmers" or "people from the countryside"). He formed the Land Authority to apportion land to the *jíbaros*. Over the next few years, more than 20,000 housing units were built.

In 1949 Muñoz Marín became the first democratically elected governor of Puerto Rico, and only the second native islander to hold the post. Prior to this, the island's

INFLUENCES AND INSPIRATION

One of the most influential people in Luis Muñoz Marín's life was his father, the poet, journalist, and politician Luis Muñoz Rivera (1859–1916).

In 1898, by the treaty signed at the end of the Spanish–American War, Spain ceded Puerto Rico to the United States. Muñoz Rivera had been a leading campaigner for independence from Spain. He was president of Puerto Rico's Liberal Party and headed the first Puerto Rican cabinet under U.S. occupation. In 1910 he was appointed resident commissioner for the island in Washington, D.C. He lobbied in Congress for Puerto Ricans to be granted U.S. citizenship and to have a self-elected legislature.

When his son, Luis Muñoz Marín, first became involved in politics, he believed in Puerto Rico's right to total independence. Over the years Muñoz Marín moved closer to his father's ideas. He became convinced that it was more beneficial for Puerto Rico to remain part of the United States. Muñoz Marín worked hard to get Puerto Rico commonwealth status, influenced by an appreciation of the United States's form of government and also by the belief that such an association would aid Puerto Rico's development.

governor had been appointed by the United States. As governor, Muñoz Marín continued to work for the industrialization of Puerto Rico.

Working for the good of his country

Muñoz Marín began a series of programs implemented during his terms as senator and governor of the island. One of these programs was Operation Bootstrap, intended to help improve the economic situation of the island. The program attracted investors from the United States by offering, among other things, tax exemption for 12 years. There were some positive results for Puerto Rico, such as higher incomes and a lower level of unemployment. Other programs included Operation Serenidad (Serenity), which encouraged enjoyment of the arts.

In 1952 Congress in the United States voted for a constitution for Puerto Rico, and on July 25 of that year Puerto Rico became an Estado Libre Asociado, or a commonwealth of the United States. Under this new status, Puerto Rico could elect its own officials without U.S. intervention; it could also create domestic laws. Puerto Rico was also allowed to fly its own flag, which had been impossible under its previous undefined political status. Muñoz Marín was governor of Puerto Rico until 1964, after which he remained in the Senate until 1968.

Legacy

Muñoz Marín was immensely popular, and his charisma and intellect helped him achieve his objectives for the island. However, Muñoz Marín also received much criticism from his opponents. The church, for example, objected to his support of birth control, and nationalists argued that Puerto Rico's status as a commonwealth was little more than a new form of colonialism. Muñoz Marín thought that commonwealth status granted Puerto Ricans autonomy without losing the support of the United States. Muñoz Marín died on April 30, 1982, in San Juan, Puerto Rico.

See also: Muñoz Rivera, Luis

Further reading: Bernierd-Grand, Carmen T. *Poet and Politician of Puerto Rico: Don Luis Muñoz Marín.* New York, NY: Orchard Books, 1995.
www.munoz-marin.org (Web page of the Fundación Luis Muñoz Marín (LMM Foundation).

KEY DATES

1898   Born in San Juan, Puerto Rico, on February 18.

1932   Joins the Partido Liberal; elected senator in Puerto Rico.

1937   Creates the group Acción Social Independentista (ASI or Social Independence Action).

1938   Helps create the Popular Democratic Party (PDP).

1940   Elected president of the Senate in Puerto Rico.

1949   Becomes the first democratically elected governor of Puerto Rico; stays in office until 1964.

1952   The Puerto Rican Constitution is drafted and approved by the U.S. Senate; Puerto Rico becomes a commonwealth of the United States.

1963   Awarded the presidential medal of freedom by President John F. Kennedy.

1980   Dies on April 30 in San Juan, Puerto Rico.

MUÑOZ RIVERA, Luis

Politician

Luis Muñoz Rivera is one of the most distinguished men in Puerto Rico's history. He dedicated his life to greater independence for his home nation, struggling first against Spanish colonial rule and then against U.S. control.

Muñoz Rivera founded a political party and used his diplomatic skills to persuade foreign statesmen to support his cause. Muñoz Rivera was also a journalist. He started several newspapers, using them to argue in favor of Puerto Rican independence. He is also considered one of Puerto Rico's best political poets. Muñoz Rivera's lasting achievement, however, was to persuade the U.S. government to grant Puerto Ricans U.S. citizenship and allow them to elect their own legislature.

KEY DATES

1859 Born in Barranquitas, Puerto Rico, on July 17.

1887 Founds the Autonomist Party.

1890 Starts *La Democracia* newspaper.

1891 Publishes *Retamas*.

1897 Autonomist Charter grants independence to Puerto Rico from the Spanish government.

1898 Appointed secretary of state and chief of cabinet of Puerto Rico on July 21. Puerto Rico comes under U.S. military control on July 25.

1899 Founds *El Territorio* newspaper.

1900 Foraker Act makes Puerto Rico U.S. territory.

1901 Founds the *Puerto Rico Herald*.

1902 Publishes *Tropicales*.

1904 Helps found the Unionist Party.

1906 Begins to serve in Puerto Rico's House of Representatives.

1910 Appointed to the U.S. House of Representatives as Puerto Rico's commissioner.

1916 Dies in Luquillo, Puerto Rico, on November 15.

1917 Jones-Shafroth Act signed into law to replace Foraker Act, giving U.S. citizenship to Puerto Ricans.

A man with a sharp pen

Muñoz Rivera was born in 1859 in Barranquitas, Puerto Rico. He attended a nearby private school, then worked in his father's store.

The island had been under Spanish rule for nearly 400 years, and from an early age Muñoz Rivera was a passionate believer in political independence. In 1887 Muñoz Rivera became a founding member of the Autonomist political party. The group sought an independent government for Puerto Rico while retaining colonial links with Spain. Three years later Muñoz Rivera started *La Democracia,* the first of several newspapers. Muñoz Rivera used the publication and his flair for writing to win supporters for the cause of Puerto Rican independence. He was also invited to write similar articles in a number of other Puerto Rican newspapers.

In 1891 Muñoz Rivera published his first collection of poetry, *Retamas*. His most important collection, *Tropicales*, followed in 1902.

National statesman

Muñoz Rivera traveled to Spain in 1893 to further his education. He took a close interest in the Spanish political system. On returning to his homeland, he helped to draft a plan, known as the Plan de Ponce, for Puerto Rican political and administrative independence.

Muñoz Rivera returned to Spain two years later accompanied by several supporters. They met the leader of the Liberal Party, Praxedas Mateo Sagasta (1825–1903). A pact was signed promising that, should Sagasta come to power, Puerto Rico would be granted autonomy.

In 1897 the Spanish prime minister was assassinated by a terrorist. Sagasta was swept to power, and proved true to his word. In November 1897 Puerto Rico was granted self-government under the terms of Muñoz Rivera's Autonomist Charter. The new government took some time to establish, and Muñoz Rivera was appointed both secretary of state and chief of the cabinet, effective from July 21, 1898.

From Spanish to U.S. control

Puerto Rico's freedom was to prove short lived. Spain and the United States went to war in 1898, and Puerto Rico was handed to the United States as part of a treaty to end the hostilities.

LEGACY

The Jones-Shafroth Act of 1917 put in place the present system of government in Puerto Rico, and awarded all islanders U.S. citizenship. The act is better known as the Jones Act for its sponsor, Congressman Walter Jones.

The act created a government that was based on that of a U.S. state. The Puerto Rico legislature has two houses. The Senate has 19 members, and there are 39 representatives in the lower house. The head of state is the governor of Puerto Rico. At first

the position was appointed by the U.S. president, who also had a final veto over any law passed by the island's legislature. In 1946 Puerto Ricans were given the right to elect their own governor. The governor now holds the veto on laws passed by the Senate.

On July 25, 1898, U.S. troops took control of Puerto Rico and established a military government. Muñoz Rivera was then replaced by a U.S.-appointed government that swept away many of the changes that Muñoz Rivera had fought so hard to secure.

Most people were pleased to see the end of Spanish rule, but opinion about the future was roughly divided into three schools of thought. The first wanted total independence, the second wanted Puerto Rico to be incorporated into the United States, while the third wanted a compromise: to have their own government with a high degree of control, yet to remain part of the United States. Muñoz Rivera lobbied the United States to allow the islanders to choose their own future.

Nondemocratic government

The Foraker Act of 1900, also known as the Organic Act, dashed Muñoz Rivera's hopes. It established that Puerto Rico was to have a governor and an executive council appointed by the U.S. president. A nonresident commissioner for Puerto Rico would be a member of the U.S. Congress, but without voting rights. The people of Puerto Rico would have the opportunity to elect representatives to an assembly with limited power. Once again, Muñoz Rivera started his campaign for full civil rights.

The United States also imposed a trade blockade preventing Puerto Rican farmers from exporting their crops. Muñoz Rivera took up their cause, and founded another newspaper in 1899, *El Territorio*, to denounce the blockade. He also traveled to the United States to try and establish a free trade agreement. He was unsuccessful and decided that a move to New York would allow him to make better progress.

U.S. resident

In 1901 Muñoz Rivera started a third newspaper in New York, the *Puerto Rican Herald*, which is still in circulation. It appeared in English and Spanish and its aim was to

teach Americans about Puerto Rico's political and economic situation. The first edition featured an open letter to President McKinley condemning the Foraker Act.

Three years later Muñoz Rivera returned to Puerto Rico, where he helped to found the Unionist Party, which became the most important political party for 20 years. Between 1906 and 1910 he served in Puerto Rico's House of Delegates.

In 1910 Muñoz Rivera was appointed to the U.S. House of Representatives as Puerto Rico's nonresident commissioner. He moved to Washington, D.C., taking up his position on January 4, 1911. Although he was a great public speaker in Spanish, he did not speak fluent English, and attended evening classes to learn to present his arguments with greater success.

The Jones Act

Thanks to Muñoz Rivera's long campaign, on May 23, 1916, the U.S. House of Representatives passed the Jones-Shafroth Act. This important act granted a large measure of independence by entitling Puerto Ricans to elect candidates to their own senate and house of representatives. It also extended civil rights to Puerto Ricans, and allowed them U.S. citizenship.

The act entitled the U.S. president and governor to veto any law passed, and the United States also maintained control over tax, immigration, and defense matters. Muñoz Rivera did not live to see the act come into effect in 1917. He died of cancer in 1916 in Luquillo, Puerto Rico. His son, Luis Muñoz Marín, accomplished the dream they shared by becoming the first elected governor of Puerto Rico in 1949.

See also: Muñoz Marín, Luis.

Further reading: Reynolds, Mack. *Puerto Rican Patriot: The Life of Luis Muñoz Rivera.* New York, NY: Crowell-Collier Press; 1969.
www.puertorico-herald.org/issues/2001/vol5n06/Profile
LMunozRivera-en.shtml (biography).

MURRIETA, Joaquín
Bandit

Joaquín Murrieta is a legendary figure from the time of the California Gold Rush in the 1850s. Also known as the Mexican Robin Hood, or the Robin Hood of El Dorado, Murrieta was either an infamous bandit or a Mexican patriot, depending on one's point of view. For his admirers, Murrieta symbolizes resistance to Anglo-American domination in California.

Early life

Although there are many legends surrounding Joaquín Murrieta, very few verifiable facts exist about his life. By most accounts, Murrieta was born in 1829 in Trincheras, in the northern part of the state of Sonora, northwestern Mexico. Other accounts place his birth near Alamos in the southern part of the state of Sonora in 1830. What is agreed, however, is that the young Joaquín eventually married Rosa Féliz and, along with Jesús Murrieta and Rosa's three brothers, went to California upon news of a great gold strike in 1849.

Accounts differ substantially about what ensued after Murrieta's arrival at the gold-mining camp. According to common legend, Murrieta's wife was raped and killed by Anglo-American miners, his brother was wrongly hanged,

◀ *A romantic watercolor of Murrieta, painted by Charles Nahl in 1859.*

and he himself was tied to a tree and severely whipped for a crime that he did not commit. However, there is little evidence to confirm that this is actually what happened. Similar things happened to other Mexicans living in California at the end of the Mexican War (1846–1848) and before and after the Treaty of Guadalupe Hidalgo (1848), which ceded a large part of Mexico's northern territory to the United States.

Whatever the truth, most writers agree that Murrieta was probably mistreated, and as a result hated Anglos. The legend describes how Murrieta tracked down and killed the five men who had raped and murdered his wife. He formed a bandit group, and began a life of robbery and murder that allegedly spanned the length and breadth of the Mother Lode region of the Sierra Nevada Mountains. Virtually every community in the Sierra foothills has one or more stories of Murrieta during the three years from 1850 to 1853. One story suggests that Murrieta may have eventually been killed by a hired gunman named Harry Love on July 25, 1853.

Fact or fiction

Admirers see Murrieta as a daring Mexican Robin Hood. Critics say that he was a vicious killer. The mystery surrounding Murrieta's life and death, his Robin Hood status as one who suffers injustices and fights against impossible odds, and his inspirational appeal to generations of Chicano activists make it difficult to separate the history from the myth and the fact from the fiction. We may never know who Murrieta really was.

Further reading: Boessenecker, J. B. *Gold Dust & Gunsmoke: Tales of Gold Rush Outlaws, Gunfighters, Lawmen, and Vigilantes.* New York, NY: John Wiley & Sons, 1999.
http://www.ameri-land.com/joaquin.htm (Ameriland Realty Web site relating some of Murrieta's legendary exploits).

KEY DATES

1829 Born in Trincheras, Mexico, at about this time.

1849 Moves to California.

1850 Arrives at Murphy's Camp on the banks of the Stanislaus River.

1852 Organizes an *"acordada"* among Mexicanos and other Latinos for self-protection.

1853 California governor John Bigler posts a $1,000 reward for the capture of Joaquin Murrieta.

1853 Captain Harry Love claims to have killed Murrieta.

MUSIC AND HISPANIC AMERICANS

Hispanic music is an important part of both Latino and mainstream U.S. popular culture. It comprises many musical genres from different Latin cultures and countries. Influenced by music from Spain, other countries in Europe, and Africa, as well as by that of indigenous native groups, Hispanic music covers a wide range of sounds from the pan-pipe music of the Andes and the *corrido*s of Mexico to Afro-Cuban salsa, Latin jazz, and Puerto Rican reggaeton.

During the 20th century Hispanic music and dance increasingly became part of mainstream U.S. culture. Latin independent record labels, such as Tico, Alegre, and Fania, and Latin music and Spanish-language radio stations helped Hispanic stars such as Tito Puente and Celia Cruz cross over to appeal to non-Hispanic U.S. audiences. Latin clubs, playing mambo, salsa, and other Hispanic music, sprang up in major U.S. cities, New York and Miami among them. Musicals such as the Oscar-winning *West Side Story* also helped popularize Hispanic music.

In the late 20th and early 21st centuries Hispanic American superstars such as Christina Aguilera and Enrique Iglesias emerged to achieve global success. Their records sold not just to the 41 million or so Hispanics living in the United States, but also to Latino and non-Hispanic audiences around the world. While these stars won international awards for their singles and albums, the U.S. music industry also implemented

award ceremonies specifically to honor Latin musicians, such as the Latin Grammys and the *Billboard* Latin Music Awards.

In 2005 the Recording Industry Association of America (RIAA) reported that Latin music was outpacing sales of all other music genres. Latin music generated huge sums of money: In 2004, U.S. music stores ordered 21.6 percent more CDs by Latin artists than in the preceding year, generating more than $650 million in sales.

Origins

Music played an important part in the culture and celebrations of indigenous groups in Latin America prior to the explorer Christopher Columbus's "discovery" of the Americas in

Conjunto music, which is extremely popular among Mexicans and Mexican Americans, particularly in South Texas, draws on many different music traditions, including Spanish classical music, Tejano, German, Czech, and Bohemian music.

1492. In Mexico, for example, the Aztecs believed that certain instruments were sacred. The vertical *huehuetl* drum was the "king" and the horizontal *teponaztli* was the "queen" of Aztec musical instruments. The Aztecs believed that they were gods banished to earth in the form of drums. Clay and reed pipes and rattles were other instruments popular among indigenous groups such as the Aztecs and the Maya.

MARIACHI AND RELIGION

Since before the Spanish arrived in Mexico, music played a vital part in religious celebrations. Native groups used instruments such as rattles, conch shells, and clay flutes to create their music. The Spanish brought with them a new religion, Roman Catholicism, and a range of new instruments such as violins and harps. Local people adopted these instruments, often making their own versions to play.

In Mexico mariachi music, which blended Spanish and native Indian styles, was often played at baptisms, weddings, and funerals. As the Catholic Church became more popular in Mexico, mariachi music was also played at other celebrations: "Las Mañanitas" is a traditional song used to celebrate saints' days, for example.

The mariachi ensemble originally played the *son* (a traditional folk song that drew on Spanish, Mexican, and African traditions). By the 1950s the mariachi group played other music such as *rancheras, cumbias, corridos,* and *huapangos*. Today a complete mariachi ensemble can include as many as eight violins, two trumpets, the *vihuela* (a round-backed guitar), a *guitarrón* (a deep-voiced guitar that serves as the bass), and a Mexican folk harp.

Since 1966 the mariachi mass has become popular in Spanish-speaking Catholic communities. Introduced by Canadian priest Father Juan Marco LeClerc to help attract more local people to Sunday mass in Cuernavaca, Mexico, the mass was accompanied by mariachi music. It proved so popular that the mariachi mass was moved to the Cathedral of Cuernavaca. Similar masses are today held all over Mexico and the United States.

After the conquest of Mexico in 1521, the Spanish began to establish settlements in Latin America. They brought with them a new culture and way of life. The romance ballad, a form popular in Spain that told epic tales of love, war, and feats of heroism, became popular in Latin America. Traveling troubadours performed these songs to audiences, playing European instruments such as the guitar and violin. The *corrido*, which emerged in the mid-19th century in Mexico and Texas, evolved from the romance ballad.

Spanish and Portuguese settlers brought millions of Africans to Latin America through the slave trade. African rhythms, vocal styles, dances, and instruments influenced and were incorporated into different Latin music styles such as mariachi music in Mexico, rumba and salsa in Cuba, and the *cumbia* in Colombia.

As different European migrant groups began to settle in Latin America, they also brought with them their own musical traditions. Germans introduced the polka and instruments such as the accordion, which became an essential part of conjunto music. In Argentina, Spanish influences, French contradancing, and Italian music all contributed to the tango.

The Southwest
From the mid-19th century, Anglo Americans became increasingly aware of Hispanic music and culture. The 1848 Treaty of Guadalupe Hidalgo ceded more than 50 percent of Mexican territory to the United States. About 100,000 Mexicans subsequently became U.S. citizens. As increasing numbers of non-Hispanic settlers moved into the U.S. Southwest a unique culture developed in the region.

The *corrido* and *canción* became popular song forms in the southwestern states. The early *corridos,* ballads sung by a *corridista* to a simple tune in fast waltz or polka time, told of the difficulties faced by Mexicans adjusting to their new lives in the United States. The "hero *corrido,*" for example, usually featured a larger-than-life Mexican hero who defended his community against the threat of hostile non-Hispanics.

The *canción* was more lyrical in tone and songs were usually about love. The *canción-corrido,* describing the experiences of life in the Hispanic Southwest, became popular there from the 1920s to the 1940s. For example, "El Deportado" ("The Deported One"), a popular song in the 1930s, told of the Mexican immigrant experience in the United States. The *corrido* later became popular with Hispanic activists, who used it to highlight their causes. The 1949 song "Discriminación a un Mártir" ("Discrimination against a Martyr") told the true story of Félix Longoria, a soldier killed in action who was denied burial rights by a Texas funeral home. It therefore brought attention to the discrimination suffered by Hispanic servicemen and women.

Two types of music were particularly popular among Mexican communities in Texas: conjunto (known as *música norteña* outside of Texas) and *orquesta tejana*, known more simply as *orquesta*.

Conjunto bands became popular at working-class dances and featured an accordionist either playing solo or accompanied by a *tambora de rancho* (ranch drum) or *bajo sexto* (12-string guitar). Conjunto drew on several music traditions, including the polka, the mazurka,

and the *huapango* (from Tamaulipas and northern Vera Cruz). Conjunto musicians such as Narciso Martínez and Santiago Almeida brought the music to wider audiences when they began to record with major record companies in the 1930s. Martínez revolutionized conjunto music by concentrating on the treble buttons on the accordion, leaving Almeida to pick up the bass on the *bajo sexto*. Martínez and Almeida's music influenced other conjunto musicians such as Valerio Longoria and Paulino Bernal.

Orquestas were also popular in the Southwest. While early *orquestas* were simple affairs, featuring a violin and a couple of guitars, by the 1920s the larger *orquesta típica* (folk orchestra) often played at local celebrations. These bands ranged in size from 5 to 20 musicians playing violins, guitars, and other instruments. The musicians often dressed up in *charro* (cowboy)

outfits, similar to those used by mariachi bands. By the 1930s these bands had been replaced by big bands. The later *orquesta* played both Latin music, such as rumbas and boleros, and American music such as swing, boogie, and the fox-trot.

In many U.S. cities such *orquestas* became extremely popular. Lalo Guerrero emerged as one of the leading bandleaders, fusing swing with different elements of Latin music and often utilizing caló, Chicano street language.

The "Latin tinge"

Hispanic music had a considerable influence on the development of jazz. The first Cuban migrants arrived in New Orleans in 1809, bringing their music and traditions with them. By the mid-1840s *habanera*, a style that has a short, repeating 2/4 rhythmic figure in the bass line, was established in New Orleans, Louisiana. In 1914 the African American composer W. C. Handy wrote "St. Louis Blues," based on Cuban *habanera* music. A few years later Jelly Roll Morton wrote another *habanera*-based jazz tune, "New Orleans Blues."

Other influential jazz and blues artists began to incorporate Latin rhythms in their work. The pianist Art Tatum called this "the Latin tinge." Some of Duke Ellington's signature tunes, such as "Perdido" and "Caravan," show the Latin roots of their composer, the Puerto Rican-born trombonist Juan Tizol.

From the 1930s increasing numbers of immigrants from Mexico, Puerto Rico, Cuba, and other Latin countries settled in the United States, particularly in big

---

KEY DATES

1848   Treaty of Guadalupe Hidalgo cedes more than 50 percent of Mexican territory to the United States; *corrido* becomes popular in the Southwest.

1914   W. C. Handy writes the "St. Louis Blues" based on Cuban *habanera*.

1930s   Spanish-language radio stations begin broadcasting; musicians such as Narciso Martínez begin recording conjunto.

1948   Tico Records founded.

1959   Ritchie Valens has hit with "La Bamba"; musical *West Side Story* a hit.

1964   Fania Records founded.

1992   Selena is the first Tejana to sell more than 300,000 albums with *Entre a Mi Mundo* (*Come into My World*).

1998   Big Pun becomes the first Latino solo rapper to have a platinum record.

1999   Christina Aguilera wins the Grammy for best new artist.

2000   Latin Grammys launched.

2005   Daddy Yankee wins a Latin Grammy.

cities such as New York, Miami, and Chicago. Big bands, featuring such stars as Eddie Palmieri, Tito Puente, and Tito Rodríguez, and performing the mambo, rumba, and other types of Latin music, flourished in these cities. Latin stars played at a range of stylish clubs such as the Palladium, which called itself "the home of the mambo." Mixed crowds of African Americans, Latinos, and Anglos gathered at these clubs to listen to new songs and learn the latest Latin dances.

The emergence of Spanish-language radio stations in the 1920s and 1930s, broadcasting Hispanic news and music, also helped bring Latin music to the attention of wider audiences. In addition, Hispanic music was featured in several hit Hollywood movies of this period. Fred Astaire and Ginger Rogers danced the rumba, while Brazilian singer and actor Carmen Miranda made her debut in *Flying Down to Rio.*

The rumba craze began in the early 1930s, with Cuban singer Antonio Machín's version of "El Manisero" ("The Peanut Vendor"). The celebrated bandleader Xavier Cugat and his orchestra maintained the craze, which flourished well into the 1940s.

Big record labels such as RCA Victor, Decca, and Columbia began recording Latin music for Hispanic and non-Hispanic audiences. In the 1940s several independent record labels specializing in Latin music were also founded, Tico Records (*see box*) and IDEAL among them. These labels helped Latin stars reach non-Hispanic audiences.

Mario Bauzá and Chano Pozo played an important part in the development of bebop jazz when they joined Dizzy Gillespie's band in the late 1940s. Several important jazz musicians such as Charlie Parker, Buddy Rich, Stan Getz, and Benny Goodman also began to work with Latin artists, including Tito Puente, Ray Barretto, and Desi Arnaz.

Changing times
In the 1950s and 1960s, Latin music began to influence and in turn be influenced by other music genres, including rhythm and blues and rock 'n' roll. Lalo Guerrero, a big swing and blues star in the 1940s and early 1950s, began recording rock 'n' roll and doo-wop songs such as "Do You Believe in Reincarnation." He also produced a string of rock 'n' roll parodies such as "Elvis Perez."

In 1958 the Mexican American singer–songwriter Ritchie Valens had hits with "Donna" and "Come On Let's Go." Valens's huge 1959 hit "La Bamba" was a reworked version of an old Mexican folk song. Valens's career was cut short when he was killed in the same plane crash that killed Buddy Holly. Despite his short career, Valens influenced many other Latin rock 'n' roll stars.

After Valens's death, his manager Bob Keane invited Chan Romero to record some sessions for his record label, DelFi. Romero recorded one of his own songs "Hippy Hippy Shake," which was later released in Britain and

Xavier Cugat (far right, in profile) was among the musicians who performed Latin music in Hollywood films such as Chicago Syndicate *(1955); Abbe Lane (center), Cugat's real wife, performed the rumba in the movie.*

TICO RECORDS

In the 1940s the first independent labels specializing in Latin music were founded. Foremost among them was Tico Records. Formed in New York in 1948 by record executive George Goldner and Art "Pancho" Raymond, host of a Latin radio show on station WLIB, the label was named after Xavier Cugat's hit song "Tico Tico No Fubá."

Among the first musicians signed by Tico were two veteran Latin stars, the percussionist Tito Puente and the singer Tito Rodríguez, who had been lead vocalist with Xavier Cugat's band and had his own orchestra, The Mambo Devils.

In 1949 Tico had its first hit, the mambo song "Abaniquito." Released by Puente, the song featured Cuban vocalist Vicentico Valdés, who also signed with Tico, and trumpeter Mario Bauzá. During his time at Tico, Puente made more than 80 recordings, including the groundbreaking album *Puente in Percussion*, featuring Mongo Santamaría, Potato Valdés, and Willie Bobo. The celebrated singer and bandleader Tito Rodríguez also had hits with his newly named band Los Lobos del Mambo, including "Chiqui Bop."

In 1950 Raymond left Tico, and Goldner formed a new partnership with New York nightclub owner Joe Kolsky. In 1957 Goldner's gambling debts led him to sell his share in Tico to Morris Levy, Kolsky's boss.

During the 1950s, Tico emerged as the leading Latin label: Its stable included Joe Loco, José Fajardo, Machito and His Afro-Cubans, and José Alfredo Jiménez. In the 1960s Tico competed successfully against other Latin labels such as Alegre, releasing records by Ray Barretto, Eddie Palmieri, Celia Cruz, La Lupe, and Rafael Cortijo and His Combo, featuring the salsa star Ismael Rivera.

From 1967 onward, many Tico stars, including Palmieri and Barretto, left to record with other labels. Although Tico recorded emerging stars such as Julio Iglesias, by the 1970s Levy wanted to offload it. In 1974 he sold it to Johnny Pacheco and Jerry Masucci's label Fania. Many people believe that they bought Tico in order to eliminate competition for their salsa-dominated label.

---

rerecorded with great success by the Swinging Blue Jeans.

Los Angeles produced dozens of Mexican American rock 'n' roll acts, including Thee Midniters, who had a hit with the instrumental song "Whittier Boulevard" in 1965. Thee Midniters were also one of the first rock acts to openly sing about Chicano themes: One of their songs was entitled "The Ballad of César Chávez." Other rock bands also incorporated the Tex-Mex sound. One was the San Antonio-based Sir Douglas Quintet, which had a hit in 1965 with "She's about a Mover."

Trini López also emerged as a star in the 1960s. Signed by Frank Sinatra's label Reprise, López had hits with such songs as "If I Had a Hammer," which was number one in 25 countries and a Top-40 hit in the United States.

Salsa

At the same time, another Latin-influenced style of music, salsa, was taking the country by storm. Fania Records, formed by Jerry Masucci and Johnny Pacheco, became one of the leading promoters of salsa, recording such stars as Willie Colón and Celia Cruz. The Fania All-Stars, the house orchestra featuring the label's top bandleaders, musicians, and singers, promoted salsa through concerts and several successful albums.

In the late 1960s, Latin soul emerged in East Harlem and the Bronx. Musicians such as Ray Barretto, Mongo Santamaría, and Machito fused elements of salsa with jazz and rhythm and blues to create groundbreaking albums such as Barretto's *Acid* and *Machito Goes to Memphis*.

These bands preceded other successful Latin groups that fused elements of different genres to create a distinctive style of music. Carlos Santana, for example, combined psychedelic rock guitar with Latin rhythms and instrumentation. Santana merged jazz and blues with Afro-Latin music from Puerto Rico, Cuba, and Brazil to create his popular and distinctive music.

In the 1970s and 1980s Hispanic bands became increasingly popular with U.S. audiences. The successful band Los

Reggaeton star Daddy Yankee performs at New York's Madison Square Garden on August 27, 2005.

Lobos, for example, blended rock, blues, soul, Afro-Latin, jazz, folk, and regional Mexican styles in their music, creating a unique sound. Los Lobos have collaborated with leading musicians such as Paul Simon.

Cuban music
Cuban musicians have contributed to the development of U.S. music across several different musical genres. Many Cuban musicians came to the United States in the first half of the 20th century, playing with such bands as Machito and the Afro-Cubans.

African American musician Dizzy Gillespie also promoted Cuban music, working with such musicians as the congo player Luciano Pozo y González. Gillespie performed in Cuba with the groundbreaking band Irakere and sponsored one of its founders, Arturo Sandoval, when he defected to the United States.

Many Cuban musicians came to the United States after Fidel Castro's rise to power in 1959. Emilio Estefan was one such star. Estefan was responsible for one of the most successful Cuban

American bands of the late 20th century, Gloria Estefan and the Miami Sound Machine. The band produced hugely successful music in Spanish and English that appealed to both Latino and non-Latino audiences.

Other successful Cubans include the rappers Sen Dog and Louis Freese, members of the band Cypress Hill.

Influence
Today Latinos and Latino musical styles continue to have a major influence on music in the United States, from non-Hispanic musicians such as Madonna, who has incorporated Latin beats in her music, to billion-dollar selling Hispanic artists such as Ricky Martin, Jennifer Lopez, Christina Aguilera, and Shakira.

In the late 1970s and early 1980s, Latinos played an important role in the development of hip-hop, particularly on the East Coast, where New York-based Puerto Ricans were among the first rappers. Artists such as Charlie Chase of the Cold Crush Brothers and Master OC were leading exponents of early rap. In the

1990s rappers such as Fat Joe and Big Pun became important. Big Pun was the first Latino solo rapper to have a platinum record.

Mexican Americans also contributed to the development of West Coast rap, incorporating traditional Mexican genres into their music. Kid Frost was the first Chicano to gain national recognition with this style when he relesed the album *Hispanic Causing Panic* in 1990. Other prominent Latino rappers include Spanish Fly, Krazy Race, Sir Dyno, and Lil Rob.

In the 1990s, musicians began fusing rap with jazz, salsa, merengue, and reggae, creating reggaeton. Important innovators include Tego Calderón, Vico C, Ivy Queen, and Daddy Yankee, who received a Latin Grammy artist of the year award in 2005.

See also: Aguilera, Christina; Big Pun; Cruz, Celia; Cypress Hill; Cugat, Xavier; Daddy Yankee; Estefan, Emilio; Estefan Gloria; Fat Joe; Hispanic Identity and Popular Culture; Iglesias, Enrique; Longoria, Félix; Lopez, Jennifer; Martin, Ricky; Martínez, Narciso; Media, Spanish-Language; Palmieri, Eddie; Puente, Tito; Queen, Ivy; Sandoval, Arturo; Santana, Carlos; Valens, Ritchie

Further reading: Habell-Pallan, Michelle, and Mary Romero (eds.). *Latino/a Popular Culture.* New York, NY: New York University Press, 2002. Stavans, Ilan (ed.). *Encyclopedia Latina: History, Culture, and Society in the United States.* Danbury, CT: Grolier, 2005. http://www.lamusica.com/music.html (site dedicated to Latin music).

NAJERA, Eduardo
Basketball Player

Establishing a loyal fan base by playing with heart and taking on bigger players, Eduardo Najera is a Mexican player in the National Basketball Association (NBA). A tough rebounder and tenacious defender, Najera is only the second Mexican ever to play in the NBA (Horacio Llamas became the first in 1996, when he joined the Phoenix Suns). Najera also receives wide praise for his strong character and his off-court charity work.

Early life
Born in 1976 in Meoqui, a suburb of Chihuahua, Mexico, Eduardo Alonso Najera was the sixth and youngest child of Servando Najera and Rose Irene Perez. His early ambition was to emulate his father, who had been the star shortstop for a local professional baseball team. However, in the ninth grade, Eduardo was barred from the school baseball team because of his height: He had grown to 6 feet 6 inches (1.98m). When Najera was 15, a neighbor set up a makeshift basketball hoop, and Eduardo soon became hooked on the game. After three years at two different Mexican high schools, Najera received a scholarship offer from Cornerstone Christian School in San Antonio, Texas, and transferred for his senior year. Najera averaged nearly 25 points a game, and earned a scholarship to the University of Oklahoma.

Tough competitor
Najera gained a gritty reputation. After his four-year career at Oklahoma, he ranked third all-time for the team in minutes played (3,856), fourth in steals (193), fifth in rebounds (910), sixth in blocks (89), and eighth in points

▲ *Eduardo Najera during a Dallas Mavericks' practice session in 2002.*

(1,646). Najera was named a third-team All-American in 2000. That June, Najera was selected in the second round (38th overall) by the NBA's Houston Rockets. His draft rights were immediately traded to the Dallas Mavericks, with whom he played his first four professional seasons. Najera was traded to the Golden State Warriors in August 2004, and in midseason was then transferred to the Denver Nuggets. In his first five NBA seasons, Najera scored in double figures 42 times, and had 12 career double-doubles.

Najera stresses the importance of education, and teaches basketball to fellow Latinos. He has a strong following among Mexican youth. In 2004, he set up the Eduardo Najera Foundation in Dallas to offer scholarships and community programs for Hispanic youth. In the summer of 2005, the NBA standout players hosted the first Eduardo Najera All-Star Game in his home state of Chihuahua. Approximately 15,000 fans attended the game, and all the money raised went to the Eduardo Najera Basketball League, a youth league for about 5,500 boys and girls that began play in six Mexican states in April 2005.

KEY DATES

1976 Born in Meoqui, Chihuahua, Mexico, on July 11.

2000 Named a third-team All-American in his senior year at Oklahoma by the Associated Press.

2003 Represents Mexico in the Tournament of the Americas in Puerto Rico.

2004 Traded by the Mavericks to the Golden State Warriors in a seven-player deal on August 24.

2005 Traded from the Warriors to the Denver Nuggets in a four-player swap on February 24.

Further reading: Wahl, Grant. "One Tough Hombre." *Sports Illustrated* Vol. 92, No. 3. January 24, 2000.
http://www.nba.com/playerfile/eduardo_najera (NBA player Web site)

Since the 19th century national organizations have played an important role in the socio-economic, political, and cultural maintenance and advancement of Latinos in the United States. Groups such as the League of United Latin American Citizens (LULAC) and the American GI Forum (AGIF) have historically been central to the Hispanic struggle for equality and the attainment of better civil rights. These organizations are important because they represent the major interests and political agendas of the Latino community and also those of particular groups within the Hispanic community.

Fighting back

Often perceived as racially and intellectually inferior by Anglo-Americans in the late-19th and early-20th centuries, Hispanics in the United States were frequently forced to accept low-paid jobs in exploitative conditions and to live in substandard housing. Similarly, Hispanics were forced to send their children to inferior, segregated schools in which the speaking of Spanish was discouraged or forbidden.

Some activists joined together to try to support their community from within. They formed mutual aid societies, or *mutualistas*, which provided a variety of insurance, burial plans, and credit unions/savings plans, as well as promoting cultural and political interests. One of the oldest of them was the Alianza Americana (American Alliance), founded in 1894 in Tucson, Arizona. By that time, Cubans had also established several *mutualistas* in Florida.

Some campaigners realized that they would only be able to bring about effective and positive change if they had greater support from the Hispanic community. From the late 19th century, many intellectuals, journalists, and philanthropists began to air their grievances in such newspapers as the Texas-based *La Crónica*, publishing articles about the evils of segregation, the brutal treatment of Hispanics by law-enforcement forces, and the second-class status of women.

In 1911, Nicasio Idar, the proprietor of *La Crónica*, organized El Primer Congreso Mexicanista, a conference to discuss issues of racial inequality. It resulted in the establishment of several civil rights organizations, including La Liga Femenil

Louis Tellez, a delegate from New Mexico, addresses the annual convention of the American GI Forum in the late 1950s.

Mexicanista (The Mexican Female League), one of the first attempts by Mexican women to unite for social and political change.

Civil rights

During the 20th century, several key national organizations were established to help Latinos address specific issues in the United States. LULAC, the AGIF, and the National Organization of La Raza (The Race) emerged as leading advocates of Hispanic rights.

Established in 1929, LULAC supports the interests of U.S. Latinos by promoting citizenship and the English language as the paths to political power and personal success. It has been key in challenging civil rights abuses in the courts: In 1954, for example, in *Hernandez v. State of Texas*, it challenged the lack of Mexican Americans serving on juries. The Supreme Court ruled the exclusion unconstitutional.

LULAC has worked hard to improve Latino voting registration. It also holds public symposiums on language and immigration issues, and has provided assistance through the LULAC National Scholarship Fund and LULAC National Educational Service Centers to about 100,000 of the more than one million Hispanic students who go to college in the United States.

American GI Forum

Among the issues that concerned Hispanics during and after World War II (1939–1945) was the treatment of Latinos serving in the military. In 1948, the AGIF was established by physician Hector P. García to promote and protect Latino veterans' rights. The AGIF, like LULAC, soon expanded its scope beyond Mexican Americans in the Southwest to include all Latinos across the country. It also began working with other

KEY DATES	
1929	LULAC established.
1948	American GI Forum founded.
1968	National Council of La Raza founded as Southwest Council of La Raza.
1979	Hispanic Chamber of Commerce founded in New Mexico.
1986	National Hispanic Media Coalition founded.
1988	Latino National Political Survey conducted.
2006	LULAC and other civil rights bodies organize marches across the United States to protest proposed immigration reform.

organizations, including LULAC, with which it collaborated on *Hernandez v. State of Texas*.

National Council of La Raza

Founded in 1968, the National Council of La Raza (NCLR) is another important organization that was formed to support Latino rights and combat such issues as discrimination and poverty. It has more than 300 affiliated community-based organizations, and reaches Latinos in 41 states and Puerto Rico. It provides research, analysis, and advice, particularly on assets and investments, civil rights and

immigration, education, employment, economic status, and health issues.

Labor unions

Another important area in which national organizations have been key in helping Latinos achieve better rights is employment.

Organizations such as LULAC have long battled to highlight the problems faced by many Latinos, particularly migrant workers, arguing for more protective legislation, but it was really through unionization that Hispanic laborers' rights and conditions improved.

U.S. HISPANIC CHAMBER OF COMMERCE

The U.S. Hispanic Chamber of Commerce (USHCC) was founded in 1979 in New Mexico to promote the interests of Hispanic business owners and Hispanic communities across the country. There are now close to 150 chapters throughout the United States, representing over one million Hispanic-owned and operated businesses. The main base of operations for the USHCC is Washington, D.C.

The USHCC provides vital assistance to small-business owners by helping them gain access to loans and government programs. It also helps create opportunities for Latinos to become involved with Hispanic-friendly corporations and promotes ethnic diversity in boardrooms and executive offices.

Some critics, however, claim the USHCC is a redundant

organization that promotes separatism since Latino business owners could become part of established local Chambers of Commerce. Many Hispanic business owners support the USHCC, arguing that its importance lies in providing Latinos with economic self-determination and also a certain amount of protection from the discrimination they previously experienced.

Latinos have often had the most dangerous jobs with the worst pay and few if any benefits. Various government policies have served to undermine Latino labor rights. The Bracero Program, for example, signed into being by Mexico and the United States in 1942, supplied cheap Mexican labor for use in southwestern industry and agriculture. The workers were denied the right to remain in the United States after their jobs were done, however.

Unions have been instrumental in changing the lives of these workers by helping them bargain collectively. They have also given workers a political voice, and a platform from which to lobby for protective legislation.

United Farm Workers
Perhaps the best known national labor union representing Latinos is the United Farm Workers (UFW),

Hector M. Flores (left), president of LULAC, meets members of migrant labor families at the Hope Migrant Workers Center in Hope, Arkansas (2005).

founded by César Chávez and Dolores Huerta in California.

Chávez organized a well-publicized protest by laborers in the 1960s that helped bring the plight of migrant farm laborers to public attention. He helped California table-grape laborers and other agricultural workers unionize. Chávez also influenced other leading Latino activists.

Another important national agricultural labor union is the Farm Labor Organizing Committee (FLOC), founded in Ohio by Baldemar Velásquez in 1968.

Similarly, in the service sector, large national unions include the Service Employees International Union (SEIU) and the Hotel Employees and Restaurant Employees Union (HERE).

Political organizations
Latinos have formed several national political organizations to increase their numbers in elected office and their successes in public policy.

One of the earliest such organizations was the Political Association of Spanish Speaking

Organizations (PASSO), which was formed in 1960. Other organizations followed, including, in 1976, the Congressional Hispanic Caucus (CHC) of the United States Congress, and the National Association of Latino Elected Officials (NALEO). The Latino National Political Survey was also established to give some insight into Latino political issues, attitudes, and behaviors.

While these organizations have supported Latinos politically, there is still a substantial gap between the numbers of Hispanics living in the United States (more than 41 million in 2005) and their political underrepresentation in local and national government.

Legal issues
Another area in which national organizations have played an important part is the law.

LULAC and other national rights organizations lent their support and financial aid to civil rights cases, often to good effect. Later, specific legal advocacy organizations, such as the Mexican American Legal Defense and Education Fund (MALDEF) and the Puerto Rican Legal Defense and Education Fund (PRLDEF), were formed to prevent legal abuses against Latinos, particularly in the areas of immigrant rights, voting, political rights, education, and housing.

Immigration has always been a contentious issue. The U.S. government has, at various points in the last 100 years or so, introduced policies to increase or decrease immigration from Latin America, and from Mexico in particular. The number of undocumented immigrants living in the United States has also

President Bill Clinton (1993–2000) receives the Lifetime Achievement Award from Rick Dovalina, then president of LULAC, on February 14, 2000, in the East Room of the White House.

caused great concern, and various organizations have evolved to help ensure that immigrants are properly protected.

Founded by Quakers in 1917, the Immigration Monitoring Project of the American Friends Service Committee now documents human rights abuses of immigrants along the U.S.–Mexico border, particularly by government agents.

Leading civil rights organizations continue to provide support for immigrants, and to fight perceived injustices, such as the cutting of welfare services and education to the children of undocumented immigrants. In 2006, LULAC joined together with other groups to help organize marches and demonstrations against proposed immigration reforms. The protest involved hundreds of thousands of Latinos, including students, in cities across the United States.

Business organizations
Hispanic entrepreneurs have often found themselves marginalized by Anglo-American business owners. The U.S. Hispanic Chamber of Commerce was one of the organizations established in the late 1970s to help small business owners assert their rights (*see box on page 43*). The Latin Business Association (LBA) promotes Hispanic business interests in the global economy. Women's rights are protected by organizations such as the Hispanic Business Women's Alliance.

Latino organizations demonstrate the importance of grassroots organizing, and the power of the ballot box.

Mobilizing on a massive scale, Hispanics have made sure that their interests are properly represented across U.S. society.

In the media, for example, the influential National Association of Hispanic Journalists has been important in helping Latinos achieve prominence in journalism and broadcasting. The National Hispanic Media Coalition (NHMC), an alliance of several Hispanic American organizations, addresses a variety of media-related issues that affect Hispanics. The NHMC has worked with other national Latino organizations, such as the National Council of La Raza, when necessary.

Organizations such as the Hispanic National Bar Association represent more than 25,000 Latino members of the legal profession. Hispanic representation in the law is important, critics argue, since it helps ensure that issues of Latino importance are addressed.

See also: Chávez, César; Civil Rights; García, Hector P.; Huerta, Dolores; Idar, Nicasio; Political Movements; Velásquez, Baldemar

Further reading: Acuña, Rodolfo. *Occupied America: A History of Chicanos.* New York, NY: Pearson Longman, 2004.
http://www.hispaniconline.com/res&res/org_ix.html (list of Hispanic organizations with contact details and Web sites).
www.agif.us (AGIF site).
www.lulac.org (LULAC site).
www.nclr.org (National Council of La Raza site).

NAVA, Gregory
Filmmaker

Gregory Nava is one of the most successful Chicano screenwriters, producers, and directors in Hollywood. He receives accolades for his ability to capture a variety of authentic Hispanic experiences, drawing in Hispanic and non-Hispanic audiences alike. Nava is best known for his blockbuster movies *El Norte, My Family (Mi Familia),* and *Selena,* and for working with the biggest Latin American names in Hollywood. Among them have been Edward James Olmos, Jennifer Lopez, Jimmy Smits, Sonia Braga, Lupe Ontiveros, and Esai Morales.

Gregory Nava was born in San Diego, California, in 1949, to Mexican and Basque parents. Growing up in San Diego on the U.S.–Mexico border, Nava saw how the great wealth of the United States contrasted sharply with the poverty and suffering in the city of Tijuana, on the Mexican side of the border. These impressions influenced Nava's work, in particular his first award-winning film, *El Norte.*

Beginnings of a film career
Nava studied at the prestigious film school at the University of California at Los Angeles (UCLA), where he wrote, directed, and produced his first film, *The Journal of Diego Rodríguez Silva.* There he also met his wife, Anna Thomas, another film student. The film won an award for the best drama at the National Student Film Festival. In 1973, Nava produced his first feature film, in collaboration with Anna Thomas, entitled *The Confessions of Amans,* which won the Best First Feature Award at the Chicago International Film Festival.

Nava continued making films for another decade until, in 1984, he achieved his greatest success so far, with the movie *El Norte.* The movie received an Academy Award nomination for best original screenplay, which Nava had written with his wife. In 1996, the movie was named an "American Classic," and slated for preservation in the Library of Congress. *El Norte* told the story of a Guatemalan brother and sister, Enrique and Rosa, who migrate through Mexico into the United States. The most memorable scene is the crawl the two make through a rat-infested tunnel between Mexico and the United States. It is a tragic look at the poverty and suffering of immigrants, without the happy ending stereotypical of many immigrant narratives in film. *El Norte* educated audiences about the dire conditions in Central America that were driving people

to migration. The film crew also faced hardship during the making of *El Norte,* being kidnapped and ransomed back in Mexico.

In 1988, Gregory Nava and Anna Thomas wrote their first Hollywood-produced film, *A Time of Destiny,* starring William Hurt and Timothy Hutton, about Italian Americans. It was a box-office failure. Nava returned to his Mexican roots. In 1995, he wrote and directed the multigenerational saga *My Family (Mi Familia),* about a Mexican American family in Los Angeles. The movie became the basis for Nava's later television serial of a similar name, *American Family,* which was shown on the Public Broadcasting System (PBS).

Actress Jennifer Lopez starred in *My Family* and received critical notice for her work, but it was Nava's next film that brought her real stardom. In 1997, Nava achieved commercial success with the movie *Selena,* about the murdered Tejana performer Selena Quintanilla-Pérez. It was a crossover success, reaching far beyond Latino audiences, and earned Lopez a Golden Globe nomination. Nava then directed Vivica A. Fox and Halle Berry in the 1998 film *Why Do Fools Fall in Love?* In 1999, Nava directed a documentary about the U.S. immigrant experience entitled *American Tapestry.* In 2002, Nava wrote the screenplay for the movie *Frida,* starring Salma Hayek, which received two Academy Awards.

From big screen to small
In 2002, Nava also made an important shift as an artist, moving from film to television. Nava created the PBS series *American Family,* which lasted two seasons. It was the first Latino prime-time drama series, and the first to

INFLUENCES AND INSPIRATION

Gregory Nava has an overwhleming ambition. He wants to see Latinos move from the fringes of U.S. society into the mainstream, and thinks that movies and television can help the transition. Hollywood is beginning not only to reflect the changes that are already taking place, but also to create changes itself. In television, Latinos have been important to many shows according to Nava, who cites the 1960s' situation comedy *I Love Lucy* as groundbreaking both technically, with its use of three cameras, and socially, by having Cuban American Desi Arnaz as one of its stars. Nava also emphasizes the universality of human experience, regardless of ethnicity, and believes it is the ability to tell stories that touch the hearts, minds, and souls of everyone that has led to his success. Nava is particularly interested in the dramatic narratives of struggle, immigration, work, assimilation, acculturation, hope, success, and failure.

▼ *Gregory Nava on the set of his successful 1995 movie,* **My Family (Mia Familia).**

feature an all-Latin American cast. Nava served as executive producer. The show was originally designed for network television, but was soon picked up by public television. It featured Edward James Olmos, Constance Marie, Raquel Welch, Sonia Braga, and Esai Morales among others. The series traced a Mexican American family in East Los Angeles, quite like the one in the movie *My Family.* It also featured a documentary section at the end of each episode entitled "Realidades," about real life for Latinos. The show was canceled owing to its high production cost and the sense that the U.S. viewing audience was not yet ready for a dramatic series on Mexican life in the United States.

Achievement

In addition to the awards his work has received from the Motion Picture Academy and others in the industry, Nava has been recognized as a leader in the Latino community. In 2001, the Hispanic Heritage Foundation gave Nava the prestigious Hispanic Heritage Award. Some critics claim that Nava's movies and television shows produce a type of ethnic separatism, dividing rather than uniting Americans, but Nava disagrees. He emphasizes that he tells stories about American families of Latin ancestry, often the same type of immigrant-to-American narratives told popularly about many other ethnic groups.

See also: Arnaz, Desi; Hayek, Salma; Lopez, Jennifer; Morales, Esai; Olmos, Edward James; Ontiveros, Lupe; Smits, Jimmy

Further reading: Rosen, David. "Crossover: Hispanic Specialty Films in the U.S. Movie Marketplace." In *Chicanos and Film: Representation and Resistance,* edited by Chon Noriega. Minneapolis, MN: University of Minnesota Press, 1992. http://www.pbs.org/now/transcript/transcript_nava.html (transcript of Bill Moyers's interview with Gregory Nava).

NAVA, Julián
Politician

Julián Nava was appointed U.S. ambassador to Mexico by President Jimmy Carter (1977–1981). He was the first Mexican American to serve in the position.

Early life
Nava was born in Los Angeles, California, on June 19, 1927. He was raised in the ethnically diverse neighborhood of Boyle Heights. Nava's parents had emigrated from Zacatecas, Mexico, during the Mexican Revolution. His family worked during the summers picking fruit in local orchards. During the Great Depression of the 1930s, nativist groups and local authorities carried out campaigns to "repatriate" or deport Mexicans. Approximately 100,000 Mexicans were involuntarily or voluntarily repatriated, and Nava's family was scheduled to be deported. Fate intervened when the eight-year-old Nava suffered a burst appendix on the eve of his family's departure, and the Navas were allowed to stay in Los Angeles.

After graduating from Roosevelt High School, Nava volunteered for military service, ranking second in his training class as a naval air machinist and gunner. Nava used benefits from the G.I. Bill to pursue a college education. He received a bachelor's degree from Pomona College in 1951, and went on to earn a doctorate in history from Harvard University in 1955. He was one of the first Mexican Americans to achieve such qualifications from those educational institutions.

Improving education for all
Nava was a founding member of the history department of California State University at Northridge, where he taught from 1957 to 2002. Nava was also the first Mexican American to be elected to the governing board of the Los

▲ *Julián Nava (left) meets with José López Portillo, president of Mexico, in 1980.*

Angeles Unified School District (1967–1979). He was elected in citywide contests to three terms, and served as president twice. He successfully campaigned for greater respect for social and cultural diversity at a time when discrimination was rife in the Los Angeles public-school system and electoral politics. Nava also promoted bilingual education programs to benefit historically underserved Mexican American students, and pushed for the recruitment of more Mexican American teachers and principals. He was president of the school board when school desegregation was ordered.

Nava played an important part in the Chicano movement, collaborating with Rodolfo Acuña to create the first Chicano studies program in the United States. He was on the advisory committee of the Mexican American Legal Defense and Education Fund (MALDEF). From 1980 to 1981, he also served as U.S. ambassador to Mexico.

Nava has taught at universities in Spain, Colombia, Puerto Rico, and Mexico. In addition to research on the historical experience of Mexican Americans and Latin American history, Nava has produced documentary films on the Basque people in Spain, contemporary Cuba, and the Zacatecas immigrant community in California. In 2002, Nava published his autobiography, *My Mexican American Journey*.

See also: Acuña, Rodolfo

Further reading: Nava, Julian. *My Mexican American Journey.* Houston, TX: Arte Público Press, 2002. http://www.hispanicvista.com/HVC/Columnist/jschmal/062005 jpschmal.htm (short biography).

KEY DATES

1927 Born in Los Angeles, California, on June 19.

1955 Receives doctorate from Harvard University.

1957 Joins California State University at Northridge.

1980 Appointed by President Jimmy Carter as U.S. ambassador to Mexico; serves until 1981.

2002 Publishes autobiography, *My Mexican American Journey.*

NAVARRO, José Antonio
Lawyer, Politician, Texas Patriot

During the Texas War of Independence in 1836, most of the Texas patriots were non-Texans. José Antonio Navarro, however, was born in San Antonio, Texas, in 1795, to parents of Corsican descent.

Navarro's father died in 1808, leaving a young widow with six children. As a young man, Navarro was home-schooled and taught himself Spanish and Mexican law. At age 17, he took up arms against the Spanish, from 1812 to 1813. After Mexican independence from Spanish rule in 1821, Texas/Coahuila was made a Mexican state in 1824, and Navarro was elected to the legislature, and later to the National Mexican Congress, representing Texas/Coahuila. Navarro championed a liberal federal constitution, however, and broke with President Antonio López de Santa Anna. He advocated Texas's independence from Mexico, befriended Stephen F. Austin (an influential founder of Anglo-American Texas), and was one of two Tejanos to sign the Texas

▼ *José Antonio Navarro was a lifelong and tireless fighter for Texas independence.*

KEY DATES	
1795	Born in San Antonio, Texas, on February 2.
1825	Marries Margarita de la Garza on February 15.
1835	Elected as a deputy to the National Mexican Congress representing Texas/Coahuila.
1836	Serves as elected senator in the Congress of the Republic of Texas.
1841	Captured and imprisoned in Mexico, but later escapes.
1871	Dies on January 13.

Declaration of Independence on March 2, 1836. Once Texas was a republic, Navarro was elected a senator. His family suffered many indignities and the theft of cattle, horses, and other property at the hands of newly arrived Anglo settlers, yet he remained loyal to the Texan cause.

Prisoner of war, statehood, and secessionist
In 1841, Navarro became part of the Sante Fe Expedition, which sought to persuade New Mexicans to secede from Mexico and join Texas. He was captured during that foray, and imprisoned for life by Santa Anna. Navarro managed to escape when Santa Anna was briefly deposed, and fled to Havana, Cuba, from Vera Cruz, Mexico, before making his way back to San Antonio via New Orleans and Galveston. By then, Texas was seeking admission as a state of the United States. Navarro supported statehood, and served as a state senator for three terms. Navarro County, Texas, is named in his honor. Navarro opposed many of Texas president Sam Houston's policies. Later, he became a secessionist, and four of his sons served in the army of the Confederacy.

Navarro died on January 13, 1871. He is buried in San Fernando Cemetery in San Antonio, Texas. The family home in San Antonio (corner of South Laredo and Nueva streets) is now a state historical park.

Further reading: Dawson, Joseph Martin. *José Antonio Navarro, Co-creator of Texas.* Waco, TX: Baylor University Press, 1969.
http://www.tsha.utexas.edu/handbook/online/articles/NN/fna9.html (Handbook of Texas Online).

NAVARRO, Max
Businessman

Capitalizing on the military demand for multidisciplinary technical services in the San Antonio area, Max Navarro cofounded a defense-contracting firm called Operational Technologies Corporation. The company became one of the nation's fastest growing Hispanic-owned high-tech businesses, making Navarro a very rich man: He is ranked the 75th richest Hispanic in the United States. Navarro has used his wealth to help empower the Hispanic community, in particular young Latinos.

Early life
Max Navarro was born into a humble working-class home in San Antonio, Texas, on October 18, 1943. His parents, who did menial work, believed that education was the key to a more prosperous life and encouraged Navarro to take his schooling seriously. Despite the discrimination that Navarro experienced growing up and the loss of his mother when he was nine, he remained in the upper echelon of his class at high school.

Making the most of life
After finishing school, Navarro volunteered to join the U.S. Army, where he met all kinds of people and experienced other cultures. Impressed by the lives of many of the high-ranking officers and privileged civilians that he encountered abroad in the 1960s, Navarro resolved to raise himself from the "bottom of the barrel" to a higher station in life.

Taking advantage of the GI Bill, Navarro worked his way through school, earning a BA in psychology from the University of Houston in 1977. He went on to complete multidisciplinary graduate studies at St. Mary's University in 1980.

Navarro spent the next few years working in the computer industry until outsourcing jeopardized his position. An acquaintance who worked for an air force

▲ *Max Navarro took advantage of the GI Bill to go to college and change his life. A successful entrepreneur, he is the 75th richest Hispanic in the United States.*

base asked Navarro to assist him with a project involving psychometrics. The scientific dimensions of the project required expert knowledge, and Navarro enlisted the help of seven highly qualified professionals. Navarro found his team's services in high demand, and in 1986 he cofounded the company Operational Technologies. By 2006 Optech employed more than 200 people, making Navarro one of the largest employers in the San Antonio Region.

In 1998 Navarro resigned as CEO of Optech. He dedicated his time to the Hispanic community, regularly visiting local schools, where he uses his own story to motivate minority students. In 2005 he was appointed to a federal committee for diversity in communications. Navarro hopes to solve the problem of existing technological inequalities between rich and poor in the United States to ensure that the country remains a place where, as he puts it, "anyone can be another Bill Gates."

Further reading: http://www.otcorp.com/default.asp (Operational Technologies Corporation Web site).

KEY DATES	
1943	Born in San Antonio, Texas, on October 18.
1986	Cofounds Operational Technologies Corporation.
2005	Appointed to the Federal Communications Commission's Advisory Committee for Diversity for Communications in the Digital Age.

NAVAS, William A., Jr.
Military Leader

Puerto Rican Major General William A. Navas, Jr., is one of the United States's most outstanding soldiers, with a distinguished record of service in both the U.S. Army and the Army National Guard, the United States's civilian militia. In 2001, William A. Navas was appointed assistant secretary of the Navy, the first Puerto Rican to serve in the post.

A military family

Navas was born in 1942 in Mayagüez, Puerto Rico, and grew up in a family in which military service was a tradition. His grandfather, Colonel Antonio M. Navas, was one of the first Puerto Ricans to be commissioned as a U.S. Army officer, while his father, William A. Navas Sr., served as a captain during World War II (1939–1945). Navas, Sr., later returned to Puerto Rico to found a successful civil-engineering company.

After high school, Navas studied engineering at the University of Puerto Rico, and graduated in 1965. His father wanted his son to follow him into the family business, but in 1966 Navas joined the U.S. Army as a second lieutenant. After a period of duty in West Germany, from 1968 to 1969, he served in the Vietnam War (1965–1973) as a commander with the 168th Engineer Battalion. In 1970, Navas resigned his commission in the U.S. Army. He returned to Puerto Rico to work in his father's engineering firm, and to raise a family of his own. Nevertheless, he continued his military service part time, working for the Puerto Rican Army National Guard, where he rose to be the director of the State Area Command Section, Headquarters and Headquarters Detachment.

To Washington, D.C.

In 1980, Navas quit his civilian job to work for the Puerto Rican Army National Guard full time. In 1987, he went to Washington, D.C., where he had been appointed deputy

▲ **William A. Navas, Jr. (in civilian dress), is one of the most senior Latinos serving in the United States's armed services.**

director of the Army National Guard Bureau. Navas became the bureau's vice chief in 1990, and in 1995 its director, managing more than 362,000 Guardsmen and a budget of $6 billion. Navas served at the National Guard Bureau until 1998, when he retired.

In 2001, President George W. Bush nominated Navas as assistant secretary of the Navy. At the Department of the Navy, Navas's special responsibilities focused on personnel issues, such as the health care of servicemen and women. Navas has been the recipient of many military decorations, including the Defense Meritorious Service Medal, two Legion of Merit awards, and a Bronze Star. In 2004, Navas won one of *Hispanic* magazine's Achievement Awards.

Further reading: "Puerto Rico Profile: William A. Navas Jr." *The Puerto Rico Herald*, July 20, 2001 (available online at www.puertorico-herald.org/issues/2001/vol5n29/ProfNavas-en.shtml).
http://www.chinfo.navy.mil/navpalib/people/assistsecnav/asn_mra/navas/navasbio.html (brief biography).

KEY DATES	
1942	Born in Mayagüez, Puerto Rico.
1965	Joins U.S. Army.
1995	Appointed director of the National Guard Bureau.
2001	Sworn in as assistant secretary of the Navy.

NEGRÓN MUÑOZ, Mercedes

Poet

Mercedes Negrón Muñoz, who wrote under the pseudonym Clara Lair, is considered by some to be one of the finest Hispanic American poets of the early 20th century. Nevertheless, very little of her work has been translated into English, and much of it is out of print even in Spanish—the language in which she wrote exclusively. Likewise, there has been no biography about the Puerto Rican writer. However, in 1996 the Puerto Rican documentary maker Ivonne Belen (1955–) made an important film about her life—*A Passion Named Clara Lair*.

Despite her relative obscurity, however, Negrón Muñoz's intensely personal and lyrically sensual poetry has been hugely influential on the generations of Puerto Rican poets who have studied her work. Perhaps her greatest influence has been on the work of the much better known writer Julia de Burgos.

A family of poets

Negrón Muñoz was born on March 8, 1895, in the inland town of Barranquitas, Puerto Rico, where she was raised and educated. She belonged to one of Puerto Rico's leading families. Both her father and one of her uncles were well-respected poets. Another uncle was the great liberal statesman Luis Muñoz Rivera, who was the leading figure in setting up the current governmental system of Puerto Rico and was himself a celebrated journalist and poet. Her cousin, Luis Muñoz Marín, was the first democratically elected governor of Puerto Rico after President Truman gave islanders the right to elect a head of state in 1948.

Writing career

Mercedes began to write when she was still very young, and pursued her love of literature through studies at the Universidad de Puerto Rico in San Juan. Like many other Puerto Rican poets of her generation, she was inspired by the innovative works of modernist French poets such as Stéphane Mallarmé (1842–1898). In around 1918 Muñoz visited New York City, and on her return began to publish her verse—notably *Amor en Nueva York* (Love in New York)—in some of Puerto Rico's flourishing literary magazines. She published her first collection of poetry, *Arras del Cristal* (Cracked Glass), in 1937, and her second, *Tropico Amargo* (Bitter Tropic), in 1950.

Love poet

The frank eroticism of some of Muñoz's poetry shocked many contemporary critics, but for fellow Puerto Rican poet Luis Llorens Torres, she was comparable to the renowned Argentine poet Alfonsini Storni (1892–1938).

Despite her reputation as an introspective love poet, however, Muñoz was also a passionate supporter of Puerto Rican independence and a determined feminist. Mercedes Muñoz died on August 26, 1973, in San Juan, Puerto Rico, aged 78.

In 1979 the Instituto de Cultura Puertorriqueña (Puerto Rican Institute of Culture) published a complete collection of Muñoz's works, including the poems that had been left unpublished at her death. A school and street on the island are named in her honor, as is a woman's refuge in Hormigueros.

See also: De Burgos, Julia; Muñoz Marín, Luis; Muñoz Rivera, Luis; Torres, Luis Llorens.

Further reading: Lair, Clara. *De la Herida a la Gloria: La Poesía Completa de Clara Lair*. Carolina, Puerto Rico: Terranova, 2003.
http://welcome.topuertorico.org/culture/litera.shtml (Essay on Puerto Rican literature).

KEY DATES

1895 Born in Barranquitas, Puerto Rico, on March 8.

1918 Visits New York City and is inspired to write one of her most famous works, *Amor en Nueva York* (Love in New York).

1937 Publishes *Arras del Cristal* (Cracked Glass).

1950 Publishes *Tropico Amargo* (Bitter Tropic).

1961 Puerto Rican Institute of Culture publishes selection of her poems.

1973 Dies in San Juan, Puerto Rico, on August 26.

1979 Complete works published by Puerto Rican Institute of Culture.

1991 Hogar Clara Lair, a women's refuge charity, is founded.

1996 Subject of documentary *A Passion Named Clara Lair*.

NIEBLA, Elvia
Scientist

Elvia Niebla is a soil scientist. She is the national coordinator for global change research in the Forest Service, a division of the Agriculture Department.

Early life
Born on March 12, 1945, in Nogales, Arizona, Elvia Niebla is of Mexican heritage. From an early age, Niebla showed great talent and aptitude for science and math. Despite the fact that teaching and secretarial work were the traditional professions for women of Hispanic origin, Niebla wanted to pursue her interest in sciences. With her parents' complete support, she continued to study biology, chemistry, calculus, and physics, graduating from high school in 1963.

Pursuing a science education
In 1965 Niebla received an associate of arts degree from Fullerton Junior College. Two years later she was awarded a bachelor of science degree in zoology and chemistry from the University of Arizona. Over the next three years Niebla worked at a high school in California, where she taught science and math to students with learning disabilities. She then decided to return to the University of Arizona, working as a research scientist and studying for a PhD. In 1979 she was awarded a doctorate in soil chemistry.

KEY DATES

1945 Born in Nogales, Arizona, on March 12.

1963 Graduatues from high school.

1965 Receives an associate of arts degree from Fullerton Junior College.

1967 Receives BS in zoology and chemistry from the University of Arizona; teaches science and math to students with learning disabilities in California.

1979 Receives doctorate in soil science from University of Arizona.

1984 Becomes soil scientist for the U.S. Environmental Protection Agency (EPA), where she examines the effects of sludge on agricultural land.

1989 Takes on role of national coordinator for the Global Change Research Program.

Niebla's first job as a qualified soil scientist was at the Western Archaeological Center. Niebla examined soil types and worked out which had been used to construct historic adobe buildings; she also advised on the best way to preserve them. One of Niebla's legacies from her time at the center was helping increase the number of minority applications for federal jobs. Before Niebla revolutionized the application process, people had to travel to Washington, D.C., to take eligibility tests, but Niebla suggested that the tests should be located in the places where the jobs were situated.

Environmental Protection Agency (EPA)
In 1984 Niebla joined the U.S. Environmental Protection Agency (EPA) as a soil specialist. Her main role was to monitor the effects of sludge (decomposed garbage) used on agricultural land. One particular project in which Niebla took part involved studying the pathways through which people could get toxin poisoning from the sludge. Niebla proposed a series of regulations that prevented the poisons in such substances from reaching humans. The EPA awarded Niebla the bronze medal for her work in this area.

The Global Change Research Program
Since 1989 Niebla has worked as national coordinator for the Global Change Research Program (GCRP), which is part of the U.S. Agriculture Department's Forest Service. Her work involves monitoring the effects of global climate patterns on forest ecosystems. She advises on scientific research, distributes funding to projects, and helps policymakers develop regulations. Niebla also represents the United States at international conferences and committees on the environment and global climate change.

Niebla strongly advises people to pursue their interests and dreams. She says, " Don't be dissuaded by the obstacles and disbelievers you will encounter. If you are dedicated to your dreams, you will always find a way to accomplish them."

Further reading: Godrej, Dinyar. *No Nonsense Guide to Climate Change.* New York, NY: Verso, 2001.
www.usgcrp.gov (the homepage of U.S. Global Change Research Program).

NIETO, Sonia
Educator

Puerto Rican American Sonia Nieto is one of the foremost educators working in the United States. She is a passionate advocate of multicultural education, and the author of several influential books that have helped forge progressive thinking in this much debated area. She became professor of education at the University of Massachusetts in Amherst.

Puerto Rican student

Sonia Nieto was born and raised in Brooklyn, New York. While attending public schools there during the 1950s, Nieto and her fellow Puerto Rican students were expected to keep their Hispanic culture and language for their home lives only. That proved a formative experience for Nieto, who came to consider that her education in the United States had devalued her cultural identity and damaged her self-esteem. Nieto looked toward a career in education, in which she hoped to be able to improve the situation for future Hispanic students by making education more inclusive and relevant to different cultural groups.

After high school, Nieto went to St. John's University, New York, where, in 1965, she received a bachelor's degree in elementary education. This was followed by a year's study in Madrid, Spain, which ended in the award of a master's degree in Spanish and Hispanic literature. Nieto subsequently began her career in New York City's public schools, teaching students in both English and Spanish.

Educational career

In 1975, Nieto, her husband, Angel, and their two daughters, moved to Massachusetts, where she studied for a further degree in education. The University of Massachusetts awarded her a doctorate in 1979, and she subsequently took up a teaching post there. Nieto taught, lectured, and published widely. Her work focused on multicultural and bilingual education, curriculum reform, teacher education, Puerto Rican children's literature, and on the education of Latinos, immigrants, and other culturally and linguistically diverse student populations. Among her most important publications are *Affirming Diversity: The Sociopolitical Context of Multicultural Education* (1992) and *The Light in Their Eyes: Creating Multicultural Learning Communities* (1999). Nieto has also written for such journals as *Educational Leadership, Theory into Practice, The Harvard Educational Review,* and *Multicultural Education.*

In her work, Nieto argues that multicultural education should mean much more than just occasional "special" lessons devoted to what she calls the "heroes and holidays" aspects of nonwhite cultures. Multiculturalism, she believes, is a philosophy that should underpin every aspect of school life, from the curriculum and the integration of staff and pupils to the kinds of food served in the canteen. In this way all children—whatever their racial or ethnic background—are encouraged to value their own culture as well as those of others. Multicultural education is fundamental to educational equity and—more broadly—to democracy, she argues.

Other activities

In addition to teaching and writing on educational equity, Nieto has served on many local, regional, national, and international bodies. Among them have been the Massachusetts Advocacy Center, an advisory committee for California Tomorrow, and the national advisory boards of both Facing History and Ourselves (FHAO) and Educators for Social Responsibility (ESR). Nieto's broad field of work has been widely recognized. In 1989, for example, she received the Massachusetts Teachers Association's Human and Civil Rights Award; in 1997, she won the Educator of the Year award from the National Association for Multicultural Education (NAME). Nieto has also been awarded honorary doctorates by Lesley University in 1999 and by Bridgewater State College in 2004.

KEY DATES

1979 Awarded doctorate in education from the University of Massachusetts, Amherst.

1992 Publication of her first book: *Affirming Diversity: The Sociopolitical Context of Multicultural Education.*

1997 Wins Educator of the Year award.

Further reading: Nieto, Sonia. *Affirming Diversity: The Sociopolitical Context of Multicultural Education.* New York, NY: Longman, 2004.

www-unix.oit.umass.edu/~snieto/index.html (University of Massachusetts Web page.)

NIGGLI, Josefina
Writer

Josefina Niggli was a prolific playwright during the 1930s. She is best known, however, for *Mexican Village*, the celebrated novel that prefigured much of the Chicano literary movement of the 1960s and 1970s. In the work, Niggli examined the nature of borders and the identity conflict experienced by many Mexican Americans.

Early life

Born Josephine María Niggli on July 13, 1910, in Monterrey, Nuevo León, Mexico, Niggli was the only child of Frederick Ferdinand Niggli and Goldie Morgan Niggli. Her father was a Texan who went to work on the Mexican railroad in 1893, and her mother was a concert violinist from Virginia. By the time of Niggli's birth, her father was the manager of a cement plant in Hidalgo, employing most of the people in the small town.

Niggli spent her early years in Mexico, but the growing instability after the start of the Mexican Revolution in 1910 led to her mother taking her back to the United States to San Antonio, Texas, in 1913. For a while, they traveled between the two countries. Niggli eventually attended the Main Avenue High School in San Antonio; her mother later taught her at home.

In 1925, Niggli attended the Incarnate Word College in San Antonio, where one professor observed that he had never had a student with such a blank mind. He intended the remark as a compliment, and insisted that Niggli's teachers should not allow her to take paper into class, so that she would be forced to remember facts. Niggli developed an excellent memory that served her well when she came to write about the Mexico of her childhood.

The emergence of a writer

At a young age, Niggli started to write poetry and short stories. Several of her early works appeared in magazines such as *Mexican Life* and *Ladies' Home Journal*. Recognizing her talent, Niggli's parents and teachers persuaded the young girl to enter writing competitions, which she did with some success. In 1928, Niggli's father paid to have a collection of her poetry privately printed. He took copies of the book, entitled *Mexican Silhouettes*, to an English-language bookstore in Mexico City, where they were put on display in the window and sold out almost immediately. In 1931, a revised edition of the book appeared in San Antonio.

▲ *Josefina Niggli worked as a stable writer for movie companies such as MGM. She later wrote for television and radio.*

During the 1920s and early 1930s, Niggli worked for KTSA Radio and studied for her BA, which she received in 1931. She went on to study drama under Coates Gwynne, the director of the San Antonio Little Theater, who suggested that Niggli become a playwright.

In 1935, Niggli went to study with Frederick H. Koch (*see box on page 56*) at the University of North Carolina at Chapel Hill. There followed a very creative period for Niggli, during which she wrote several one-act plays. *Tooth or Slave* (1935), *The Cry of Dolores* (1935), *The Red Velvet Goat* (1936), *Sunday Costs Five Pesos* (1936), *Soldadera* (1936), and *Azteca* (1936) were all about aspects of the Mexican Revolution and Mexican life. In 1936, Niggli also wrote two full-length plays, *The Fair God* and *Singing Valley*.

Like many of Niggli's plays, *Sunday Costs Five Pesos*, her most performed work, was written as a folk comedy. It captures Mexican rural or village life with great wit and a sense of irony. *Soldadera* is unique in portraying women soldiers of the revolution. It was included in Margaret Mayorga's collection *The Best One-Act Plays of 1937*.

INFLUENCES AND INSPIRATION

The drama educator Frederick H. Koch (1877–1944) was very influential in developing Niggli's talent for writing folk plays. Following an English degree, Koch studied in a theater arts program at the Emerson School of Oratory in Boston. After graduating in 1903, he accepted a position in the English department of the University of North Dakota, where he developed an interest in folk drama. He was asked to bring his skills and experience to the University of North Carolina at Chapel Hill in 1918. Koch created a dramatic composition class at the university that encouraged students to write original plays with an emphasis on bringing tradition and folklore into the present.

During his 25 years at the University of North Carolina, Koch encouraged many students, including Josefina Niggli, to write more than 400 original one-act folk plays. He is widely regarded by critics as a founding father of the American folk drama, and as a man who fostered many talented writers, including Thomas Wolfe.

Niggli's plays showed her talent for dialogue, plot, and characterization. Her portrayal provided a realistic depiction of contemporary Mexico since Niggli refused to sentimentalize or patronize her characters.

During the late 1930s, Niggli received a number of awards, including two from the Rockefeller Foundation. The Fellowship of the Bureau of New Plays, which she received in 1938, allowed Niggli to move to New York.

Mexican Village

While Niggli's plays were based on the Mexican Revolution, her first novel, *Mexican Village* (1945), dealt with its aftermath. The book provides a good overview not only of life in Mexico but also of the problems created by living along the border and the identity crisis that came from being a mestizo (a person of mixed-race heritage). The story, which centers on Bob Webster, the novel's half-American and half-Mexican protagonist, was dismissed by some contemporary U.S. critics as being nothing more than a naïve tale of Mexican innocence. Niggli's supporters, however, believe that such criticism misunderstands Niggli's intention and execution. Niggli shows how Webster is reconciled to his Mexican heritage and how, as a mestizo, he comes to symbolize the future of the village and of Mexico itself. *Mexican Village* remained in print until 1978, and has recently been reissued. It has also been translated into a number of languages.

In the late 1940s, Niggli moved to Hollywood, where she worked as a stable writer fixing scripts. Although the job was well paid, stable writers worked anonymously. Niggli also wrote scripts of her own, including *Sombrero*, the unsuccessful 1953 movie version of *Mexican Village*.

In 1956, Niggli settled in the United States, after spending time in England and Ireland. She was hired to teach at Western Carolina University, and worked there until her retirement in 1975. While teaching, she also wrote for radio and television, contributing to such popular shows as *Laramie*. She published her last novel, *A Miracle for Mexico,* in 1964. Set in 1531, the book describes Mexico's turbulent history following the Spanish conquest.

Legacy

Niggli wrote in English. She wanted to educate North Americans about Mexico, and to break down the myths and stereotypes that were prevalent in the United States in the early and mid-20th century. She believed that by writing in English she was better able to reach her target audience. Literary historians and critics have reevaluated her work, and now see it at the forefront of Chicano studies. Niggli, who never married, died in 1983.

Further reading: Niggli, Josefina. *Mexican Village.* Albuquerque, NM: University of New Mexico Press, 2001. www.tsha.utexas.edu/handbook/online/articles/NN/fnitt.html (comprehensive biography).

KEY DATES

1910	Born in Monterrey, Nuevo León, Mexico, on July 13.
1928	Publishes first book, *Mexican Silhouettes*, privately.
1935	Studies at the University of North Carolina.
1945	Publishes first novel, *Mexican Village*; it was made into a film, *Sombrero*, eight years later.
1956	Teaches at Western Carolina University.
1964	Publishes *A Miracle for Mexico*.
1983	Dies in Cullowhee, North Carolina, on December 17.

NOGALES, Luis G.
Businessman, Philanthropist

One of the most successful Latino businessmen in the United States, Luis Guerrero Nogales is the founder and managing partner of Nogales Investors, a private equity investment firm. Nogales also sits on the boards of Edison International, Arbitron, KB Home, and Kaufmann & Broad (France). A well-known supporter of the Hispanic community, Nogales has worked over the years to promote its interests—as a member of the student activist organization MEChA (Movimiento Estudiantil Chicano de Aztlán) in the late 1960s, through to his support of various Hispanic rights organizations. In 2003 Nogales was featured on *Hispanic Business* magazine's most influential Hispanic Americans' list.

Early life
Born in 1944, Nogales grew up in the agricultural valleys of Calexico, California, where he worked as a farmworker. An intelligent young man, Nogales realized that he needed a proper education in order to make a success of his life. He studied hard and was able to go to college. Nogales received a BA from San Diego State University, after which he graduated from Stanford Law School in 1969.

The Chicano movement
In the 1960s Nogales became influenced by the Chicano movement, which promoted the rights, culture, and education of Mexican Americans. Nogales set up a chapter of MEChA, a student organization dedicated to progressive change for the Chicano community, at Stanford. After graduating, Nogales was appointed Stanford's first assistant to the president for Mexican American Affairs, a position that gave him the opportunity to promote and defend Latino students' interests.

White House fellow
Between 1972 and 1973 Nogales was a White House fellow. More than 1,000 people apply each year for the prestigious post that President Lyndon B. Johnson established in 1965. Johnson wanted candidates to receive first-hand experience of the workings of the federal government. Nogales worked full time as a special assistant to White House staff and top-level government officials. He studied U.S. domestic and international policy, and took part in discussions on key issues such as education. Nogales used this experience, together with his own natural business acumen, to help establish himself as a leading force in U.S. commerce in the 1980s.

United Press International (UPI)
Employed by the news agency United Press International (UPI), Nogales was a member of the management team that promised to make the ailing UPI profitable by 1985.

▲ *Businessman Luis G. Nogales has served on the boards of numerous prestigious firms. A great believer in giving back to the Hispanic community, Nogales had contributed large sums to leading Latino activist groups, such as MALDEF.*

LEGACY

Luis G. Nogales believes in supporting organizations that protect the Hispanic community's rights. In 2002 Nogales made headlines when he pledged $1 million to MALDEF (Mexican American Legal Defense and Educational Fund) for the protection of immigrant rights. It was the largest gift made by an individual in MALDEF's history.

Established in 1968 in San Antonio, Texas, MALDEF is one of the leading nonprofit U.S. Hispanic litigation, advocacy, and educational outreach institutions.

It fights to protect the rights of and empower the millions of Hispanics currently living in the United States.

MALDEF's Immigration Rights Program has challenged several discriminatory laws and programs. Its successes include the striking down of California's Proposition 187, which would have denied education, health care, and social services to undocumented immigrants living in the state. In the final settlement of the case, *Gregorio T. v. Wilson*, Governor Gray Davis and the state of

California officially agreed to dismiss their appeal of the district court's decision to strike down Proposition 187.

MALDEF's defense of immigrant rights led Nogales to make his donation. He said, "It's always taken great uphill effort to secure the rights of new immigrants. This donation demonstrates my faith in the capacity of our institutions to give new Americans the full measure of their civil and human rights and the opportunity to pursue the American Dream."

A year before that date, Nogales was chosen to replace William J. Small as president and chief operating officer of UPI. He eventually rose to become UPI's chair and CEO. Nogales's leadership of UPI is described in the award-winning book *Down to the Wire*, which was chosen by *Business Week* as one of the best books on U.S. business.

Moving on

In 1986 Nogales left UPI to become president of the leading Spanish-language television network Univision Communications, Inc., a post he stayed in until 1988. In

1990 he set up his own company, Nogales Investors, which was dedicated to investing in companies in minority and underserved communities. He also maintained interests in other businesses, and from 1992 to 1997 was chair and CEO of Embarcadero Media, Inc.

A dedicated man

Nogales has also served on several boards of directors of commercial, charitable, and educational organizations. He sits on the boards of Levi Strauss, Stanford University, and the Bank of California, and is a trustee of the Ford Foundation and the J. Paul Getty Trust. Nogales has been appointed to several presidential commissions and is a member of the Council on Foreign Relations

Nogales's commitment and dedication to protecting the rights of others has earned him great respect in the U.S. business community. Following the announcement that Nogales had donated $1 million to the Hispanic organization MALDEF to use for the protection of immigrant rights, Bruce Karatz, president and CEO of KB Home, stated that he was proud of Nogales's example of "community dedication and generosity." John Bryson, CEO of Edison International, also said that Nogales was a natural leader who cared deeply about equal opportunity and the future of the state of California.

KEY DATES	
1944	Born in about this year in California.
1969	Graduates from Stanford Law School; becomes assistant to Stanford's president for Mexican American Affairs.
1972	Becomes a White House fellow.
1984	Becomes president of United Press International.
1986	Becomes president of Univision Communications, Inc., until 1988.
1990	Sets up Nogales Investors.
1992	Appointed chair and CEO of Embarcadero Media, Inc.
2002	Donates $1 million to MALDEF to defend the rights of immigrants.
2003	Named an influential Hispanic American by *Hispanic Business* magazine.

Further reading: Gordon, Gregory, and Ronald E. Cohen. *Down to the Wire: UPI's Fight for Survival.* New York, NY: McGraw-Hill, 1989.

http://www.nogalesinvestors.com/team.htm (short biography on Nogales's investors site).

NOLOESCA, Beatriz
Actor

Beatriz Noloesca was the stage name of Beatriz Escalona Pérez, a popular Mexican American comic and actor who performed in Spanish-language vaudeville (song, dance, and sketch) shows in the early 20th century. Noloesca's sharp-tongued, irreverent style drew on the rambunctious Mexican tradition of *carpa* (tent) theater, which mixed bawdy humor and clowning with satirical allusions to contemporary events. Noloesca was also affectionately known as La Chata or La Chata Noloesca, after a character she played of the same name.

Early life
Beatriz Escalona Pérez was born in San Antonio, Texas, on August 20, 1903, the daughter of poor Mexican immigrants. From early childhood, Noloesca loved the theater. As a teenager, she worked as an usherette and box-office cashier in San Antiono's Hispanic theater houses. While working at the Teatro Nacional, she won a "beautiful legs" contest and came to the attention of the Mexican impresario José Areu, who invited her to join the Variedades Hermanos Areu, his family troupe. Escalona and Areu later married.

Finding an audience
Escalona made her stage debut at the Teatro Colón in El Paso in 1920, adopting the stage name Noloesca. During the 1920s, the Hermanos Areu became one of the most popular touring troupes of the Southwest, performing *zarzuelas* (comic operettas) for Hispanic audiences on both sides of the border. Although Noloesca also sang and danced, she became best known for her comic routines and, above all, for her onstage character La Chata. A quick-witted, pigtailed Mexican maid, La Chata always got the better of the people whom she served. The character became so popular with audiences, particularly working-class Mexican Americans, that the Hermanos Areu

▲ **Noloesca's character La Chata often satirized contemporary events in entertaining monologues.**

were able to rent their own theater in Los Angeles, where they showcased other Hispanic musical and acting talent.

In 1930, Noloesca and Areu divorced, after which Noloesca founded her own company, Atracciones Noloesca, made up predominantly of women from her native San Antonio. The group performed comedy sketches and song-and-dance routines. The Great Depression of the 1930s, and the forced repatriation of many Mexicans to their homeland, combined with the growing popularity of movies, led theater attendances to decline, however, and many troupes were forced to disband. Noloesca survived by taking her company, now called the Companía Mexicana, to play in Puerto Rican communities in such places as New York and Chicago.

Between 1941 and 1950, Noloesca lived in New York, and her company became one of the most important in Hispanic vaudeville. In the early 1950s, Noloesca retired, returning home to San Antonio, where she settled down with her daughter and second husband, the musician Rubén Escobedo. She continued to perform until her death on April 4, 1979.

KEY DATES	
1903	Born in San Antonio, Texas, on August 20.
1920	Makes debut performance with Los Hermanos Areu.
1930	Forms her own company, Atracciones Noloesca.
1979	Dies in San Antonio, Texas, on April 4.

Further reading: http://www.tsha.utexas.edu/handbook/online/articles/EE/fes26.html (biography).

NORIEGA, Carlos
Astronaut

Carlos Noriega has had a distinguished career as an astronaut and computer scientist. He has visited the Russian space station Mir and helped assemble the International Space Station (ISS).

Early life

Born in Lima, Peru, on October 8, 1959, Noriega moved to California with his parents and two sisters in 1964. He studied at Wilcox High School, graduating in 1977. Early on, he developed a thirst for knowledge and decided to go on to college. Noriega studied at the University of Southern California, funded by the military ROTC. After graduating with a bachelor of science degree in computer science in 1981, he was commissioned into the Marine Corps. During his time with the Marines, Noriega graduated with two masters degrees in computer science and space systems operations from the Naval Postgraduate School. Noriega also gained valuable experience flying CH-46 Sea Knight helicopters (1983 to 1985) at the Marine Corps Air Station (MCAS) in Kaneohe Bay, Hawaii.

Following a dream

Like many other children who have dreamed of becoming astronauts, Noriega first became intrigued by space at a young age while watching Neil Armstrong land on the moon in 1969. As a child, struggling to speak English, Noriega did not believe that he would ever be able to travel to space, but as a Marine it seemed possible. He submitted his application for astronaut candidacy to NASA.

Upon graduation from the Naval Postgraduate School in September 1990, Noriega was assigned to the United States Space Command in Colorado Springs, Colorado,

▲ **Carlos Noriega discourages students from using ethnicity as a crutch to achieve success. He says: "You have to work for yourself to do the things you want."**

where he served as Space Surveillance Center Commander and was responsible for a number of software development projects. In December 1994 Noriega was selected by NASA to train as a mission specialist at the Johnson Space Center, a position he achieved in May of 1996. Noriega later held technical assignments in the Astronaut Office EVA/Robotics and Operations Planning Branches, and flew on space shuttle missions STS-84 in 1997 and STS-97 in 2000. In July 2004 Noriega served as manager of the Exploration Systems Engineering Office at Johnson Space Center.

In the course of his illustrious career, Noriega has received various medals and awards, including a Defense Superior Service Medal, Navy Achievement Medal, and the NASA Exceptional Service Medal. Noriega visits schools to talk about his work.

Further reading: Cassutt, Michael. *Who's Who in Space.* New York, NY: Macmillan, 1999.
http://www11.jsc.nasa.gov/Bios/astrobio_activemgmt.html
(NASA biography).

KEY DATES	
1959	Born in Lima, Peru, on October 8.
1990	Receives two master of science degrees from the Naval Postgraduate School.
1994	Selected as an astronaut candidate by NASA.
1997	Gains first space flight experience aboard the Space Shuttle *Atlantis*.
2004	Appointed manager of the Exploration Systems Engineering Office at Johnson Space Center.

NOVARRO, Ramon
Actor

Ramon Novarro was a popular romantic lead actor of the 1920s and 1930s, often billed as the "Latin Valentino" (after the famous silent-era screen lothario, Rudolph Valentino). Novarro appeared in more than 50 films, successfully making the transition from silent movies to talking pictures. His best-known roles include the lead in *Ben-Hur: A Tale of the Christ* (1925) and the part of Lieutenant Alexis Rosanoff opposite Greta Garbo in *Mata Hari* (1931). Novarro won a Golden Globe Special Award in 1959, and was given a star on the Hollywood Walk of Fame.

Early life
Ramón Gil Samaniego was born in 1889 in Durango, Mexico. His father, Mariano Nicolas Samaniego, was a successful dentist, and his mother, Leonor Gavilán, raised 13 children. During the unrest of the Mexican Revolution in 1910, Novarro's family decided to immigrate to the United States, settling in Los Angeles, California, in 1916. Novarro took casual work as a cinema usher and singing waiter, and between 1917 and 1922 began to find work as an extra in Hollywood movies.

Novarro's first major role came in *The Prisoner of Zenda* in 1922. Promising actor Ramón Samaniego became

▼ **Actor Ramon Novarro plays the title role in the 1925 film Ben-Hur.**

screen idol Ramon Novarro, and parts followed in *Trifling Women* (1922) and *Where the Pavement Ends* (1923). It was his part in the swashbuckling romance *Scaramouche* in 1923, however, that proved to be his breakthrough role, establishing Novarro as the "Latin Valentino."

Among Novarro's best-known performances is the lead role in *Ben-Hur: A Tale of the Christ*. Actor Rudolph Valentino's death in 1926 confirmed Novarro as the new Hollywood heartthrob. Further lead roles followed in *The Student Prince in Old Heidelberg* (1927), *Forbidden Hours* (1928), and *The Flying Fleet* (1929). During the period, Hollywood made the transition from silent films to talking pictures, and *Devil-May-Care* (1929) provided Novarro with his first speaking role. With his excellent speaking and singing voice Novarro easily adapted, playing leading speaking roles in *Call of the Flesh* (1930), *Mata Hari* (1931), *The Barbarian* (1933), and *A Desperate Adventure* (1938).

A brutal end
Novarro appeared in *The Big Steal* in 1949. However, as Hollywood began to favor action stars such as John Wayne, Novarro's popularity began to fade. He had a brief Broadway career and made his final film in 1960 *(Heller in Pink Tights)*, before making the transition to television. His television appearances include *Rawhide* (1964), *Dr. Kildare* (1964), and *The High Chaparral* (1968). Novarro died on October 30, 1968, murdered in his Hollywood Hills home by two brothers who wrongly believed he had a fortune hidden in his house.

Further reading: Soares, A. *Beyond Paradise: The Life of Ramon Navarro.* New York, NY: St Martin's Press. 2002. http://www.ramonnovarro.com (photographs, filmography, and a brief biography).

NOVELLO, Antonia
Doctor

Puerto Rican–born Antonia Novello was the first woman and first Hispanic American to become the Surgeon General of the United States. As a specialist in pediatrics, Novello's term in office was marked by high-profile campaigns against alcohol and tobacco use by children.

Ill health as a child

The chosen career of Novello is little surprising given her traumatic childhood experiences. She was born Antonia Coello in Fajardo, Puerto Rico, in 1944. Her parents, Antonio and Ana Delia Coello, soon discovered that their daughter suffered from a congenital abnormality of the large intestine. Although the condition required surgery to correct, the procedure was never performed during her childhood. Instead, Novello endured frequent visits to the hospital for temporary treatment. Novello's childhood was further blighted by the death of her father in 1952. Her widowed mother struggled to raise Novello alone.

Medical career

Despite her problems, Novello excelled at school. Novello graduated from high school aged just 15 and accepted a place at the University of Puerto Rico at Rio Pedras. During her undergraduate studies, Novello underwent long-awaited surgery to correct her condition. However, complications continued, and Novello was forced to visit the hospital regularly until after her 20th birthday. She then traveled to the world-famous Mayo Clinic on the U.S. mainland for a final operation that met with success.

Novello graduated from the University of Puerto Rico in 1965. Galvanized by her own experience of the medical establishment, Novello immediately applied for a place to study medicine. With the financial support of her mother, who had remarried by then, Novello earned her medical doctor degree in 1970. The same year, she married Navy flight surgeon Joseph R. Novello.

The couple then moved to Ann Arbor, Michigan, to take up residencies at the University of Michigan Medical Center. There, Novello specialized in pediatric kidney

▶ *Antonia Novello answering questions at a press conference in Washington, D.C., in 1999. She is dressed in the uniform of the Public Health Service Commissioned Corps, one of the seven uniformed services of the United States.*

disorders, becoming the first woman to win the pediatrics Intern of the Year award. She then moved to Georgetown University Hospital, in Washington, D.C., completing her training in pediatrics in 1975.

In 1979 Novello joined the Public Health Service Commissioned Corps, the uniformed division of the Public Health Service. Its members are doctors and other

INFLUENCES AND INSPIRATION

Antonia Novello knows what is is like to be let down by a public health system. She suffered with intestinal problems for the first 18 years of her life until the Puerto Rican health service could finally provide her with necessary surgery. Even then, she was forced to travel to the U.S. mainland two years later for further surgery. Novello battled through the discomfort and hardship and excelled in school. She became determined to spare other children the neglect she had suffered for so long.

During her time as Surgeon General, Novello sought to reduce underage drinking, smoking, and the incidence of AIDS. She also endeavored to focus attention on the health problems of women, children, and minorities. Novello helped launch the Healthy Children Ready to Learn Initiative. She also promoted child immunization programs and worked to reduce childhood injuries. Novello pressured the inspector general of Health and Human Services to look into ways of reducing underage drinking and made similar efforts to discourage illegal tobacco use by young people. She was an outspoken critic of the tobacco industry for appealing to children through the use of cartoon characters such as Joe Camel.

professional health workers who swear to protect and promote the health of the nation. The corps is one of seven uniformed services in the United States, along with the Army, Navy, Marines, Air Force, and Coast Guard, and the NOAA Corps, which operates the ships and aircraft of the National Oceanic and Atmospheric Administration.

KEY DATES

1944	Born in Fajardo, Puerto Rico, on August 23.
1952	Her father dies.
1964	Her intestinal problems are finally resolved after surgery at the Mayo Clinic.
1965	Graduates from the University of Puerto Rico.
1970	Receives her medical doctor degree from the University of Puerto Rico.
1975	Completes medical training and begins private pediatric practice.
1978	Joins Public Health Service Commissioned Corps.
1979	Begins work as project officer for the Public Health Service National Institutes of Health.
1982	Receives master's degree in public health from Johns Hopkins University, Baltimore, Maryland.
1986	Becomes deputy director of the National Institute of Child Health and Human Development.
1990	Sworn in as Surgeon General of the United States.
1993	Becomes UNICEF special representative.
1999	Becomes state health commissioner for New York.

Novello began work for the National Institute of Arthritis, Metabolism, and Digestive Diseases in 1979. Determined to further her qualifications, Novello studied for a master's degree in public health at Johns Hopkins University, in Baltimore, Maryland. She graduated in 1982.

Political role

By this time Novello was serving as a congressional fellow, guiding public health policy on issues such as organ transplantation. In 1986 Novello combined her roles as a pediatrician and public health policy advisor by accepting the post of deputy director of the National Institute of Child Health and Human Development. The position offered Novello the chance to draw public attention to the plight of AIDS-infected children.

In 1989 President George H. W. Bush nominated Novello for the position of Surgeon General of the United States. She began work in March 1990 and served for three years. Novello's legacy as Surgeon General lies in her campaigns to raise awareness of children's health-care issues. She continued her work with AIDS-infected children and also campaigned against teenage alcohol and tobacco use.

Following her term as Surgeon General, Novello worked as a United Nations International Children's Emergency Fund (UNICEF) special representative. Since 1999 she has been health commissioner for New York.

Further reading: Hawxhurst, Joan C. *Antonia Novello, U.S. Surgeon General.* Brookfield, CT: Millbrook Press, 1993.
http://www.achievement.org/autodoc/page/nov0bio-1 (biography).
http://www.achievement.org/autodoc/page/nov0int-1 (interview).

NÚÑEZ CABEZA DE VACA, Álvar

Explorer, Geographer

Álvar Núñez Cabeza de Vaca was one of the first Europeans to travel through what is now the southern United States. He landed on the Texas coast in November 1528, and began to explore areas of Texas, New Mexico, and other neighboring regions. Cabeza de Vaca's journey would last eight years and involve war, slavery, and death. The chronicle of Cabeza de Vaca's incredible journey, his escape from captivity, and his return to Spain is an epic tale of exploration and survival that has captured the imaginations of generations since.

Early life

Born in Spain in about 1490, Cabeza de Vaca was the son of Francisco de Vera and Teresa Cabeza de Vaca. His mother's unusual last name means "Cow's Head." The name was bestowed on the family by King Sancho of Navarra after the Battle of Las Navas de Tolosa in 1212. During the battle, one of Teresa's ancestors, a shepherd boy, helped the Spanish army by marking with a cow's skull the mountain pass through which the enemy would pass.

Cabeza de Vaca joined the military as a young man, and fought with distinction for Spain at the Battle of Ravenna (1512) during the Italian Wars (1494–1559). He was promoted to ensign, and went on to serve as an aide to the Duke of Medina Sidonia, Spain's most important grandee.

Ill-fated expedition to Florida

In 1527 Cabeza de Vaca was appointed royal treasurer on an expedition to Florida. Commanded by Pánfilo de Narváez, the objectives of the expedition were to explore some of the southern mainland of North America and to settle a Spanish colony.

Narváez left Spain in June 1527 with five ships. Three months later, the fleet reached Santo Domingo (now the capital of the Dominican Republic). Almost immediately, Cabeza de Vaca's ship and two of the other vessels sailed

▼ *Spanish explorer Álvar Núñez Cabeza de Vaca (second right) surveys the landscape during his ill-fated expedition in 1535.*

INFLUENCES AND INSPIRATION

Álvar Núñez Cabeza de Vaca's detailed accounts of the native tribes he encountered during his travels, as well as his descriptions of the geographical landscape through which he passed, appear in *La Relacion de Cabeza de Vaca*. Written by Cabeza de Vaca in 1537, the book recounts his experiences in the southwest United States and describes everything from the almost two dozen native American tribes he spent time among to the search for gold, and the question of human rights in native societies. Read by Spanish explorers during the 16th century, *La Relación de Cabeza de Vaca* provided a roadmap for notable later explorers of the Southwest, such as Francisco Vásquez de Coronado, Pedro de Alvarado, and Don Juan de Zaldívar.

on to Cuba in search of further supplies. Cabeza de Vaca decided to remain on the island until good weather returned the following spring, but during the winter two of his ships were destroyed in a hurricane.

Narváez's ships had also suffered storm damage in Cuba. When they were repaired, all the explorers reunited and sailed on together to the west coast of Florida. On landing, Narváez, Cabeza de Vaca, and more than 300 other men set off to explore the land in search of the Río Panuco (River of Palms), which Narváez believed to be nearby. The expedition was, in fact, more than 1,500 miles (2400km) away from the river, and soon became lost. Over the next three months the party traveled to northwestern Florida. Confronted by hostile native peoples, and running low on supplies, the explorers lived off the land and melted down any metal items to fashion saws, axs, and other equipment. They built five boats, using their clothing for sails and hair from the manes and tails of horses to make rope.

In 1528 the stranded expedition set sail. Its luck did not improve, however. A storm soon forced the voyagers to separate from each other. Narváez was drowned, but Cabeza de Vaca made it to the safety of an island near the westernmost point of Galveston Island. He and his men named their discovery Isla de Malhado (Island of Misfortune).

KEY DATES

1490 Born in Jerez de la Frontera, Spain, at about this time.

1527 Appointed as treasurer in the American expedition of Panfilo de Narváez.

1536 Arrives at Culiacan, a Spanish outpost in Mexico, after seven years in Texas and parts of the southwestern United States.

1540s Appointed governor of Paraguay.

1556 Dies in Spain.

At death's door

Soon after landing on Isla de Malhado, Cabeza de Vaca became seriously ill and was near death. In fact, the rest of his party thought he had died and continued along the coast. Remarkably, however, Cabeza de Vaca survived his illness and managed to make a modest living by trading with local peoples in shells from the coastal waters and the beans that grew on mesquite trees. Cabeza de Vaca also became widely revered as a healer and remained in the area that was later known as Galveston for several years.

Another man who survived the storms was Lope de Oviedo. In 1532 both men traveled along the Texas coast to Panuco, Mexico. Oviedo turned back along the way, but Cabeza de Vaca went on, and caught up with three other men from the original Narváez expedition. At what was probably the Guadalupe River, the four men were captured and enslaved by Mariame Indians. The men had to wait another two years before they were able to make their escape. They traveled from Galveston to Culiacan, an outpost along the coast of Mexico. They finally returned to Europe in 1536.

Cabeza de Vaca reaches home

At the end of his seven-year expedition through Texas to the Rio Grande in Mexico, Álvar Núñez Cabeza de Vaca became the first Spaniard to describe that part of North America. In the 1540s Cabeza de Vaca was made governor of what is now known as Paraguay. He was accused of misconduct during his rule and sent to Africa. Later, he was cleared of the charge and returned to Spain.

Further reading: Krieger, Alex D. (editor). *We Came Naked and Barefoot: The Journey of Cabeza de Vaca.* Austin, TX: University of Texas Press. 2002.
http://www.cah.utexas.edu (Web site of Texas history at the University of Texas at Austin).

OBEJAS, Achy
Writer

Achy Obejas is a Cuban American writer from Chicago, Illinois. She is also a lecturer in creative writing and a literary critic and journalist.

Coming to America
Obejas was born in Havana, Cuba, in 1956. In 1962, after the Cuban revolution, her family went into exile to the United States, making the journey to their new home in a small boat. The Obejas family were of Sephardic Jewish ancestry. (The Sephardim were Jews who lived in Spain, Portugal, North Africa, and the Middle East. In the 1490s they were expelled from Spain and Portugal.)

Obejas spent her childhood in Michigan City, Indiana. Since 1979 she has lived in Chicago, Illinois, but divides her time between Chicago and Havana.

Hispanic and Jewish
Obejas has a multifacted identity. She is an immigrant, an exile, a Cuban American, a Hispanic American woman, a Sephardic Jew, and a lesbian. These labels have been the focus of her writing as she explores her reaction and resistance to a mainstream U.S. culture where all things and people are categorized and marginalized.

However, Obejas is in no doubt about the significance of her Cuban identity: "I was born in Havana and that single event pretty much defined the rest of my life. In the United States, I'm Cuban, a Cuban American, Latina by virtue of being Cuban, a Cuban journalist, a Cuban writer, somebody's Cuban lover, a Cuban dyke, a Cuban girl on a bus, a Cuban exploring her Sephardic roots, always and endlessly Cuban. I'm more Cuban here than I am in Cuba, by sheer contrast and repetition."

Groundbreaking achievements
Obejas's collection of short stories, *We Came All the Way from Cuba so You Could Dress like This?* (1994), was the first publication by an openly lesbian Cuban writer. She is the author of two novels: *Memory Mambo* (1996), which deals with the intricacies of memory, and *Days of Awe* (2001), the story of a Sephardic Jewish family in Cuba and the United States.

Both works have been awarded the prestigious Lambda Award for lesbian fiction. *Days of Awe* was also acclaimed Best Book of the Year by both the *Los Angeles Times* and *Chicago Tribune*. Literary critics and historians have also

KEY DATES	
1956	Born in Havana, Cuba.
1962	Moves to the United States.
1979	Settles in Chicago, Illinois.
1994	Publishes *We Came All the Way from Cuba so You Could Dress like This?*
1996	Publishes *Memory Mambo*.
2001	Publishes *Days of Awe*.

prized and recommended the book as an invaluable source of accurate information about the long-neglected Sephardic Jewish history in Cuba and the rest of the Americas. (Most American Jews are Ashkenazim, descended from communites originating in northern Europe.)

Obejas's poems have been published in magazines and journals such as *Revista Chicano-Riqueña, Third Woman, Conditions, Bilingual Review,* and *Beloit Poetry Journal*. Her short stories have been widely anthologized in collections, including *By Heart: De Memoria: Cuban Women's Journeys In and Out of Exile* (2003), *Chicago Works: A New Collection of Chicago Author's Best Stories* (2003), *Crossing into America: The New Literature of Immigration* (2003), *The Vintage Book of International Lesbian Fiction* (1999), *Little Havana Blues: A Cuban-American Literature Anthology* (1996), *Latina: Women's Voices from the Borderlands* (1995), *The Way We Write Now: Short Stories from the AIDS Crisis* (1995), *West Side Stories* (1992), and *Discontents: New Queer Writers* (1992).

Her journalistic essays and critical articles on the arts and culture have appeared in *Vogue, Playboy, The Village Voice, Los Angeles Times, Chicago Reader, The Nation, Chicago Tribune, Windy City Times,* and *High Performance*. In 2001, Obejas shared the Pulitzer Prize with her team for their work on the *Chicago Tribune*. Her incisive journalism has also made her the recipient of the Studs Terkel Journalism Prize and the Peter Lisagor Award.

Further reading: Obejas, Achy. *Days of Awe*. New York: Ballantine Books, 2001.
http://voices.cla.umn.edu/vg/Bios/entries/obejas_achy.html (biography).

OBLEDO, Mario
Attorney

Mario Obledo is a Mexican American lawyer who became prominent in the civil rights movement of the 1960s.

Early life
Obledo was one of 12 children from a family of poor Mexican immigrants. He attended public schools in San Antonio, Texas, and then studied pharmacy at the University of Texas at Austin. Shortly after he arrived at the university, however, the Korean War (1950–1953) began, and Obledo joined the U.S. Navy. After the conflict, Obledo returned to full-time education, and completed his degree in 1957. While an undergraduate, he joined the League of United Latin American Citizens (LULAC).

Obledo began practicing pharmacy, and also pursued a law degree at St. Mary's University law school in San Antonio. He became a lawyer in 1960, and joined the staff of the Texas attorney general. In 1966, Chicano farmworkers held a march to demand a minimum wage of $1.25 an hour. The attorney general and the state governor tried to stop the protest, and their conduct so disgusted Obledo that he quit his job to help set up a legal defense fund for Mexican Americans. Around the same time, he also cofounded the La Raza Lawyer Association, the National Hispanic Bar Association, and the National Coalition of Hispanic Organizations.

MALDEF's general counsel and president
Obledo was appointed as general counsel of the Mexican American Legal Defense and Education Fund (MALDEF).

▲ **President Bill Clinton presents Mario Obledo with a Presidential Medal of Freedom in 1998.**

He was active in the ultimately successful legal struggles for the implementation of single-member districts in Texas, and for the extension in 1975 of the Voting Rights Act (1965) to cover speakers of minority languages. When MALDEF relocated its national office to Los Angeles, California, Obledo became the fund's national president.

Political involvement
On the election of liberal Democrat Jerry Brown as California governor in 1975, Obledo accepted an appointment to head the Department of Health, Education, and Welfare. After his retirement, Obledo became national president of LULAC. He ran for governor of California, and protested the use of a Chihuahua dog with a comic Spanish accent in an advertisement for the Taco Bell Corporation. Obledo opposed Mexican guest worker programs and the nominations of Miguel Estrada to the D.C. Court of Appeals and Alberto Gonzales as U.S. attorney general. In 1998, Mario Obledo was awarded a Presidential Medal of Freedom for his lifetime of civil-rights work.

See also: Estrada, Miguel A.; Gonzales, Alberto

Further reading: http://www.lulac.org/advocacy/press/archive/obledo.html
www.tsha.utexas.edu/handbook/online/articles/MM/jom1.html

KEY DATES

1915 Born in San Antonio, Texas, to Mexican parents who had migrated to the United States.

1968 Becomes cofounder of the Mexican American Legal Defense and Education Fund (MALDEF) and serves as its general counsel.

1975 Becomes California's Secretary of Health, Education, and Welfare, and national president of MALDEF.

1983 Becomes national president of the League of United Latin American Citizens (LULAC).

1998 Awarded a Presidential Medal of Freedom by President Bill Clinton.

OBREGÓN, Eugene Arnold
Medal of Honor Recipient

Private First Class (PFC) Eugene Arnold Obregón is one of 40 Latino servicemen who have been awarded the Congressional Medal of Honor, the United States's highest military award. Obregón's outstanding act of bravery during the Korean War (1950–1953) highlights the committed service that many Hispanic Americans have given to their country, not only in that conflict but in U.S. military engagements throughout history.

Private "Obri"
Eugene Arnold Obregón was born on November 12, 1930, in Los Angeles, California, and attended Roosevelt High School. In 1948, at age 17, Obregón enlisted in the U.S. Marine Corps. Following recruit training at San Diego, he was assigned to the Marine Corps Supply Depot at Barstow, where he served as a fireman.

As is popular in the military, PFC Obregón was soon given a nickname, and became known to his fellow Marines as "Obri." During his time at Barstow, his closest friend was a Texan from Grand Prairie, PFC Bert "Bobo" Johnson. Little did the men know that their friendship would soon be put to the ultimate test.

War in Korea
In June 1950, Communist North Korea launched a full-scale invasion of South Korea, and the United Nations (UN) sent in troops—composed largely of U.S. Army and Marine Corps personnel—to halt the attack. Both Obregón and Johnson were sent to Korea almost immediately as part of the 1st Marine Division. Their unit departed the United States on July 14, 1950, and arrived at Pusan, Korea, on August 3. By August 8, Obregón and Johnson were involved in their first action, along the Naktong River. In mid-September, they were involved in the successful landing

at Inchon, as a result of which UN troops were able to establish themselves within 25 miles (40km) of Seoul, the occupied South Korean capital.

A gallant death
On September 26, 1950, during the assault on Seoul, came the act of heroism in which Obregón would sacrifice his life. Obregón was serving as a machine-gun ammunition carrier. As the U.S. Marines fought their way along one of the broad boulevards that led into the city, Johnson was wounded by enemy fire. Obregón, armed only with a pistol, ran from his position of cover to his friend's aid. Firing with one hand and dragging his friend with the other, Obregón reached the side of the road where, still under fire, he began to bandage Johnson's wounds. The two soldiers now came under attack from a whole advancing North Korean platoon, so Obregón shielded Johnson with his own body and, picking up his friend's rifle, fired back accurately and effectively at the enemy. Obregón was eventually struck in the face by two bullets and was killed. Nevertheless, he had gained enough time with his actions for Johnson to be rescued by their fellow Marines.

Commemorating a war hero
On August 30, 1951, the secretary of the Navy, Daniel A. Kimball, presented Eugene Obregón's parents with his posthumous Medal of Honor. Obregón was also awarded several other decorations, including a Purple Heart and a Korean Service Medal with three bronze stars. In subsequent years, a U.S. naval vessel, a Los Angeles elementary school, parks, and barracks have all been named in Obregón's honor. More recently, two Hispanic American veterans set up a fund with the object of raising a memorial to commemorate Latino Medal of Honor recipients in Los Angeles's Pershing Square. The proposed statue for the monument depicts Obregón's heroic defense of his fallen comrade.

See also: Military

Further reading: www.homeofheroes.com/moh/citations_1950_kc/obregon_eugene.html (Citation for Medal of Honor). hqinet001.hqmc.usmc.mil/HD/Historical/Whos_Who/Obregon_EA.htm (short biography of Eugene Arnold Obregón).

KEY DATES

1930 Born in East Los Angeles, California, on November 12.

1948 Enlists in the U.S. Marine Corps.

1950 Sent to South Korea with the 1st Marine Division in June, at the beginning of the Korean War; killed in action in Seoul, South Korea, on September 26.

1951 Awarded the Congressional Medal of Honor.

O'BRIEN, Soledad
Journalist

S oledad O'Brien is a respected U.S. broadcaster. The coanchor of the popular CNN program *American Morning*, O'Brien has received several awards for her work.

Early life
María de la Soledad O'Brien was born in St. James, New York, on September 19, 1966. Her Irish Australian father, Edward, was a mechanical engineering professor, and her Afro-Cuban mother, Estrella, was a teacher. O'Brien grew up in a family of six children on Long Island. She went to Smithtown High School East in St. James.

Becoming a broadcaster
In 1989 O'Brien graduated from Harvard University with a BA in English and American Literature. As a student she worked as an intern at the NBC-Boston affiliate WBZ-TV. O'Brien went on to work as an associate producer and newswriter for the station. In 1993 she moved to California to work at the San Francisco-based KRON-TV, also an NBC

affiliate. O'Brien worked as an on-air reporter before cohosting *The Know Zone* with Don Bleu. The program earned O'Brien an Emmy in 1995.

In 1996 O'Brien got her big break when she was asked by MSNBC to work on *The Site*, a new show aimed at Internet users. The program was very successful, and O'Brien became a national TV personality, leading *Salon* magazine to call her the "goddess of the geeks."

O'Brien moved on to anchor the *Morning Blend*. Her good looks combined with a sharp journalistic style soon made her a popular broadcaster with audiences.

In 1999 she joined NBC to coanchor the *Weekend Today*. Her reports of significant events, such as the death of John F. Kennedy, Jr., the Space Shuttle *Columbia* disaster, and the U.S. war with Iraq, received critical acclaim. In July 2003 O'Brien was appointed to present CNN's *American Morning* with Miles O'Brien (no relation). Her reports on such important events as the 2004 U.S. presidential election, the December 2004 tsunami, and the July 2005 terrorist bombings in London, England, have confirmed her status as one of the United States's top journalists.

O'Brien is a member of both the National Association of Hispanic Journalists and the National Association of Black Journalists. She also made *Irish American Magazine*'s Top 100 Irish Americans list. O'Brien is married to investment banker Bradley Raymond.

▲ *Soledad O'Brien has reported on a number of breaking stories of international importance, such as the July 2005 terrorist bombings in London, England.*

KEY DATES	
1966	Born in St. James, New York, on September 19.
1989	Works as an intern for WBZ-TV.
1993	Goes to work for KRON-TV, San Francisco.
1995	Wins an Emmy award for *The Know Zone*.
1996	Becomes anchor for the Internet program *The Site*.
1999	Becomes coanchor (with David Bloom) of *Weekend Today*.
2003	Becomes coanchor (with Miles O'Brien) of *American Morning*.

Further reading: http://www.cnn.com/CNN/anchors_reporters/obrien.soledad.html (biography on CNN).

OCAMPO, Adriana
Scientist

Adriana Ocampo is a leading research scientist at the headquarters in Washington, D.C., of the National Aeronautics and Space Administration (NASA).

Early life

Ocampo was born in 1955 in Baranquila, Colombia. She grew up in Buenos Aires, Argentina, and was fascinated by outer space from an early age. In 1969 she moved with her family to Pasadena, California. Three years later recruiting officers from NASA's Pasadena-based Jet Propulsion Laboratory (JPL) visited Ocampo's high school in search of prospective space scientists. In 1973, after graduating from high school, Ocampo took up an offer of a job at JPL, but meanwhile continued to study at Pasadena Community College.

Space missions

In 1976 Ocampo became a full-time member of the team responsible for the Viking missions to Mars. She worked as a programmer for the imaging equipment used to survey the planet's two moons, Phobos and Deimos. Having spent so much time studying rocks on the surface of Mars as part of the Viking missions, Ocampo opted to study geology and planetary science at California State University. In 1983 she received her bachelor's degree and returned to work at JPL, again specializing in imaging. Ocampo subsequently worked on a range of high-profile planetary explorations, including the Voyager missions to the outer planets and the Galileo mission to Jupiter.

Chicxulub crater

In 1988 Ocampo produced valuable research on the Chicxulub impact crater in Belize. Throughout the 1990s she conducted several expeditions to the site, formed about 65 million years ago when an asteroid hit the Earth. Ocampo's work, funded by NASA and the Planetary Society, earned her a master's degree from California State University, Northridge, in 1997.

In 1998 Ocampo moved to NASA headquarters in Washington, D.C. There, in addition to her duties as research scientist in the offices of space science and earth science, she worked as desk officer for international space science missions in the Office of External Relations. As part of her job, Ocampo regularly met with space scientists from Japan, Russia, and Europe.

KEY DATES	
1955	Born in Baranquila, Colombia, on January 5.
1969	Moves to Pasadena, California.
1973	Starts work at NASA's Jet Propulsion Laboratory.
1980	Becomes a U.S. citizen.
1983	Receives BA degree in geology and planetary science from California State University.
1988	Starts research on Chicxulub crater in Belize.
1997	Receives MA in geology.
1998	Relocates to NASA headquarters in Washington, D.C.

Science for all

One of Ocampo's ambitions was to introduce space science to a wider audience, particularly people from developing countries. In 1987, again funded by the Planetary Society, she set up a workshop in planetary science in Mexico City, Mexico. It was so successful that the United Nations set up similar workshops in countries all over the world.

Ocampo is a director of the Society of Hispanic Professional Engineers (SHPE). She also serves on the Planetary Society Advisory Council and is a member of the Association of Women in Geoscience, the American Institute of Aeronautics and Astronautics, and the Society of Women Engineers.

In 1990 Ocampo organized the first Space Conference of the Americas to be held in Costa Rica. The conference takes place every three years and aims to increase the peaceful use of space science and technology among Pan-American countries.

In recognition of her contributions to science, Ocampo has received many accolades, including the 1996 JPL Advisory Council for Women Award for outreach and community work.

Further reading: Hopping, Lorraine Jean. *Space Rocks: The Story of Planetary Geologist Adriana Ocampo.* New York, NY: Franklin Watts, 2005.
www.jpl.nasa.gov/tours/women/ocampo.html (brief profile of Ocampo from the JPL Web site).

OCHOA, Ellen
Astronaut

A noted inventor and scientist, Ellen Ochoa was the first female astronaut of Hispanic descent in the NASA program.

Early life
Ochoa was born on May 10, 1958, in Los Angeles, California. When Ochoa was in junior high, her parents separated, and she lived with her mother, sister, and three brothers. Ochoa was always encouraged to excel in school, and during her teenage years developed an interest in math. She was also a noted classical flutist. Ochoa graduated from high school at the top of her class; her ambition was to complete a college degree.

In 1975 Ochoa entered San Diego State University and pursued a bachelor's degree in physics, graduating in 1980 with honors. She studied electrical engineering at Stanford University, completing a master's degree in 1981 and a doctorate degree in 1985. During this period, Ochoa also performed with the Stanford Symphony Orchestra as a soloist. It was during this time that Ochoa first realized that she wanted to become the first Latina astronaut accepted by NASA.

Realizing a dream
In 1985 Ochoa and other fellow students at Stanford applied to the NASA astronaut training program. She was finally selected as an astronaut candidate in 1987. From 1985 to 1988 Ochoa worked as a researcher at Sandia National Laboratories in Albuquerque, New Mexico, and subsequently at the NASA Ames Research Center in Mountain View, California. Ochoa gained experience in optical systems development and in information processing performance for space exploration applications.

▲ **Ellen Ochoa is not only a talented scientist and astronaut but a recognized solo flutist as well.**

She also coinvented an optical inspection system, an optical object recognition device, and a noise-reducing method.

In 1990 Ochoa began her astronaut training at the Johnson Space Center in Houston, Texas. This demanding program consisted of physical exercises and academic training in the fields of meteorology, astronomy, oceanography, and space and orbiter systems. Ochoa had her first opportunity to be on a space mission aboard the space shuttle *Discovery* in April 1993, after which she was part of the team aboard *Atlantis* in November 1994. She operated a remote robotic arm to deploy and capture a satellite containing data on solar activity. Ochoa's third space flight was as a mission specialist and flight engineer aboard *Discovery* in May 1999; as part of those duties she was involved in the docking of the space shuttle with the International Space Station (ISS) for the first time, and the transfer of supplies from the vehicle to the station.

Ochoa has also worked in various technical support positions with NASA at Houston, serving as crew representative for robotics, checking flight software, and working at Mission Control as spacecraft communicator. She is a member of the American Institute of Aeronautics and Astronautics. Ochoa has received several awards for her contributions to the space program and for her scholarship, including NASA's Exceptional Service Medal.

Further reading: Cassutt, Michael. *Who's Who in Space.* New York, NY: Macmillan, 1999.
http://www11.jsc.nasa.gov/Bios/index.html (official NASA biography).

KEY DATES	
1958	Born in Los Angeles, California, on May 10.
1985	Receives a doctorate in electrical engineering from Stanford University.
1987	Becomes the first Hispanic female to join NASA's astronaut training program.
1993	Serves on the first of three space missions.
1997	Receives NASA's Exceptional Service Medal.

OCHOA, Estevan
Entrepreneur, Politician

Tucson, Arizona, became part of the United States when the United States and Mexico negotiated the Gadsden Purchase in 1854. In the years after the annexation, Mexicans remained a majority in Tucson, making contributions to the political, economic, and cultural life of southern Arizona. One of the most famous Mexicans of the time was Estevan Ochoa, a diminutive man who made such an impact that modern-day Tucson still benefits from the influence of his legacy.

The land of opportunity

Estevan Ochoa was born in 1831 in Chihuahua, Mexico, to a well-to-do family. As a boy, he accompanied his brother's freight trains from Chihuahua to Independence, Missouri. He quickly acquired a command of English but retained his native Spanish. Early in life, Ochoa developed a sense of business and human relations, dealing with both Mexican and U.S. business people.

At age 28, Ochoa moved to Mesilla, New Mexico, where he started a business with a Mexican partner. Within a year, however, this first business venture fell apart and Ochoa decided to relocate to Tucson.

Ochoa the entrepreneur

Immediately upon his arrival in Tucson, Ochoa formed a company that became known as Tully, Ochoa and Co. It was soon to become one of the largest, most diversified economic empires in early territorial Arizona. At the time Ochoa started the firm, freighting was already Arizona's most important industry. With the skills he had developed in the field, Ochoa soon became one of Arizona's leading entrepreneurs, trading and transporting goods all over the Southwest. Tucson became the center for upper- and middle-class Mexican society. Ochoa was the epitome of

▲ *This photograph shows Estevan Ochoa as a Wells Fargo agent in Pantano, Arizona, in 1870.*

the nascent Mexican elite. He was a merchant, freighter, and philanthropist, and in 1875 became the only Mexican elected mayor of Tucson after the Gadsden Purchase. He also served as justice of the peace and served in the fifth, sixth, and seventh Arizona territorial legislatures.

Ochoa the philanthropist

Ochoa was a strong believer in education. One of his greatest contributions was in the area of public education. He introduced a bill in the territorial legislature to levy a property tax to support public schools in Arizona. In 1871, he was chairman of the education committee and introduced a bill to establish Arizona's first public schools. Ochoa served as the president of the Tucson School Board, and donated the land and supervised the construction of the first modern public school in Arizona.

KEY DATES

1831 Born in Chihuahua, Mexico, on March 13.

1859 Founds Tully, Ochoa and Co., in Tucson, Arizona.

1872 Is instrumental in opening Tuscon's first public school.

1875 Elected mayor of Tucson.

1888 Dies in Las Cruces, New Mexico, on October 27.

Further reading: Sheridan, T. E. *Los Tucsonenses: The Mexican Community in Tucson, 1854–1941.* Tucson, AZ: University of Arizona Press, 1986.
http://parentseyes.arizona.edu/mexamer-bios.html (Tucson regional history Web site).

OCHOA, Severo
Scientist

Severo Ochoa was a pioneer in the fledgling fields of biochemistry and molecular biology. Official recognition of his work came in 1959, when he became the first Hispanic American to receive the Nobel Prize in medicine or physiology for his work with Arthur Kornberg.

Early life

Severo Ochoa de Albornoz was born in Luarca, Spain, on September 24, 1905. He was named after his father, a lawyer and businessman who died when Ochoa was seven years old. His devoted mother, Carmen de Albornoz, moved her seven children to Málaga, southern Spain. Ochoa, who was the youngest, attended high school there, before studying for a BA at Málaga College.

Ochoa was introduced to Spanish physician and neurologist Santiago Ramón y Cajal (*see box on page 74*), who became a great influence. Absorbed by Cajal's pioneering work on histology and the anatomy of the nervous system, Ochoa enrolled at the medical school of the University of Madrid in the hope of studying under his

▼ *A renowned biochemist, Severo Ochoa won the Nobel Prize in 1959 for his work on the metabolism of carbohydrates and fatty acids.*

idol. Unfortunately for Ochoa, the great scientist had retired by the time that he began studying at the university. Ochoa received his medical degree in 1929.

Working abroad

Over the next 12 years, Ochoa worked with some of Europe's leading academics. With funding from the Spanish Council of Scientific Research, Ochoa first went to the Kaiser Wilhelm Insitut at the University of Heidelburg in Germany. There he studied biochemistry and physiology under the German biochemist Otto Meyerhof (1884–1951).

In 1931 Ochoa moved back to Spain to work as a physiology lecturer at the University of Madrid; in that year he also married Carmen García Cobián. The year after their marriage, Ochoa and his wife traveled to London, where he worked as a researcher at the National Institute for Medical Research under H.A. Dudley (1887–1935). In 1934 Ochoa returned to Madrid and took up a post as head of the Physiology Division of the Institute of Medical Research.

In 1936 Ochoa was forced to leave Spain following the outbreak of the Spanish Civil War (1936–1939). He accepted a post as guest research assistant under Meyerhof at the Kaiser Wilhelm Insitut. A year later, he moved back to England to work at the Plymouth Marine Biological Laboratory. Between the years 1938 and 1941, Ochoa studied at the University of Oxford under Professor R.A. Peters (1889–1982). Ochoa's research involved studying the structure and function of vitamin B1, but his time at Oxford also marked the start of the work that would lead to a Nobel Prize.

Life in the United States

In 1941 Ochoa moved to the United States. Nobel Prize-winning biochemists Carl (1896–1984) and Gerty Cori (1896–1957) invited him to work as a research associate in pharmacology at the Washington University School of Medicine in St. Louis. He worked on problems to do with enzymology. In the following year, Ochoa accepted a job as a research associate at the New York University School of Medicine; he became assistant professor of biochemistry in 1945, professor of pharmacology in 1946, and finally professor of biochemistry and chair of the biochemistry department in 1954.

INFLUENCES AND INSPIRATION

In 1959 Severo Ochoa won the Nobel Prize in medicine or physiology with U.S.-born scientist Arthur Kornberg (1918–). After training with Ochoa in enzymology at the New York University School of Medicine in 1946, Kornberg worked with Professor Carl Cori at Washington University School of Medicine. Ochoa and Kornberg were the first scientists to identify the enzyme catalyzing the synthesis of DNA, polymerase I.

Ochoa acknowledged the people who had been major influences in his work during the acceptance speech he gave at the Nobel banquet in Sweden on December 10, 1958. He first paid homage to the pioneering work of Santiago Ramón y Cajal, the Nobel laureate of 1906. Cajal published a huge volume of work during his illustrious career as a physician and academic, stimulating Ochoa's early interest in biology and

medicine. Another important role model was Otto Meyerhof, Ochoa's "admired teacher and friend," and another Nobel laureate of 1929. Meyerhof tutored Ochoa at Heidelburg, Germany. Meyerhof's exceptional enthusiasm and talent as both an academic and mentor influenced Ochoa's choice of career. Ochoa also thanked renowned biochemists Carl and Gerty Cori for enlarging his "intellectual experience."

Nobel work

Most of Ochoa's research dealt with enzymology. In 1955 Ochoa made the discovery for which he earned his Nobel Prize four years later. With his colleague and former pupil Arthur Kornberg, Ochoa identified an enzyme in bacteria responsible for the synthesis of ribonucleic acid (RNA), a molecule used by cells to make proteins. The

discovery marked an important step in the understanding of how genes encoded in deoxyribonucleic acid (DNA) direct the manufacture of proteins. Ochoa also became a U.S. citizen during this time.

Between 1974 and 1985, Ochoa worked as a distinguished researcher at the Roche Institute of Molecular Biology in Nutley, New Jersey. He then moved back to Spain, where he spent his final years as honorary director of the newly formed Center of Molecular Biology Severo Ochoa (part of the Autonomous University of Madrid), which he had helped to create. He also advised the Spanish authorities on science policy. Ochoa died in Madrid on November 1, 1993.

For services to science

Ochoa held several honors and awards during his lifetime. In addition to his Nobel Prize, other awards included the Neuberg Medal in Biochemistry (1951), the Medal of New York University (1959), and the Medal of the Société Chimie Biologique (1959). He was an active member of several respected international societies, including the International Union of Biochemistry. Ochoa was also awarded several honorary doctorates by prestigious universities around the world, including the University of Glasgow, Scotland; University of Oxford, England; and Wesleyan University.

KEY DATES

1905   Born in Luarca, Spain, on September 24.

1929   Graduates with honors from the medical school of the University of Madrid; works under Otto Meyerhof at the Kaiser Wilhelm Insitut für Medizinische Forschung.

1931   Marries Carmen García Cobián; becomes a lecturer in physiology at the University of Madrid.

1938   Accepts three-year post at the University of Oxford under Professor R.A. Peters.

1941   Moves to the United States.

1954   Becomes professor of biochemistry and chair of the biochemistry department at the New York University School of Medicine.

1956   Becomes a U.S. citizen.

1959   Wins Nobel Prize in medicine or physiology with Arthur Kornberg.

1974   Works as a researcher at the Roche Institute of Molecular Biology.

1985   Moves back to Madrid, Spain.

1993   Dies of pneumonia in Madrid on November 1.

Further reading: Garretson, Gregory. *Severo Ochoa.* Oxford, England: Raintree, 2005.

http://nobelprize.org/medicine/laureates/1959/index.html (official site of the Nobel Prize; includes a biography of Ochoa and transcripts of his Nobel lecture and banquet speech; also includes information on Kornberg).

OCHOA, Víctor
Artist

Víctor Ochoa is a major figure in the Chicano art movement. Part of the first generation of artists who shared the aims of the Chicano civil rights movement, he paints educational murals in barrios and produces political posters.

Early life

Ochoa was born in 1948 in Los Angeles, California, and raised there until 1955, when his Mexican American parents were deported to Mexico. He returned to the United States in 1963. His early experiences gave him first-hand experience of alienation in two cultures, and had a lasting effect on his life and work. Settling in San Diego, Ochoa supported himself through school. He received a BA in fine art from San Diego State University in 1974. The following year his work was displayed at Chicanarted, a seminal exhibition of Chicano work organized by the Los Angeles Municipal Art Gallery.

Community art

Meanwhile, in 1970, Ochoa had cofounded the Centro Cultural de la Raza. During his two terms as its director—first from 1970 to 1973, and then from 1988 to 1990—he

▼ *This portable mural, entitled* **Border Realities,** *was created by Ochoa in 1985.*

KEY DATES

1948 Born in Los Angeles, California.

1955 Deported with family to Mexico.

1963 Returns to the United States.

1970 Cofounds the Centro Cultural de la Raza in San Diego to help nurture Chicano art.

1980 Unveils *Geronimo*, his first major mural.

was instrumental in the establishment of community murals in San Diego's Chicano Park. The Centro Cultural de la Raza became the main establishment for Chicano art in the city.

Geronimo (1980), on the round façade of the Centro Cultural de la Raza building, consolidated Ochoa's reputation as a muralist. The work, which depicts an Apache warrior as a freedom fighter, had a lasting impact, and was subsequently included in *Chicano Art: Resistance and Affirmation (CARA) 1965–1985*, a major retrospective held in 1991 at the Wight Art Gallery of the University of California, Los Angeles (UCLA).

Teaching and painting

In 1984 Ochoa cofounded the Border Arts Workshop/Taller de Arte Fronterizo (BAW/TAF), an art collective that carried out projects along the U.S.–Mexico frontier itself and in Tijuana. His series of posters entitled *Border Bingo/Lotería Fronteriza* (1987), which caricatured border politics, were a central feature of *Just Another Poster: Chicano Graphic Arts*, an exhibition held in 2001 at the University Art Museum, Santa Barbara.

Since 1988 Ochoa has been an instructor in the department of crosscultural studies at Grossmont College, El Cajon, California. He taught at the University of California, San Diego, between 1995 and 1996. The Victor Ochoa Papers' Archive was established in 1997 at the University of California, Santa Barbara.

Further reading: Keller, Gary D., et al. (eds.). *Contemporary Chicana and Chicano Art: Artists, Works, Culture, and Education*. Tempe, AZ: Bilingual Press/Editorial Bilingüe, 2002. http://www.chicanozauruz.com (Web site dedicated to the work of Ochoa).

OCHOA, Victor L.
Revolutionary, Inventor

In the 1890s, Chicano Victor L. Ochoa led one of the many uprisings against the authoritarian Mexican president Porfirio Díaz (1830–1915), and subsequently gained a reputation as one of the folk heroes of the U.S.–Mexico borderlands. Later in life, however, Ochoa settled down to a quieter career as an entrepreneur and inventor, responsible for a somewhat eccentric range of prototypes, including an early kind of airplane.

The El Paso rebel

Victor Leaton Ochoa was born in 1850 in the Mexican border town of Ojinaga, of mixed Mexican and Scottish ancestry. His father was a well–to–do timber merchant who owned large estates in northern Mexico and west Texas and a lumber mill at Fort Davis, Texas. Ochoa grew up largely in El Paso, Texas.

In 1889, Victor Ochoa became a U.S. citizen. By this time, he had become an important figure in El Paso's Tejano community. Around 1891, Ochoa helped set up a "sociedad mutualista," or self-help organization, as a way

▼ *Victor Ochoa led an unlikely life as a revolutionary soldier who became an eccentric inventor.*

KEY DATES

1850 Born in Ojinaga, Mexico.

1889 Becomes a United States citizen.

1893 Leads a revolt in northern Mexico.

1897 Leaves prison and begins inventing career.

1945 Thought to have died in Sinoloa, Mexico.

of promoting community solidarity and cultural pride. Ochoa also remained interested in Mexican affairs and was a vehement opponent of President Porfirio Díaz. In 1893, Ochoa gathered a band of Mexican and Mexican American rebels and stirred up unrest across northern Mexico. Díaz was worried enough to promise a $50,000 reward for his capture "dead or alive."

The following year, Díaz's troops surrounded Ochoa and his soldiers in the northern mountains, and in the ensuing fight only Ochoa survived among the rebels. Disguising himself in the uniform of a Mexican soldier, he escaped across the border. Soon after, however, he was captured by the Texas Rangers, and was sent for trial in New York City, accused of trying to raise an army on U.S. territory. In 1895 he was found guilty and sentenced to a two–year prison sentence.

The New York inventor

After his release from prison, Ochoa remained in New York City, where he turned his back on politics to raise a family and to concentrate on his career as an inventor. His earliest obsession was with inventing a flying machine, and during the early 1900s he created a succession of models, culminating in the Ochoa Plane, based on two bicycles. In order to manufacture his invention, he set up the International Airship Company in Patterson, New Jersey, though without any long–term success. Other inventions were less ambitious and more profitable: In 1907, Ochoa sold a patent for an electric brake for streetcars and, in 1922, he sold a patent for an adjustable wrench.

Further reading: www.smithsonianeducation.org/scitech/impacto/graphic/victor/index.html (Smithsonian biography focusing on Ochoa's career as an inventor).

O'FARRILL, Arturo "Chico"
Musician

Arturo "Chico" O'Farrill was one of the leading Latin jazz musicians and composers of the 20th century.

Early life
O'Farrill was born to an Irish father and a Cuban mother in Havana, Cuba, in 1921. He was educated at a military academy in Georgia in the United States. His parents wanted him to become a lawyer, and were horrified when he began to play the trumpet. When they realized how passionate he was about music, however, they paid for him to study with Cuban composer Félix Guerrero.

O'Farrill played with numerous Cuban bands in the 1930s and into the mid-1940s. When he discovered jazz, however, his life changed dramatically. O'Farrill moved north to New York City in 1948, where he was hired by Benny Goodman, for whom he composed "Undercurrent Blues" and "Shiskabop." Later, O'Farrill went to work with renowned jazz trumpeter Dizzy Gillespie, who was in the process of integrating Cuban rhythms with jazz. One of O'Farrill's key contributions came in 1947, when he

composed "Manteca" with Gillespie and Chano Pozo. The song initiated a trend known as Cubop, and set the stage for Latin jazz in the 1950s.

Collaborations
In 1950, O'Farrill teamed up with Charlie Parker, Flip Phillips, and Buddy Rich to record *The Afro-Cuban Jazz Suite*, a successful blend of Cuban rhythms and bebop. In 1954, O'Farrill arranged a new version of "Manteca" for Gillespie. O'Farrill continued to compose, and two notable pieces were "The Aztec Suite" and "Six Jazz Moods" for jazz trumpeter Art Farmer.

In 1965, O'Farrill moved to Los Angeles, California. There he wrote music for the new Glenn Miller Orchestra, helped record an album of Hawaiian music, and recorded a jazz album under his own name. He also arranged several albums for Count Basie.

O'Farrill later joined Gillespie and singer Machito on *Afro-Cuban Jazz Moods*, then spent the next 20 years working as a commercial composer. He arranged several tracks for David Bowie's *Black Tie White Noise* (1993). In 1995, he returned to center stage with *Pure Emotion*. The album was critically acclaimed, and nominated for a Grammy award. O'Farrill recorded two further albums, *Heart of a Legend* in 1999 and *Carambola* in 2000. He appeared in a Latin jazz film, *Calle 54* (2000), and led a regular big band session at the Birdland Club in New York. O'Farrill's son, also named Arturo, is a respected jazz pianist.

◀ *Arturo "Chico" O'Farrill performs in New York City in 2000.*

See also: Machito; Pozo, Chano

Further reading: http://www.allaboutjazz.com/php/article.php?id=14972 (short biography).

OLIVAS, John
Engineer

John Daniel "Danny" Olivas is an engineer employed by the National Aeronautics and Space Administration (NASA). He has won several awards for his work. He often speaks at schools and colleges, promoting NASA's work.

Early life
Born on May 25, 1966, in North Hollywood, California, Olivas first wanted to be an astronaut at the age of seven, when he toured the Johnson Space Station during a vacation. He studied at Burges High School in El Paso, Texas, after which he went on to study mechanical engineering at the University of Texas–El Paso, graduating with a bachelor of science degree in 1989.

Moving toward space
After graduating, Olivas worked as a mechanical/materials engineer for the Dow Chemical Company in Freeport, Texas, until 1994. He studied for a master's degree from the University of Houston. While working toward his doctoral degree in mechanical engineering and materials science at Rice University, Olivas helped with engine-coating evaluations for maintenance operations at Kelly Air Force Base. In the summer of 1995, he worked as a Summer Faculty Fellow for the Crew and Thermal Systems Directorate at NASA–Johnson Space Center.

After completing his doctorate in the spring of 1996, Olivas moved to Los Angeles, California, where he was offered a senior research engineering position in quality assurance at the Jet Propulsion Laboratory (JPL) in Pasadena, California. Not long afterward, Olivas was promoted to Program Element Manager of the JPL Advanced Interconnect and Manufacturing Assurance Program. He finally realized his dream of entering the NASA space program to train as an astronaut on June 4, 1998.

▲ *John Olivas believes that space exploration has opened the doors for many advances in medical and pharmaceutical technology.*

Olivas's training included basic orientation briefings and tours, as well as numerous scientific and technical briefings. He also received intensive instruction in Space Shuttle and International Space Station (ISS) systems, and physiological training and ground school in order to prepare for flight school. From 1999 to 2002, Olivas was chosen to lead the Special Purpose Dexterous Manipulator Robot and the Mobile Transporter projects. Subsequently, from 2002 to 2005 he was assigned to the EVA (Extravehicular Activities) Branch to help support focused research on in-orbit shuttle repair. He leads the Hardware Integration Section of the Space Station Branch, a group responsible for ensuring proper configuration and integration of future station modules and visiting vehicles.

Honors
Olivas has received several awards, including four NASA Class One Tech Brief Awards (1997, 1998), five JPL-California Institute of Technology Novel Technology Report Recognitions (1997, 1998), and the HENAAC Most Promising Engineer award. He also belongs to a number of organizations, including the American Society of Materials International (ASM International).

Further reading: Cassutt, Michael. *Who's Who in Space.* New York, NY: Macmillan, 1999.
http://www11.jsc.nasa.gov/Bios/index.html (NASA biography).

KEY DATES

1966	Born in North Hollywood, California, on May 25.
1996	Receives a doctorate degree in mechanical engineering and materials science from Rice University.
1998	Joins the NASA astronaut training program.
1999	Receives HENAAC Most Promising Engineer award.

OLLER, Francisco
Artist

Francisco Oller is acknowledged as a leading Puerto Rican painter. He is best known for his work in the European realist and impressionist styles of the late 19th century, but he brought to both styles a native sensibility that marked him as an early advocate of Puerto Rican nationalism.

Early life

Born in Bayamón, Puerto Rico, on June 17, 1833, Francisco Manuel Oller y Cesteros came from a prosperous and cultured Creole family. As a young child, Oller showed early promise in both music and art: He studied drawing and painting with a local painter and sang at the opera.

The emergence of an artist

In 1851 Oller was sent to Madrid, Spain, to complete his studies at the Real Academia de Bellas Artes de San Fernando. In 1858 he moved to Paris, France, where he studied in the ateliers of Thomas Couture and Charles

▼ **Artist Francisco Oller was a nationalist and a vocal advocate of art education in Puerto Rico.**

KEY DATES

1833 Born in Bayamón, Puerto Rico, on June 17.

1851 Studies at the Real Academia de Bellas Artes de San Fernando, Madrid, Spain, for two years.

1858 Studies in Paris, France, for five years.

1893 Paints his masterpiece *El Velorio*.

1913 Dies in Cataño, Puerto Rico, on May 17.

Gleyre and at the Academie Suisse and the École Impériale et Spéciale de Dessin. He exhibited in the official Paris Salon Exhibits in 1864, 1865, and 1867. Oller was influenced by the work of the realist painter Gustave Courbet, and became close friends with the impressionist painters Camille Pissarro and Paul Cézanne.

Returning to Puerto Rico, Oller founded the Academia Gratuita de Dibujo y Pintura, an art school, and published an art manual, *Conocimientos Necessaries para Dibujar de la Natureza: Elementos de Perspectiva al Alcance de Todos* (1869). An important artist, he was named Pintor de La Real Câmara (court painter) by King Amadeus I of Spain.

Between 1873 and 1884, Oller traveled again to Europe. In 1887 he moved decisively toward nationalism, concentrating on painting his native Puerto Rico. He captured the atmosphere of the tropics in landscapes such as *Paisaje Palma Real* (1897) and *Hacienda Aurora* (1898). He also recorded scenes of Puerto Rican life in such work as *La Escuela del Maestro Rafael* (1892). A statement of Oller's liberal values, the painting shows the dignified figure of Rafael Cordero (1790–1868), the son of freed slaves and a pioneer of public education, surrounded by children of different races. Oller's masterpiece *El Velorio* (1893) depicts a wake, a mixing of African and Christian customs, following the death of a child. Oller exhibited the painting in Paris in 1895.

Oller taught art at the Escuela Normal and also in municipal schools in Bayamón. He died in 1913. Many critics consider Oller to be the first Puerto Rican painter to have consciously tried to create a national art.

Further reading: http://www.geocities.com/gloriaespada/ historypainting.html (introduction to the history of Puerto Rican painting and artists).

OLMOS, Edward James
Actor

A native "Angeleño" (born in Los Angeles), Edward James Olmos is a successful actor. Recognized for his craggy face and authoritative demeanor, Olmos has appeared in more than 50 films and television shows. He has earned critical acclaim, including winning an Emmy award and being nominated for an Academy Award. Olmos is equally known for his political activism. He once said that he would rather be well known as an activist than as an actor. Olmos protested to help end U.S. naval test bombing at Vieques in Puerto Rico.

Olmos won the Emmy and also a Golden Globe award for his role as Lieutenant Martin Castillo in the stylish and successful TV police drama *Miami Vice* in 1985. He won another Golden Globe award for his role in the 1994 TV

▼ *A film still from the movie* **American Me** *(1992), which starred and was directed by Edward Olmos.*

movie *The Burning Season.* Olmos also won acclaim for his portrayal of Mexican American prison life in California in the 1992 film *American Me,* which was also his feature directorial debut. Among other roles, Olmos is often recognized for his origami-fixated detective in the popular 1982 science fiction movie *Blade Runner.* However, it was Olmos's role as real-life school teacher Jaime Escalante, teaching calculus to Latinos and Latinas in Los Angeles in the feature film *Stand and Deliver*, that earned him an Oscar nomination in 1989. Early in his career, Olmos struggled to overcome being typecast as an "ethnic" character, and today he is noted as a strong spokesman for the Latino community.

Early life in Los Angeles

Edward Olmos was born on February 24, 1947, in the Boyle Heights section of East Los Angeles. The area was predominantly Mexican American; however, there were also Russians, Native Americans, and Koreans, which gave Olmos a broad view of the world. Olmos's parents met during World War II (1939–1945), when his mother, Eleanor, was visiting Mexico City, where his father, Pedro, ran a pharmaceutical distribution business. Pedro, one of 13 children, decided to turn the business over to one of his brothers and move across the border to marry Eleanor. Pedro first worked in a slaughterhouse, then became a welder. Pedro and Eleanor moved to a house in Boyle Heights, where Olmos was raised as the middle child of three (he has an older brother and a younger sister).

The future actor's first love as a child was baseball. However, by age 13, Olmos had become enthusiastic about music, which would eventually steer him into acting. Olmos formed several "garage" bands, and soon was an accomplished singer, songwriter, and producer. The Los Angeles club scene was in its heyday during the 1960s, and Olmos formed a group called Pacific Ocean. Olmos played five half-hour sets per night while attending college. He went to East Los Angeles College and Cal-State Los Angeles from 1964 to 1968, studying psychology, criminology, and even some dance. After college, Olmos pursued his love of music. He went from producing albums for Kris Kristofferson and B. B. King to engineering to songwriting for plays. During the late 1960s and early 1970s, Olmos played the most famous clubs on Sunset Boulevard (better known as the Sunset Strip), including

INFLUENCES AND INSPIRATION

The making of Olmos's socially conscious drama *The Ballad of Gregorio Cortez* was a labor of love. Olmos called upon close friend and award–winning filmmaker Robert M. Young for assistance. Young had cast Olmos in his second film role as a drunken man in the 1977 film *Alambrista!* Young directed *The Ballad of Gregorio Cortez*, the true story of a Hispanic man who was unjustly killed in the early 1900s over the mistranslation of a word. When the film was completed, Olmos found it hard to find distribution from major studios, so the film aired on the Public Broadcasting Service. *The Ballad of Gregorio Cortez* was the first of many collaborations between Young and Olmos, who later formed a production company together. The two also teamed up on 1989's *Triumph of the Spirit* (about a Greek-Jewish boxer sent to Auschwitz during World War II) and 1991's *Talent for the Game* (starring Olmos as a baseball scout). Later, Young coproduced Olmos's directorial feature debut, *American Me,* and served as cinematographer. Young, who straddles the world of independent and major studio films, has often tackled controversial material and was a strong influence on Olmos; the two remain close friends.

Gazzarri's and The Factory. Around this time, Olmos married Kaija Keel, the daughter of MGM film star Howard Keel (they later divorced). While continuing his musical aspirations, Olmos began to take acting classes. Soon, he gained small TV roles in shows such as *Hawaii Five-O* and *Kojak*, but they were often ethnic hooligan roles. Olmos finally got his first big acting break when he was cast as El Pachuco, the lead in Luis Valdez's musical *Zoot Suit* in 1978. The play eventually went to Broadway. Although it only had a brief seven-week run, Olmos received a Tony award nomination for the part.

Finding a vocation

Olmos's fortunes gradually rose as he received more and more acting jobs. Ultimately, he achieved iconic status in director Michael Mann's hit series *Miami Vice* on NBC. The role almost did not happen; Olmos turned Mann down four times before finally agreeing to take the role with a "nonexclusive" contract that allowed him to do other acting work. Olmos is very concerned with the roles he accepts and their portrayal of Latinos and Latino culture. In 1988, Olmos appeared in the real-life drama *Stand and Deliver*, depicting Jaime Escalante, a Bolivian-born math teacher who helped 18 of his Hispanic students in East Los Angeles pass the Advanced Placement calculus test. When the students are accused of cheating, Olmos's character has them take the test again; the students pass with comparable or higher scores. In early 1989, Olmos received an Oscar nomination for the role. The nomination gave Olmos the clout to make *American Me*, a personal project he had wanted to do for several years. Olmos served as producer and director (his feature debut) and hired a largely Hispanic cast and crew. The cautionary tale detailed the history and troubles of Hispanic gang and prison life. Both *Stand and Deliver* and *American Me* enabled Olmos to double as actor and spokesman.

A man of the people in his native East Los Angeles, Olmos memorably went into the thick of the 1992 Rodney King riots to help quell the violence. In January 1994, Olmos married his second wife, actress Lorraine Bracco (that marriage also ended in divorce). In 2001, Olmos was arrested and jailed for protesting the U.S. Navy's test bombing at Vieques in Puerto Rico. President George W. Bush eventually agreed to halt the bombing there.

See also: Cortez, Gregorio; Escalante, Jaime

Further reading: Carrillo, Louis. *Edward James Olmos* (Contemporary Biographies). Orlando, FL: Raintree Steck-Vaughn Publishers, 1997.

KEY DATES

1947 Born in Boyle Heights, East Los Angeles, California, on February 24.

1985 Wins an Emmy for his role as Lieutenant Castillo in the NBC series *Miami Vice.*

1989 Nominated for an Oscar for his role as Jaime Escalante in the film *Stand and Deliver.*

1992 Stars in and directs the film *American Me.*

1995 Wins a Golden Globe award for his role in the TV movie *The Burning Season.*

2001 Spends time in jail after protesting the U.S. Navy's test bombing at Vieques in Puerto Rico.

ONTIVEROS, Lupe
Actor

With a career that spans three decades, Lupe Ontiveros is one of the most recognized and accomplished Latinas in film and television. She has received critical acclaim for her work and been nominated for numerous awards, including an Emmy. Although she has played a maid over 150 times in her career, her goal is to break down stereotypes and create better opportunities for other Hispanic American actors in Hollywood.

Life before acting

Born in 1942 in El Paso, Texas, Ontiveros graduated from Texas Women's College with a double major in psychology and social work. She married Elías Ontiveros and moved to Los Angeles, California, where she served as a social worker for 18 years, helping the elderly, children, and the disabled.

Ontiveros began acting as a way to earn extra income between jobs. She saw an ad in the newspaper looking for movie extras. She enjoyed the experience so much she decided to pursue an acting career in the evenings after putting in a full day as a social worker and a second shift as mother and wife. Ontiveros performed in Los Angeles's theaters backed by Nosotros, a support organization for Hispanic American actors and other media figures founded by Hispanic American actor Ricardo Montalban.

▲ *Lupe Ontiveros has appeared in more than 40 motion pictures and many more television programs.*

KEY DATES	
1942	Born in El Paso, Texas, on September 17.
1962	Marries and begins work as a social worker.
1980	Stars as Dolores in the Broadway production of Luis Valdez's *Zoot Suit*.
1985	Stars in Steven Spielberg's *Goonies*.
1987	Stars in *Born in East L.A.*, directed by Cheech Marin.
1995	Appears in Gregory Nava's *My Family/Mi Familia* alongside Jennifer Lopez.
1997	Stars as Louisa in television series *Veronica's Closet*.
1997	Stars as Yolanda Saldivar in *Selena*, a biopic.
2002	Stars as Carmen Garcia in *Real Women Have Curves*.
2005	Receives an Emmy nomination as Best Guest Actress on the television series *Desperate Housewives*.

Big break

Ontiveros's first credited movie role was as a prostitute in the 1977 film *The World's Greatest Lover*. In 1978 the playwright Luis Valdez gave her the role of Dolores, the mother, in the popular Teatro Campesino production of *Zoot Suit*. When the production moved to New York, Ontiveros continued her role, and also played the character

INFLUENCES AND INSPIRATION

The struggle for Mexican women in Hollywood cinema has been a long one, dating back to silent-era actresses such as Lupe Velez, and later stars such as Carmen Miranda and Maria Montez. Ontiveros faced the same stereotyping of Latinas as her predecessors. In a 2005 interview, she discussed having to battle the typecasting. While actresses such as Salma Hayek were cast in "hot tamale" stereotypes, Ontiveros was commonly placed in roles as a domestic servant: "It wasn't made easy for me—no way in hell. I didn't come in with the looks or the body. I literally pounded the pavement. The indignities that I suffered as a woman, as a Latina, were incredible."

Despite the struggles and indignities, and the fact that she got into acting because she needed the money, Ontiveros has retained a lifelong enthusiasm and commitment to her trade.

for the 1981 film version. *Zoot Suit* was the first Hispanic American production on Broadway, but it failed miserably, and became one of the biggest financial flops of all time.

Ontiveros returned to Los Angeles and took work in a medical clinic. She contemplated leaving show business but never did. Her next important role was in Gregory Nava's Oscar-nominated film *El Norte* (1983), about Guatemalan immigrants to the United States. Steven Spielberg recognized her talent in *El Norte* and wanted her to be in his movie *Goonies* (1985). Ontiveros did not relish the opportunity to play another maid, but wanted to work with Spielberg, so she took the part. She moved on to other Latino-themed movies such as Cheech Marin's *Born in East L.A.* (1987) and Gregory Nava's *My Family/Mi Familia* (1995), starring Jennifer Lopez. Ontiveros was invited to the White House by President Bill Clinton for a screening of *My Family/Mi Familia*.

Memorable roles

In 1997 Ontiveros worked with Nava and Lopez again, along with Edward James Olmos with whom she had worked on *Zoot Suit*. She played the role that brought her more attention than any before, that of Yolanda Saldivar (1960–), the fan-club president who murdered popular Tejana crossover singer Selena.

Later that year Ontiveros worked with Jack Nicholson in the movie *As Good as It Gets*. One of her most challenging film roles came in 2002, when she played a Portuguese widow in the film *Passionada*, having to learn the Portuguese language for the part.

Ontiveros has also had a number of recurring roles on television such as in *Desperate Housewives* (2005), *Veronica's Closet* (1997), *Hill Street Blues* (1981–1984), *Pasadena* (2001), and *Greetings from Tucson* (2002). She has also done voice-over work for a number of cartoons, such as *King of the Hill* (2002) and the PBS children's series *Maya and Miguel* (2004).

Throughout her career Ontiveros has received many awards for her stage, film, and television work. At the 2002 Sundance Film Festival, she earned a Best Dramatic Actress Award for her role as Carmen García in *Real Women Have Curves*. Two years earlier at Sundance she had earned the National Board of Review Best Supporting Actress Award and a Special Acting Award for her performance in *Chuck and Buck*. In 2005 she was nominated for the Best Guest Actress Emmy for her appearance on *Desperate Housewives*. Ontiveros has also been asked to judge film festivals in Cuba, France, Canada, and the Dominican Republic.

Community interests

Ontiveros was a special invited guest to the 2005 League of United Latin American Citizens' (LULAC) convention in Little Rock, Arkansas. The event highlighted the concerns of new Hispanic American communities that were emerging across the southeastern United States.

In her spare time, Ontiveros mentors other Hispanic Americans making a career in acting. Through this activity she hopes to destroy the stereotypical images of Hispanic Americans in the media. She also commits time to AIDS awareness and education, and preventing domestic violence in the Hispanic American community. Of particular concern to her, however, is advocacy for the deaf. Her second son was born clinically deaf and currently works as a counselor to deaf and emotionally disturbed children, following his mother's interest in social issues.

See also: Hayek, Salma; Lopez, Jennifer; Marin, Cheech; Miranda, Carmen; Montalban, Ricardo; Montez, Maria; Nava, Gregory; Olmos, Edward James; Selena; Valdez, Luis M.; Vélez, Lupe.

Further reading: Hadley-García, George. *Hispanic Hollywood: The Latins in Motion Pictures.* New York, NY: Carol Pub. Group, 1990.

ORENDAIN, Antonio
Farmworker, Union Leader

In the early 1960s, Antonio Orendain became involved in organizing unrepresented workers in California's agricultural fields. He was elected secretary–treasurer of the fledgling National Farm Workers' Association (NFWA) in 1962, along with César Chávez as president and Dolores Huerta and Gilberto Padilla as vice presidents. Within a year, the NFWA had merged with other farmworker groups to become the United Farm Workers of America (UFW), a larger union with greater influence and power. Over the next four years, Orendain was a major organizer for the UFW. He stood out from other organizers by always wearing a big black hat, jeans with a big buckle, and boots, just like many *jornaleros nortenos* (northern Mexico farm laborers and cattlemen). In 1966, Chávez tasked Orendain to organize a 300-mile (480km) march from Delano to Sacramento, California, to publicize the union's cause.

Other people became interested in organizing or affiliating with Chávez and the UFW. Eugene Nelson, an early Chávez organzer, was sent to Texas. Once Nelson was in the Rio Grande Valley of Texas and saw the conditions of farmworkers there, he began forming a local union and began a melon strike against La Casita Farms of Rio Grande City. Chávez sent money and Orendain to help. After a while, Orendain was called back to California and assigned other duties for the remainder of the 1960s. Orendain, however, wanted to return to Texas.

Texas Farm Workers Union

In 1975, Antonio Orendain ended his association with the UFW in order to devote himself to organizing Texas farmworkers in a separate and locally accountable union.

▲ *Antonio Orendain was an organizer and leader for farmworkers' unions in both California and Texas.*

In August of that year, he formed the Texas Farm Workers Union (TFWU). The TFWU organized a melon strike in West Texas that resulted in a wage increase for farmworkers, and began publication of a newspaper *El Cuhamil*. In 1977, Orendain pressed for the establishment of a state agricultural board to oversee unionization efforts and ensure fair elections. When this failed, Orendain undertook a long march from the Rio Grande Valley to Austin, the state capital, in protest. Unfazed by legislative inaction, Orendain's union members decided to walk to Washington, D.C., and press Congress and the president. They arrived at the Lincoln Memorial on Labor Day 1977, but President Jimmy Carter refused to meet them, and Orendain went on a hunger strike for 30 days. Dejected, union members returned to organizing in South and West Texas but with less success. Although the TFWU brought attention to the plight of Texas farmworkers, it did not win any collective bargaining agreements.

See also: Chávez, César; Huerta, Dolores

Further reading: http://www.tsha.utexas.edu/handbook/online/articles/TT/oct3_print.html (Handbook of Texas Online article about the TFWU).

KEY DATES

1956 Immigrates to California from Mexico, aged about 30.

1975 Founds and leads the Texas Farm Workers Union (TFWU).

1977 Leads a 420–mile (675km) march from the Rio Grande Valley of Texas to Austin, the state capital. The march lasts from February 26 to April 2.

1977 Leads a 1,600-mile (2,570km) march from Austin to Washington, D.C., between June 18 and September 5.

1986 TFWU disbanded after failure to make collective bargaining agreements.

ORLANDO, Tony
Singer

Tony Orlando has been a leading figure in the music industry and Hollywood since 1970, selling more than 30 million records and performing for five U.S. presidents. Orlando has received three American Music Awards and a People's Choice Award, in addition to having three number-one hit songs and six top–ten hits. His song "Tie a Yellow Ribbon Round the Old Oak Tree" has become a national anthem for veterans' families and ensured his popularity for more than 30 years.

Early life
Orlando was born Michael Anthony Orlando Cassavitis in 1944 in New York City. By age 16, he was performing national chart hits, but preferred the production side of the recording industry. Eventually, however, Orlando returned to singing with the 1970 number-one hit "Candida," which he recorded as a demo for Bell Records. The song was released under the name of the record's promotion director's daughter, Dawn. This became the name of Orlando's backing singers, Telma Hopkins and Joyce Vincent Wilson.

Recording star
In 1971, Tony Orlando and Dawn recorded "Knock Three Times," which was the best-selling record of the year, selling over six million copies. Orlando's greatest success followed in 1973, with the song "Tie a Yellow Ribbon Round the Old Oak Tree." Other hits, such as "Sweet Gypsy Rose" and "He Don't Love You," followed. The threesome hosted their own musical variety show from 1974 to 1976, reuniting in 1988 and periodically since then. In 2005, Tony Orlando and Dawn released a Christmas album, their first recording together in 28 years.

▲ *Tony Orlando and Joyce Vincent Wilson, one–half of his backing duo, Dawn.*

Orlando took a break from show business in 1977 to get clean and sober, quitting cigarettes, cocaine, and caffeine. The story was told in the VH1 program *Behind the Music* in 1998. After 1977, Orlando performed solo projects in music, television, film, and theater, including a 1981 stint on Broadway in *Barnum*. In 1993, Orlando opened his own music theater in Branson, Missouri, where he lives with his family. He performed more than 400 shows per year until the theater closed in 1999.

Popular influence
The sentiments behind Tony Orlando and Dawn's hit "Tie a Yellow Ribbon Round the Old Oak Tree" were inspirational. The song was first adopted by Americans looking for the return of Vietnam prisoners of war. It is now played whenever soldiers or hostages come home, veterans are honored, or missing loved ones are being sought. Although Orlando originally disliked it, "Tie a Yellow Ribbon" became his theme song and the name of his Branson music theater.

Further reading: http://www.imdb.com/name/nm0650027 (Internet Movie Database article about Tony Orlando).

KEY DATES	
1944	Born in New York City on April 3.
1973	Records number–one hit song "Tie a Yellow Ribbon."
1974	First Tony Orlando and Dawn variety show.
1981	Stars on Broadway in *Barnum*.
1990	Awarded a star on Hollywood's Walk of Fame.
1994	Appears in the movie *Forrest Gump*.

ORTEGA, Katherine
Politician

Katherine Ortega rose from a childhood in poverty to become the U.S. treasurer in the administrations of both presidents Ronald Reagan and George H. W. Bush. She was the first treasurer to work for two presidents since the early 1960s. Today she is a director of the third-largest retailer in the United States.

Early life
Katherine Ortega was born in Tularosa, New Mexico, in 1934. She was the youngest in a family of nine children. Her father was a blacksmith but the demand for his profession was in a steep decline. Her parents took a change of direction and opened a restaurant and operated a dance hall. As a child Ortega joined the family struggle to make ends meet, working at both of her parents' businesses until her high-school years. She then got a part-time job at the local bank while she finished high school and entered college.

At college she chose to pursue her long-held interest in business. She opted to major in economics at Eastern New Mexico University in Portales. She selected the college over New Mexico State University in Alamogordo, which was much nearer to her hometown. Portales is in a part of the state with a large agricultural industry, while Ortega's home was in desert country.

Becoming a business woman
Ortega had several entry-level jobs in New Mexico's banking and financial services businesses, but she longed for greater challenges in the industry and to live in a larger city. She left New Mexico for California to join Peat, Marwick, Mitchell & Company. She studied to become a

▼ *Katherine Ortega accepts the applause after making a keynote address at the 1984 Republican convention in Dallas, Texas.*

INFLUENCES AND INSPIRATION

The treasurer of the United States has responsibility for managing the production of U.S. currency. His or her signature, along with that of the Treasury's secretary, appears on all paper bills. In 1949 President Harry S. Truman appointed Georgia Neece Clark as treasurer, the first woman to take the position. Every U.S. treasurer since that time has been a woman, with successive presidents being eager to include women in high-ranking positions. In 1971 President Richard Nixon appointed Romana Acosta Bañuelos as the first Hispanic American treasurer. Since that appointment, four of the subsequent eight treasurers have been Latinas.

certified public accountant and also became a tax supervisor at the company. She continued to do consulting work in New Mexico with the Otero Savings and Loan Association in Alamogordo. After gaining valuable experience in auditing, tax matters, and the analysis of revenues and expenditures, plus budgets, she took a job with the Pan American National Bank in Los Angeles. She joined as head cashier, but was soon promoted to an executive role. While still in her early thirties, Ortega became very active in politics during the years of Ronald Reagan's governorship of the state.

Politics

When Reagan was elected U.S. president in 1980, he appointed Ortega to a federal advisory committee and then made her commissioner of the Copyright Royalty Tribunal.

KEY DATES

1934 Born in Tularosa, New Mexico, on July 16.

1957 Receives bachelor of arts degree.

1972 Named vice-president of Pan American National Bank, Los Angeles, California.

1975 Elected president of the Santa Ana State Bank, first woman selected in California to head a bank.

1982 Appointed by President Ronald Reagan as commissioner of the Copyright Royalty Tribunal and member of the presidential advisory committee on small and minority business ownership.

1983 Appointed 38th U.S. treasurer by Ronald Reagan.

1984 First woman as keynote speaker at the national Republican convention in Dallas, Texas.

1990 Alternate U.S. representative at the 45th General Assembly of the United Nations.

2000 Featured in the *Notable American Women* exhibition at the Women's Museum, in Dallas, Texas.

When Angela Marie Buchanan handed in her resignation as treasurer of the United States in 1983, Ortega expressed an interest in the role. Her political work during the president's previous election campaigns stood her in good stead. She garnered support from those who recognized her work on behalf of small business and minority business owners and made sure the president became aware of these contributions to his administration. Ortega was duly appointed to the post, the second Hispanic American to take up the job.

Treasurer of the United States

Ortega signed the plate for the printing of her signature on paper currency as treasurer of the United States with both the Davalos and Ortega surnames to honor her mother and father. Secretary of the Treasury Donald T. Regan swore her into office on October 3, 1983. Ortega took on the responsibilities of supervising more than 5,000 employees and managing a budget of $340 million. Ortega's signature eventually appeared on an unprecedented $60-billion-worth of various denominations over her six-year Treasury career.

The United Nations and beyond

In 1990, President George H. W. Bush accepted her resignation as treasurer. He then appointed her as part of the team of U.S. representatives to the United Nations in New York City.

Within a year, Ortega had decided that she preferred working in business rather than diplomacy. Major corporations invited her to serve on their boards of directors. Investment companies also sought her participation as trustee for various funds. She chose to join the board of the supermarket company Kroger.

See also: Bañuelos, Ramona Acosta

Further reading: http://www.horatioalger.com/members/ member_info.cfm?memberid=ORT02 (biography).

ORTEGO Y GASCA, Felipe de
Academic

The academic Felipe de Ortego y Gasca is considered to be the founder of Chicano literary history. He has dedicated much of his career to gaining recognition for the cultural heritage of Hispanic Americans, which, he argues, dates back to the 16th-century Hispanic Southwest. He is also a published poet and playwright.

Early career

Ortego y Gasca was born and raised in Blue Island, Illinois. As a young man he enlisted in the Army in 1943 and served in World War II (1939–1945) and the Korean War (1950–1953). In 1959 he graduated from Texas Western College of the University of Texas in El Paso with a BA in English. Ortego y Gasca was awarded his master's degree in 1966 and his PhD at the University of New Mexico at Albuquerque. After that he taught French but switched to English when he moved to New Mexico State University in 1964. He moved again to the University of Texas at El Paso, where he created the Chicano studies program, the first program of its type in the state.

In 1969 Ortego y Gasca taught the first course in Chicano literature in the United States at the University of New Mexico. Over the next three decades, Ortego y Gasca continued to push for the inclusion of Chicano studies in schools across the nation.

Leading academic

During the 1970s and 1980s, Ortego y Gasca worked mainly outside academia. In 1982 he was the first chairman of the Hispanic Foundation in Washington, D.C., formerly the Institute for the Study of Hispanic Cultures. In 1983 Ortego y Gasca and fellow Hispanic Americans founded *The National Hispanic Reporter*, the first Hispanic American newspaper published in English. He served as its first editor-in-chief and then publisher until 1992.

Ortego y Gasca returned to academia in 1986 to become the founding dean of the Hispanic Leadership Institute in Phoenix, Arizona. He moved back to Texas in

▲ *Felipe de Ortego y Gasca was the first U.S. academic to teach a course in Chicano literature.*

1993 to take up a position as the first scholar in residence in social and behavioral studies at Sul Ross State University in Alpine, Texas. He left the university as a tenured professor of English in 1999. He is now professor emeritus at Texas A&M University at Kingsville.

In addition to his academic career, Ortego y Gasca has written widely, often publishing under the name of Philip D. Ortego. He has published poetry, and his plays include *Elsinore* (a musical adaptation of Shakespeare's *Hamlet*, 1968) and *Madre del Sol* (1981), the story of the conquest of Mexico. In 2005 Ortego y Gasca received the Patricia and Rudolfo Anaya Crítica Nueva award in recognition of his contribution to Chicano literature.

Further reading: Ortega y Gasca, Philip D. *The Tejano Yearbook, 1519–1978: A Selective Chronicle of the Hispanic Presence in Texas*. San Antonio, TX: Caravel Press, 1978. http://www.kingsvillerecord.net/opinion.shtml (article by Ortego y Gasca).

KEY DATES

1926 Born in Blue Island, Illinois, on August 23.

1969 Teaches first U.S. course on Chicano literature.

1999 Retires from Sul Ross State University.

ORTIZ, Carlos
Boxer

Carlos Ortiz was one of the all-time boxing greats. He first became junior welterweight champion, then reigned as world lightweight champion between 1962 and 1968. Ortiz held a final record of 61 wins (including 30 knockouts) and 7 losses. He is an inductee of the International Boxing Hall of Fame.

Early Years

Ortiz was born in Ponce, Puerto Rico, in 1936, and moved to New York when he was ten. Soon afterward, he attracted the attention of the police. To stay out of trouble, he was warned to keep off the streets, and it was suggested he should join the nearby Madison Square Boys' Club. Although Ortiz could not afford the monthly 25-cent membership fee, he was allowed to join. On his first visit Ortiz saw a boy training with a punching bag, and he was captivated. He returned two days later, and a trainer offered to teach him to box.

Knockout

Ortiz became a professional boxer at age 18, with a knockout victory against Harry Bell. That was the first of 20 straight wins. One of his key contests came in England against Dave Charnley, one of the toughest boxers of the day. Ortiz won on a 10–round decision. He now felt confident enough to make a bid for a world title.

In June 1959, Ortiz took on Kenny Lane in New York for the world junior welterweight title. By knocking out Lane in two rounds, avenging a loss to the same opponent a couple of months earlier, Ortiz became Puerto Rico's second world boxing champion. The welterweight title had not been contested for some years, however, and was not considered highly prestigious. Ortiz successfully defended the title twice, winning matches against Duilio Loi and

▲ *A highly successful boxer, Carlos Ortiz became both world lightweight and junior welterweight champion.*

former world lightweight champion Raymundo "Battling" Torres, but then fell to Duilio Loi in Milan, Italy. While many boxers respond to defeat by gaining weight, Ortiz instead chose to move down a weight division.

Later career

In 1962, Ortiz gained a new world title in the lightweight division by defeating the former world champion Joe Brown in a 15-round decision. This, he claimed, was one of the greatest moments of his life. Victories followed over Teruo Kosaka, Doug Valiant, and Gabriel Elorde. In 1965, Ortiz lost to Ismael Laguna in 15 rounds, but avenged the defeat later that year at New York's Shea Stadium in another 15-round decision.

In 1968, Ortiz finally lost his world lightweight title to Carlos Cruz in a 15-round decision. A rematch was planned, but Cruz died in a plane crash on his way to the fight. After briefly retiring, Ortiz made a comeback in 1971. He won nine fights before losing to Ken Buchanan at Madison Square Garden in his only defeat by knockout. Ortiz has since continued to promote boxing, and gives regular speeches at various events.

Further reading: Fleisher, Nat, Sam Andre, Nigel Collins, and Dan Rafael. *An Illustrated History of Boxing*. New York, NY: Citadel Press, 2002.
http://www.ibhof.com/ibhfhome.htm (International Boxing Hall of Fame Web site).

KEY DATES	
1936	Born in Ponce, Puerto Rico, on September 9.
1955	Becomes a professional boxer.
1959	Wins world junior welterweight title for the first time.
1962	Becomes world lightweight champion.
1968	Loses lightweight title to Carlos Cruz.

ORTIZ COFER, Judith
Writer, Academic

Award-winning writer Judith Ortiz Cofer is an acclaimed author of poetry, short stories, novels, and essays. Nominated for a Pulitzer Prize, Ortiz Cofer often writes about her attempts to negotiate her native Puerto Rican and adopted American cultures. Ortiz Cofer was one of the first Puerto Rican authors writing in English to gain national recognition in the United States. Since 1984 she has taught English at the University of Georgia.

Early life

Born in Puerto Rico on February 24, 1952, Ortiz Cofer was two when her family moved to Paterson, New Jersey, where the U.S. Navy had stationed her father. Her family made regular visits back to Puerto Rico, where she spent a lot of time with her beloved grandmother. Ortiz Cofer later said that her love of writing came from her grandmother, who taught her that storytelling was a way of empowering women by teaching each generation how to deal with life in a world that marginalized them. The constant shifts in language and culture also had a deep impact on Ortiz Cofer's identity and literary style.

In 1968 the family moved to Augusta, Georgia, where Ortiz Cofer completed high school. She went on to study for a BA in English at Augusta College. After receiving an

▼ *Judith Ortiz Cofer first wrote poetry, which she claims contains the "essence of language."*

MA from Florida Atlantic University in 1977, Ortiz Cofer went abroad to study literature at Oxford University, England, for a year.

Literature

Ortiz Cofer's work spans many genres and explores issues of gender, race, and diaspora as well as art and the literary world. Her writing, whether it be poetry such as *Terms of Survival* (1987) or prose such as *Silent Dancing* (1990) often challenges the machismo, or extreme masculinity, in Puerto Rican culture and examines female empowerment, while also portraying the ways in which immigrants overcome the challenges they face when adapting to a new culture.

Ortiz Cofer's first novel, *The Line of the Sun* (1989), tells the story of Marisol, a 13-year-old girl whose family moves from Puerto Rico to Paterson, New Jersey, mirroring the author's own life. The novel was nominated for the Pulitzer Prize, one of several awards for which Ortiz Cofer's work has been nominated. In 2003 Ortiz Cofer published *The Meaning of Consuelo* to critical acclaim.

Further reading: Ortiz Cofer, Judith. *Silent Dancing: A Partial Remembrance of a Puerto Rican Childhood*. Houston, TX: Arte Público Press, 1990.
http://www.georgiaencyclopedia.org/nge/Article.jsp?id=h-488 (an informative entry on Judith Ortiz Cofer in the New Georgia Encyclopedia; includes photos and video clips of the author).

OTERO FAMILY
Politicians, Landowners, Businessmen

During the late 19th and early 20th centuries, the Oteros of New Mexico were one of the most influential Hispanic families in the United States. Its members included judges, congressional representatives, a territorial governor, a prominent suffragist, and some of the wealthiest landowners in the Southwest.

Origins

The Oteros traced their roots back to Spain. According to official family history, a Spaniard named Pedro Otero settled in Nuevo México, then a province of Spanish-ruled Mexico, in the 18th century. However, the story may not be true. Genealogical research suggests that Pedro was in fact an orphan, born Pedro Durán y Chávez. One theory is that he was adopted by a local priest, Fray Cayetano Otero, and took his last name.

Pedro grew up and married a woman named Maria, and they had several children. One, Vicente Antonio, born in 1781, served as a mayor and as a judge for many years. He married Gertrudis Aragón and had at least nine children.

Miguel Antonio Otero I

One of Don Vicente's sons, Miguel Antonio Otero, born June 21, 1829, in Valencia, Nuevo México, followed his father into politics. As a boy, he spoke Spanish and probably learned English in St. Louis, Missouri, where his parents sent him to high school. He went on to earn a law degree in New York. During Miguel's school years, the United States defeated Mexico in war, so when he arrived back home in the early 1850s, his hometown had become

◄ *Miguel Antonio Otero I trained as a lawyer in the United States and became one of the leading politicians in New Mexico when he returned in the 1850s to what was now U.S. territory.*

part of New Mexico territory, a U.S. controlled region. The territory was eventually split into the states of New Mexico and Arizona in 1912.

Otero threw himself into U.S. politics, first as the territorial governor's personal secretary and then as a member of the territorial legislature. A term as New Mexico attorney general followed, before running for Congress in 1855. Otero narrowly lost the election, but he challenged the result, accusing his opponent of relying on illegal votes from Mexican citizens. The House of Representatives agreed and voted to give him his congressional seat.

Otero devoted his efforts in Washington, D.C., to obtaining a railroad link to New Mexico, an essential aid to the growth of the territory's population and economy. Politicians from the Southern states backed his plans. In return Otero agreed to support the extension of slavery to New Mexico. In Washington Otero married Mary Josephine Blackwood. When the Civil War broke out, Otero's Southern connections ended his political career.

Miguel Antonio Otero II

After leaving office in 1861, Otero and his wife moved to Kansas and went into business. They had four children. Miguel Antonio Otero II was born on October 17, 1861. The young Miguel Antonio enjoyed growing up on the American frontier, where he met men like "Wild Bill"

LEGACY

Even though the Oteros were successful politicians and entrepreneurs, they suffered some discrimination as Hispanos—New Mexicans of Spanish descent. At one time, the Otero family owned more than one million acres of land. A Bostonian named James Whitney challenged the Oteros' ownership and the dispute escalated into a gun battle. Whitney and one of Miguel Antonio II's cousins were killed. The resulting lawsuit ended up in the U.S. Supreme Court. In 1909 the court ruled that the Spanish land grant owned by the Oteros was invalid, allowing Anglo settlers to take over the property. After World War II (1939–1945), the influence of the Oteros waned. Today the town of Otero, New Mexico, built near the first railroad tracks into the state, is gone, but the family name lives on in Otero County in the south of the state.

Hickok and "Buffalo Bill" Cody. As a teenager, his parents sent him and his brother Page to various boarding schools. Miguel Antonio stopped attending school at 17, and he and his brother joined their father in New Mexico. The railroad had finally come to New Mexico, and the first stop was named Otero to honor Miguel Antonio Otero I.

A few years later, the Oteros founded the San Miguel National Bank, with father and both sons serving as officers. The family prospered and expanded into new businesses, including a telephone service in New Mexico and northern Mexico. Miguel Antonio I died suddenly of pneumonia in 1882. Newspapers reported that he was a millionaire, though Miguel Antonio II said his wealth was mostly on paper.

In the 1880s, Miguel Antonio II went into politics, winning several local elections. He married Caroline Virginia Emmett, the daughter of a prominent judge, in 1888, and started a family. Their first son, Miguel Antonio Otero III, died after a few days; a second son, Miguel Antonio Otero IV was born a year later, on August 30, 1892. Miguel Antonio II, a third-generation politician and prominent businessman, would soon make history as the first Hispanic American U.S. governor. In 1897 President William McKinley appointed him to lead the New Mexico Territory, a position he held for nine years.

Otero remained well known and respected in New Mexico until his death on August 7, 1944. After leaving the governor's office, he remained active in politics and returned to his businesses. In retirement, he wrote the two-volume memoir *My Life on the Frontier* (1935 and 1939), followed by *My Nine Years as Governor of the Territory of New Mexico* (1940). Miguel Antonio IV became a judge and ran unsuccessfully for Congress.

Other prominent Oteros

Mariano S. Otero, Miguel Antonio's cousin, was another influential New Mexican in the 19th century. Like his cousin, he, too, served in Congress. He had run against one of his many uncles in the election. Mariano also had extensive business interests. In 1890, the *New York Times* called him the richest man in New Mexico. He died on February 1, 1904.

In the 1880s Manuel Otero married into the Luna family, another prominent New Mexico family. The ties were further strengthened when Manuel's brother-in-law Solomon Luna married an Otero. The powerful Otero-Luna family based themselves at the Luna Mansion, at Las Lunas in Valencia County, New Mexico.

In the early 20th century, Adelina "Nina" Otero Warren was the most notable family member. The granddaughter of Vicente and Gertrudis Otero, she was a leading suffragist.

See also: Luna, Solomon; Otero Warren, Adelina

Further reading: Otero, Miguel Antonio. *Otero: An Autobiographical Trilogy.* New York, NY: Arno Press, 1974. http://www.ancestry.com/search/SurnamePage.aspx?html=b&ln=Otero&sourcecode=13304 (genealogy of Otero family).

KEY DATES

1829 Miguel Antonio Otero I born in Valencia, Nuevo México, on June 21.

1848 Most of Nuevo México becomes the U.S New Mexico Territory.

1856 Miguel Antonio I becomes a representative in the U.S. Congress, serving until 1861.

1879 Mariano Sabino Otero follows his cousin into Congress.

1897 Miguel Antonio Otero II appointed governor of New Mexico.

1936 Nina Otero Warren writes *Old Spain in Our Southwest.*

OTERO WARREN, Adelina
Activist

Adelina "Nina" Otero Warren came from a long line of politicians who, since Spanish colonial times, had helped shape what is now New Mexico. She herself became one of the state's most influential female political leaders and literary figures.

One of the family

Nina María Adelina Isabel Emilia Otero was born in Las Lunas, New Mexico, to an important, wealthy, political family, in 1881. Her family traced its roots to 11th-century Spain and carried this heritage proudly as politicians and landowners in the New Mexico Territory, which had only been acquired by the United States in 1848.

Otero attended Marysville College in Saint Louis, Missouri, from 1892 until 1894. In 1908 she married Rawson Warren in Santa Fe, New Mexico, where her uncle Miguel Otero was territorial governor. The marriage to Warren failed, and although she had no children of her own, Otero raised her siblings after her mother's death. Otero Warren and a friend purchased a ranch near Santa Fe overlooking the Sangre de Cristo Mountains, called Los Dos (The Two). She lived and worked at the ranch until her death in 1965.

Political work

As an educated bilingual woman from a well-known family, Otero worked on the 1914 women's suffrage campaign in New Mexico that attempted to gain the vote for women. (New Mexico had become a state two years earlier.) Otero rose to a leadership position in the state's Congressional Union (CU; a radical suffrage movement) in 1917, attracting both English- and Spanish-speaking women. In 1920, when the U.S. Congress voted on the Nineteenth Amendment, which enshrined women's right to vote in the U.S. Constitution, the New Mexico delegation voted in favor, largely because of Otero's efforts.

▲ *Nina Otero Warren was a member of the Otero-Luna family, powerful New Mexico landowners and politicians of Spanish descent.*

Between 1917 and 1929, Otero Warren served as the Santa Fe superintendent of instruction and chair of the State Board of Health, making her one of the first women to hold government office in New Mexico. In 1922 she won the Republican nomination to run for the U.S. House of Representatives. She was the first Hispanic American woman to run for Congress, and carried four of the five Hispanic counties in the state, but lost all the Anglo ones.

Literary figure

Otero Warren was also a scholar of the unique contributions of the Spanish and Native Americans to the culture of the Southwest. She helped preserve historic structures, working with artists who flocked to the state in the 1930s and 1940s. She wrote her own book in 1936 entitled *Old Spain in Our Southwest*, which was a memoir of her life as a member of an elite family of political leaders, such as her uncle Solomon Luna, a prominent author of New Mexico's constitution.

See also: Luna, Solomon; Otero Family.

Further reading: www.autry-museum.org/explore/exhibits/suffrage/oterowarren_full.html (biography).

KEY DATES	
1881	Born in Las Lunas, New Mexico.
1917	Superintendent of instruction in Santa Fe County.
1936	Writes *Old Spain in Our Southwest.*
1965	Dies at her ranch outside Santa Fe, New Mexico.

PACHECO, Johnny
Musician

Latin music legend Johnny Pacheco is not only a respected and popular musician, but also a composer, arranger, bandleader, and producer. Pacheco cofounded the leading record label Fania Records with music producer Jerry Masucci (1935–). Grammy-nominated Pacheco has worked with the leading Hispanic American names in showbusiness, including Charlie Palmieri, Willie Colón, Rubén Blades, and Cheo Feliciano.

Early life

Born in Santiago de los Caballeros, Dominican Republic, in 1935, Pacheco grew up in a musical household. His father was the clarinettist Rafael Azarias Pacheco, bandleader of the Santa Cecilia Orchestra. Pacheco first learned to play the harmonica when he was seven years old.

In 1946 Rafael moved his family to New York. Pacheco learned to play the accordion, violin, saxophone, and clarinet. He performed with his brothers and father at private dances, raising money to help overthrow the Dominican dictator Rafael Trujillo (1891–1961). Pacheco attended a Bronx school, before studying percussion at the Julliard School of Music, where he made his own congas. Musician Gilberto Valdés gave Pacheco his first flute. Pacheco taught himself to play it and is thought by many to be one of the leading flutists of his generation.

A leading musician

In 1960 Pacheco formed the acclaimed orchestra Pacheco y su Charanga. Pacheco's band was credited with popularizing the Pachanga dance craze, which became popular on the East Coast in the early 1960s. Their first album, *Johnny Pacheco y Su Charanga, Vol 1*, sold more than 100,000 copies in its first year of release.

▲ *Johnny Pacheco (right) guests with Puerto Rican musician Willie Colón in 2002 during a surprise appearance at a concert in Santo Domingo, Dominican Republic.*

The band was also the first group of Hispanic American performers to get top billing at the famous Apollo Theater in Harlem, New York.

In 1964 Pacheco founded Fania Records with Masucci. As creative director and musical producer, Pacheco not only recorded his own material but also launched the careers of many leading Hispanic American stars. Pacheco was also responsible, along with his friend Bobby Valentin, for launching the famous Fania All-Stars, which consisted of Fania's best musicians.

Award winner

Pacheco has received many awards including the presidential medal of honor from the president of the Dominican Republic in 1996. In that same year Pacheco became the first Latin music producer to win the National Academy of Recording Arts and Sciences (NARAS) governor's award. He was also inducted into the International Latin Music Hall of Fame in 1998.

See also: Blades, Rubén; Colón, Willie; Fania All-Stars; Feliciano, Cheo; Palmieri, Charlie; Valentin, Bobby.

Further reading: www.johnnypacheco.com (Pacheco's Web site).

KEY DATES

1935 Born in Santiago de los Caballeros, Dominican Republic.

1960 Forms Pacheco y Su Charanga.

1961 Introduces dance craze, the Pachanga.

1968 Forms the Fania All Stars.

1996 Receives the Dominican Republic presidential medal of honor.

PACHECO, Romualdo, Jr.
Politician

A congressman and diplomat, José Antonio Romualdo Pacheco, Jr., was the first California native to be state governor. Pacheco was born in Santa Barbara, California, on October 31, 1831, to a prominent couple. His father was Captain José Antonio Romualdo Pacheco, a Mexican who went to California in 1825 as an assistant to Governor José María Echeandía. When Pacheco, Jr., was five weeks old, his father was killed in battle. A few years later, his mother married John Wilson, a Scottish sea captain. Pacheco and his older brother were sent to Honolulu in 1838 to attend an English school.

In 1843, at age 12, Pacheco returned to California and began working on his stepfather's ships. Pacheco left the sea in 1848 to engage in ranching operations at the family's large estate. By 1850, he was showing great interest in politics and government.

A career in politics

Pacheco began his political career in 1853, when he was elected judge of the San Luis Obispo superior court. He served several terms in the state Senate and also as judge of the superior court of his county. In 1863, Pacheco was appointed state treasurer and, in 1871, lieutenant governor under Newton Booth. Pacheco was a Democrat early in his

José Antonio Romualdo Pacheco, Jr., was a sailor, rancher, judge, and United States representative.

political career, but later became a Republican, joining the party in 1863. In 1875, when Governor Booth was elected to the United States Senate, Pacheco served as acting governor of California. He stayed in the governor's office from February 27 until December 9, 1875. As governor of California, he emphasized the importance of higher education and worked for the development of the University of California. Although his stay in the governor's office was brief, he made political history as the first Hispanic governor in the United States.

Into the U.S. Congress

In 1876, Pacheco was elected to serve in the U.S. House of Representatives by a margin of one vote. His opponent contested the election in every available judicial and legislative forum, and was eventually selected by the House to fill the seat. Pacheco went back to California, but was reelected the next year, and held the position until 1883. On retiring from Congress, Pacheco accepted an appointment from President Benjamin Harrison to serve as ambassador to the Central American States from 1891 to 1893.

Romualdo Pacheco was an excellent horseman, and the only governor of California who was known to have roped a grizzly bear. He also worked in mining projects during the California Gold Rush. At the end of his service, he returned to Oakland, California, where he died in 1899.

KEY DATES

1831 Born in Santa Barbara, California, on October 31.

1863 Accepts appointment as California state treasurer.

1871 Becomes lieutenant governor of California.

1875 Becomes governor of California.

1877 Serves first term as a United States representative.

1899 Dies in Oakland, California, on January 23.

Further reading: Garraty, John and Mark Carnes (eds.). *American National Biography. Vol. 16.* New York, NY: Oxford University Press, 1999.
http://www.militarymuseum.org/Pacheco.html (California State Military Museum Web site).

PALÉS MATOS, Luis
Writer

Luis Palés Matos was perhaps the most important poet Puerto Rico has produced. His admiration for the African culture of Puerto Rico is reflected in his unique poetry. Written in Spanish, the verse is almost impossible to translate. However, in the original Spanish, it captures the rhythms of African music and dance.

Early life

Palés Matos was born in 1898 in Guayama, Puerto Rico, a small village with a predominantly African Caribbean population. He came from an illustrious family of writers. His father and two brothers were all poet laureates of Puerto Rico. Palés Matos self-published his first volume of poetry, *Azaleas*, in 1915 at the age of just 17. He had to leave school to get a job to pay back the debts he had run up through the venture.

He later attended college, but when his father died suddenly during a poetry recital, Palés Matos was forced to quit his studies to support his family. He married his fiancée, Suliveres, in 1918, and they settled in the town of

▼ *Luis Palés Matos's poetry reflected his upbringing in a Hispanic Caribbean community.*

KEY DATES

1898 Born in Guayama, Puerto Rico, on March 20.

1915 Publishes first volume of poetry, *Azaleas*.

1921 Moves to San Juan, Puerto Rico, and publishes the poem "El Imparcial."

1942 Appointed poet-in-residence at the University of Puerto Rico.

1959 Dies at home in Santurce, Puerto Rico, on February 23.

Fajardo, where he worked as a journalist. Later that same year Suliveres gave birth to their son. Palés Matos celebrated all these events in his poetry. He also wrote about his wife's tuberculosis, which killed her in 1919.

Experiments with words

In 1921 Palés Matos moved to San Juan, Puerto Rico, to work as a journalist. Along with the writer José Isaac de Diego Padró (1899–1974), he created a new literary movement, using onomatopoeia and musical rhythms, which they called "Diepalismo," a name coined from their two names. They only published one poem written in the style, "El Imparcial" (The Impartial).

Palés Matos had also been writing a number of poems celebrating the peasant dialect, which had traditionally been portrayed as being the language of the poor and uneducated. He put together a collection of 13 poems that were published as *Tuntún de Pasa y Grifería: Poemas Afroantillanos* (Drumbeats of Kinky Hair and Blackness: Afro-Antillean Poems) in 1937.

The poems proved a turning point in Palés Matos's career. The language mixed African, Spanish, and Caribbean idioms in what became known as the Antillean or African-Antillean style. In 1942 Palés Matos was appointed poet-in-residence at the University of Puerto Rico. He started work on an autobiographical novel that remained unfinished, with 29 of the chapters being serialized in the newspaper *El Diario de Puerto Rico* in 1949. A new edition of *Tuntún de Pasa y Grifería* appeared in 1950, containing three new poems. Palés Matos died of a heart attack in 1959.

Further reading: Palés Matos, Luis. *Selected Poems = Poesía Selecta*. Houston, TX: Arte Público Press, 2000.

PALMEIRO, Rafael
Baseball Player

One of the most prolific home-run hitters of all time, Rafael Palmeiro was born in 1964 in Havana, Cuba. In 1971, he fled with his parents and brother to escape the communist dictatorship of Fidel Castro. The family immigrated to the United States.

Hitting form

The left-handed Palmeiro started in the major leagues with the Chicago Cubs in September 1986, after being the 22nd pick in the 1985 free agent draft. Early in his career, Palmeiro was considered primarily a singles hitter and, in 1988, the Cubs traded him to the Texas Rangers, with whom he played the next five seasons. During the 1993 season, at age 29, Palmeiro began to exhibit the explosive home-run power for which he would become famous. That season he hit 37, and exceeded 100 runs batted in (RBIs).

▼ *Rafael Palmeiro of the Baltimore Orioles heads to first after hitting against the Florida Marlins in 2004.*

KEY DATES	
1964	Born in Havana, Cuba, on September 24.
1986	Drafted by the Chicago Cubs.
1993	Exceeds 100 runs batted in (RBIs) in a season for the first time.
1998	Begins the highest scoring five seasons of his career, with the Texas Rangers.
2005	Tests positive for steroids.

After the 1993 season, Palmeiro signed with the Baltimore Orioles. He spent the next five seasons there, hitting 23, 39, 39, 38, and 43 home runs, respectively. After the 1998 campaign, "Raffy," as he was known to his fans, returned for a second stint with the Texas Rangers. The next five seasons were the most productive of his career, as he hit a total of 214 home runs and drove in 508 runs. After the 2003 season, Palmeiro rejoined the Baltimore Orioles.

Controversial ending

Rafael Palmeiro's impressive batting accomplishments were called into question during 2005, when he tested positive for steroids. Palmeiro, who was playing for the Baltimore Orioles at the time, was suspended for 10 games. The announcement of his suspension came just a few weeks after he became one of only four baseball players to hit 500 home runs and gather 3,000 hits in a career. The steroids revelation was all the more shocking given the fact that, in March 2005, Palmeiro passionately denied ever using steroids during a congressional hearing. Despite the mounting evidence, Palmeiro continues to deny "intentionally" ingesting an illegal substance.

Before the steroids controversy, the hallmarks of Palmeiro's career had been impressive steadiness and consistency, although he never led the league in any major hitting category. In addition to his prowess with the bat, Palmeiro was a four-time All–Star and the recipient of three Gold Glove Awards.

Further reading: Canseco, Jose. *Juiced: Wild Times, Rampant 'Roids, Smash Hits and How Baseball Got Big.* New York, NY: Regan Books, 2005.
http://www.raffy25.com (official Web site).

PALMIERI, Charlie
Musician

Charlie Palmieri has an important place in the history of Latin music, in particular in the genres that developed in New York City in the 1940s and 1950s. He was instrumental in the growth of salsa and a pioneer of Latin jazz. He has been hailed as the greatest pianist of the genre and was called "El Gigante de las Blancas y las Negras" (The Giant of the Whites and Blacks), a nickname that referred to a piano's keyboard.

Early life
Palmieri was born in 1927 of Puerto Rican parents in New York City. He grew up in El Barrio, or Spanish Harlem. He started piano lessons at the age of seven and later studied at the Juillard School of Music. Palmieri started to play

▼ *Charlie Palmieri and Dagmar Jarvel, a choreographer, demonstrate the steps of the Pachanga dance made popular by Palmieri's music in the early 1960s.*

piano in bands in 1943 and formed his own group, Conjunto Pin Pin, in 1948. However, lack of work meant that he also accompanied Tito Puente and several other leading Hispanic American stars.

Hitting the big time
In 1958 Palmieri formed the band Charanga Duboney with Johnny Pacheco. The band's innovative use of flute and violins instead of the usual trumpets was a big hit in the 1960s, and established Palmieri's career as a bandleader. In 1961 he became the music director of the Alegre All Stars ensemble. Their album *Salsa Na M*a of 1963 pioneered the use of term *salsa* for the music evolving in New York.

By 1969 Palmieri's popularity had declined and he was back accompanying Puente on his television show *El Mambo*. During the 1970s, Palmieri performed with various artists, including his younger brother Eddie. His best album of the period was *El Gigante del Teclado*.

Final years
Palmieri lived in Puerto Rico between 1980 and 1983, leading a successful orchestra. In 1983 he suffered a heart attack during a stay in New York and resumed his career there performing with small ensembles. On his return from a trip to Puerto Rico on September 12, 1988, Palmieri suffered another heart attack, which this time was fatal.

The Charlie Palmieri Memorial Piano Scholarship was established in his memory in 1989 by Tito Puente. A tribute concert was held in New York in 2004.

See also: Pacheco, Johnny; Palmieri, Eddie; Puente, Tito

Further reading: Leymarie, Isabelle. *Cuban Fire: The Saga of Salsa and Latin Jazz.* New York, NY: Continuum, 2002. http://www.latinjamradio.com/profiles.html#CharliePalmieri (biography).

PALMIERI, Eddie
Musician

Eddie Palmieri is one of the great Latin pianists in the United States. He contributed to the development of salsa with his improvisional approach. He has been called "the salsa eccentric." His long career has enabled him to develop increasing links with jazz and become an innovator of the genre.

Prodigy

Born in 1936 in New York City of Puerto Rican parents, Palmieri is a native of Spanish Harlem, or El Barrio, in northern Manhattan. Like his older brother Charlie, Palmieri was a musical prodigy. He started piano lessons at the age of eight and played at New York's Carnegie Hall as a child. He began his professional career at the age of 13, playing percussion in his uncle's band. He returned to the piano in the early 1950s. He played with Eddie Forrester's orchestra and then moved to Johnny Segui's group in 1955. He replaced his brother as the pianist for singer Vicentico Valdés (1921–1995) in 1956, and played with Tito Rodríguez's band from 1958 to 1960.

In 1961 Palmieri formed his own group, Conjunto La Perfecta, an eight-piece ensemble that made a mark with its innovative use of trombones instead of trumpets. La Perfecta lasted until 1968 and contributed a hard New York edge to the Cuban sound that later became known as salsa. The group recorded eight albums, the most famous of which was *El Sonido Nuevo* (1966).

Living legend

In the 1970s, Palmieri experimented further. This included a Latin-R&B fusion with the group Harlem River Drive in 1971. *Sun of Latin Music* (1974) won him his first Grammy Award in 1976, following the creation of a Latin Music category. After a sojourn in Puerto Rico in 1983, Palmieri returned to New York and collaborated increasingly with

▲ *Eddie Palmieri has received numerous awards for his music, including seven Grammys.*

jazz musicians such as trumpeter Brian Lynch (1956–), trombonist Conrad Herwig (1959–), and saxophonist Donald Harrison (1960–), combining salsa rhythms with jazz improvisation.

Palmieri has become a living legend of Latin music and has been the recipient of numerous awards. He has received seven Grammy Awards, including two for the recording *Obra Maestra/Masterpiece* (2000) with Tito Puente. Two of his recordings have been included in the Smithsonian Institution's catalog of recordings. Other awards included the Eubie Blake Award (1991), a doctorate from the Berkelee College of Music of Puerto Rico (1998), a Chubb Fellowship from Yale University (2002), a Harlem Renaissance Award (2005), and a Lifetime Achievement Award from the Jazz and Blues Foundation. Palmieri's album *Listen Here* was released in 2005.

See also: Palmieri, Charlie; Puente, Tito; Rodríguez, Tito

Further reading: Leymarie, Isabelle. *Cuban Fire: The Saga of Salsa and Latin Jazz.* New York, NY: Continuum, 2002. http://www.eddiepalmierimusic.com (Palmieri's Web site).

KEY DATES

1936 Born in New York City on December 15.

1961 Forms Conjunto La Perfecta.

1976 Wins first Grammy Award for *Sun of Latin Music*.

2005 Wins Lifetime Achievement Award from Jazz and Blues Foundation.

PALOMINO, Carlos
Boxer

Carlos Palomino is a former world welterweight boxing champion who became a successful actor. Born in 1949 in San Luis de Colorado, Mexico, Palomino moved to Los Angeles, California, at the age of 10. He attended high school in Orange County.

Army champion
Palomino served in the U.S. Army between 1971 and 1972 in the 1st Cavalry Division based at Fort Hood, Texas. He learned to box as part of his training, partly to please his father and partly to avoid being posted to the war in Vietnam. Palomino lost his first bout, but two months later he won the Fort Hood championship, thanks to his sharp left hook and powerful body attack. Soon he became the All-Army welterweight champion.

World champion
In 1972 Palamino defeated the Olympic gold-medalist Sugar Ray Seales (1952–). Having been discharged from the Army, Palomino turned professional and also started attending college. Palomino's first fight was a success, which he won in four rounds.

Palomino remained undefeated until 1974, when he lost a 10-round fight against Andy Price (1953–). In 1976 Palomino traveled to London, England, to face World Boxing Council (WBC) champion John Stracey (1950–). Following a defeat in March, Palomino won a June rematch in 12 rounds, becoming the world welterweight champion. Having graduated from California State University in recreational administration, Palomino was the first boxing world champion to hold a degree.

▲ **Carlos Palomino (right) poses with champion John Stracey before their second fight in 1976. Palomino won in 12 rounds to take the world title.**

Palomino held the world title for three years. He lost the title in 1979 to Puerto Rican fighter Wilfred Benítez. Palomino also lost his next fight that year, to Roberto Duran (1951–). Palomino decided to keep a promise to himself and he retired before his 30th birthday.

Acting career
Palomino soon began a successful acting career, with roles in *Taxi*, *Hill Street Blues*, *NYPD Blue*, and many other television shows. He also appeared in numerous films, and is well known for an appearance in beer commercials.

Palomino returned briefly to boxing in 1997. He won four bouts and lost one. His final record stood at 31 wins (20 by knockout), 4 losses, and 3 draws. Palomino still acts and works as a boxing commentator. He also runs a boxing program for at-risk children.

See also: Benitez, Wilfred

Further reading: http://www.ringsidereport.com/ Berkwitt6282005.htm (interview with Palomino).

KEY DATES	
1949	Born in San Luis de Colorado, Mexico, on August 10.
1971	Joins U.S. Army and learns to box.
1972	Turns professional.
1976	Wins world welterweight title in London, England.
1979	Loses title to Wilfred Benítez, and soon retires.
1989	Becomes one of the youngest boxers inducted into the Boxing Hall of Fame.
1997	Returns to boxing for one year.

PANTOJA, Antonia
Activist

Antonia Pantoja was a leading Latina civil rights leader and educator. She founded Aspira, an organization that helps Hispanic Americans achieve high standards of education. It operates in Puerto Rico and several U.S. states.

Early life
"Tonita" Pantoja was born in 1922 to Alejandrina, an unmarried mother. She grew up in the slum of Puerta de Tierra in Old San Juan, Puerto Rico, and was raised by her grandparents, Conrado Pantoja Santos and Luisa Acosta Rivera, to save her the stigma of illegitimacy. Her grandfather died when Pantoja was only six.

Her biological mother was absent from her life while she grew up in Puerto Rico. She was undernourished as a child, and could not enjoy a full social life with her school friends because she was too poor to buy shoes and dresses. During high school Pantoja contracted tuberculosis and was confined for months. Finally managing to graduate, Pantoja enrolled at the University of Puerto Rico and qualified as a teacher. She worked in Puerto Rico for two years and then moved to New York in 1944.

Good works and poor health
Within moments of arrival in New York, Pantoja was confronted with racism. She was seen as black because, although light skinned, she had kinky hair. Pantoja quickly learned about segregation, and of the second-class citizenship status afforded to Puerto Ricans. Her teaching credentials were not valid in New York, and her first job was welding lamps in a factory.

A roommate helped Pantoja get a job at a community center. There she blossomed into an able organizer and community activist. She also won a scholarship to study

▲ *Antonia Pantoja battled poor health to be a leading Latina civil rights activist.*

at Hunter College in New York City, beginning a 21-year academic career that culminated in receiving a PhD from the Union Graduate School in Ohio.

Pantoja founded many important social-justice organizations, including the National Puerto Rican Forum in 1957 and Aspira in 1961. The hard work took its toll on her health, and doctors advised her to move out of cold New York and back to warm Puerto Rico. She tried that, but returned within a year. She moved to Washington, D.C., but it was just as cold. Pantoja then moved to San Diego, California, in 1978, where the weather suited her and she regained her strength. When she decided it was time to retire, she headed for Puerto Rico again but that was not home. Pantoja realized she was a Nuyorican (Puerto Rican New Yorker) and moved back to New York to finish out her life. She died in the city in 2002.

Further reading: Pantoja, Antonia. *Memoir of a Visionary: Antonia Pantoja.* Houston, TX: Arte Publico Press, 2002.

KEY DATES

1922	Born in San Juan, Puerto Rico, on September 13.
1957	Founds National Puerto Rican Forum.
1961	Founds Aspira.
1996	Receives Presidential Medal of Freedom from President Bill Clinton.
2002	Dies in New York City on May 24.

PAOLI, Antonio
Singer

Antonio Paoli is considered to be the first internationally known Puerto Rican performer. He sang opera across the world as one of the leading tenors of his day.

Love of music

Paoli was born in 1871 in Ponce, Puerto Rico, a town in the south of the island. While at school, the young Paoli developed an interest in music. This attraction deepened after attending a concert performance by the Italian tenor Pietro Bacceri, in Ponce.

Paoli's older sister, Amalia, was a successful singer in Spain. She encouraged her brother's musical talent and arranged for him to study in Europe. In 1881 Paoli became the protégé of Queen María Cristina of Spain, and with two scholarships obtained by Amalia, he enrolled in the Real Monasterio del Escorial, north of Madrid.

By 1883 Paoli's parents had both died and he remained in Spain until 1897, when he moved to Italy to attend the singing school Academia de Canto La Scala in Milan. Two years later Paoli debuted in Rossini's opera *William Tell* in Paris, France. During the early stages of his career, Paoli used the name Ermogene Imleghi Bascarán.

Rising star

Paoli soon gained recognition across Europe, performing on various occasions at the Royal Opera House in London, England. As Paoli's fame grew, Puerto Ricans began to suspect that he was ashamed of his Caribbean roots. To counter these suggestions, Paoli made the island his home for the rest of his career.

In 1901 Paoli joined a world tour led by Italian opera star Pietro Mascagni. Once more Paoli captured the attention of opera critics. Two of his most acclaimed

▲ **In his day, Antonio Paoli was known as the "king of tenors and the tenor of kings." A theater at San Juan's Centro de Bellas Artes is named for him.**

performances were in Wagner's *Lohengrin* and in Verdi's *Il Trovatore*, which he sang in Russia, Argentina, and Poland throughout 1904. After his debut as *Othello* in Madrid in 1905, Paoli performed the same role another 570 times and subsequently gave other performances in Hungary, Belgium, Venezuela, Egypt, Chile, Colombia, Cuba, Haiti, Brazil, Canada, and the United States.

In 1907 Paoli recorded Leoncavallo's *Clown*, becoming one of the first opera artists in the world to record an entire opera. This marked the beginning of a successful career as an internationally acclaimed recording artist. With the start of World War I in 1914, Paoli left Europe for the Americas. Not being able to perform at New York's Carnegie Hall owing to his rivalry with fellow tenor Enrico Caruso, Paoli eventually returned to Puerto Rico. There, he established a singing school with his sister Amalia. Paoli also planned a music conservatory, a dream that became reality after his death in 1946.

Further reading: http://www.musicofpuertorico.com/en/antonio_paoli.html (biography).

KEY DATES

1871 Born in Ponce, Puerto Rico, on August 14.

1899 Debuts in Rossini's opera *William Tell* in Paris.

1904 Performs in Wagner's *Lohengrin* and in Verdi's *Il Trovatore*.

1907 Records entire Leoncavallo opera, *Clown*.

1946 Dies of cancer in San Juan, Puerto Rico, on August 24th.

PAREDES, Américo
Folklorist

Américo Paredes was a pioneering expert in corridos—Mexican folk ballads. In his seminal book, *With His Pistol in His Hand,* which was about Gregorio Cortez—the bandit, Tejano folk hero, and the subject of many corridos—Paredes brought attention to Hispanic American oral history of the U.S.–Mexican borderlands. Paredes's other novels, essays, poetry, and research into Mexican Americans helped overturn decades of stereotyping of Hispanic Americans, and made him a leading scholar in the field of Chicano studies.

Born into violent conflict

Américo Paredes was born in 1915 in Brownsville, Texas, in the middle of a bloody conflict between Mexican Americans and Anglo Texans. A revolutionary manifesto entitled Plan de San Diego had been published a few months before. The document called for Mexican Americans and other non-Anglo groups in the Southwest to rise up and take control of Texas and the other states from the United States. The resulting unrest left hundreds, perhaps thousands, of people dead on both sides.

▼ *Américo Paredes used the contents of Mexican folk songs to develop a fuller history of Mexican Americans.*

KEY DATES

1915 Born in Brownsville, Texas, on September 3.

1956 Earns PhD in English and folklore at the University of Texas at Austin.

1958 Begins teaching anthropology and English at the University of Texas at Austin.

1990 Receives El Orden de Aguila Azteca, Mexico's highest honor for foreigners.

1999 Dies in Austin after a lengthy illness on May 5.

Academic success

Paredes experienced racism personally when his high school counselor discouraged his aspirations to go to college because of his ethnicity. After serving briefly in the U.S. Army during World War II (1939–1945), Paredes entered the University of Texas at Austin. He graduated summa cum laude and continued his education at UT Austin, earning doctoral degrees in English and folklore studies in 1956.

Aside from his writings and research, Paredes used his time at the University of Texas to develop several Chicano studies programs. He was instrumental in founding the Center for Intercultural Studies of Folklore and Ethnomusicology in 1967. In 1972 he created a Mexican American studies program. His lifetime of work on Mexican Americans was recognized in 1990 when he received El Orden de Aguila Azteca (The Order of the Aztec Eagle) from the Mexican government.

Major achievements

Prior to Paredes's work, the popular perceptions of Hispanic Americans in Texas were overtly racist, a view perpetuated by several Anglo writers in the early part of the 20th century. Paredes's work impacted generations of Hispanic Americans, most notably the scholar and folklorist José Limón.

See also: Cortez, Gregorio; Limón, José

Further reading: Paredes, Américo. *Folklore and Culture on the Texas-Mexican Border.* Austin, TX: CMAS Books, 1993. http://www.lib.utexas.edu/benson/paredes (Américo Paredes Archives at the University of Texas at Austin).

PARRA, Derek
Speed Skater

▲ **Derek Parra achieved success on roller skates before winning Olympic gold on ice.**

Derek Parra set a new world record for speed skating at the 2002 Winter Olympic Games and won a gold medal. He had started speed skating on ice just six years earlier, and is the most successful Hispanic American speed skater in history.

Parra was born in 1970 and grew up in a Hispanic area of San Bernardino, California. After his parents separated, he was raised by his father, a prison worker. Parra spent his pocket money at a local roller rink, where he raced to win hot-dog prizes.

Inline champion

Despite his short stature, Parra's skating skills soon attracted the attention of a coach. During a school vacation, he managed to attend the U.S. Olympic Training Center in Colorado Springs, Colorado. He met in-line skating's leading coach, Virgil Dooley, who invited him to train with his team after leaving high school.

Aged 17, Parra arrived unannounced in Florida to train under Dooley. He embarked on a grueling training schedule, and supported himself by working shifts at a fast-food restaurant.

Between 1990 and 1996, Parra became the national and then world in-line skating champion. (In-line skates have wheels arranged in a line, and are also known as roller blades.) Parra won 18 titles and set several world records in the 1,500-meter event.

However, Parra's ultimate dream was to win an Olympic medal, so he was deeply disappointed when in-line skating was not chosen as a new Olympic sport for the 1996 games in Atlanta, Georgia. Now 26, Parra made the difficult decision to change to the winter sport of speed skating in the hope of achieving his Olympic goal.

Immediate success

Within weeks of the switch, Parra won two medals at the U.S. speed skating championship. He earned a place on the 1998 U.S. Olympic Team traveling to Nagano, Japan. However, once there an administrative glitch prevented Parra from competing.

Parra committed to skating in the next Olympics. He took a part-time job at a store, and combined work with training for up to six hours a day. These sessions included exercises involving jumping while wearing 40-pound weights. Parra became the leading U.S. speed skater, but was still not considered world class. However, in 2001 Parra surprised many by taking silver in the 1,500 meters at the speed skating world championships.

In the 2002 Winter Olympic Games in Salt Lake City, Utah, Parra surpassed all expectations again by taking a silver medal in the 5,000 meters. A week later he took gold in the 1,500 meters, also setting a new world record of 1:43:95 seconds.

Further reading: http://www.latinosportslegends.com/ interviews/interview_with_derek_parra-081002.htm (interview).

KEY DATES	
1970	Born in San Bernardino, California, on March 15.
1995	Most decorated athlete at the Pan-American Games.
2001	Silver medalist in the 1,500-meter world championship.
2002	1,500 meter gold medalist and 5,000-meter silver medalist at Winter Olympics at Salt Lake City, Utah.
2003	Wins overall title at 2003 World Cup, Germany.

PAU-LLOSA, Ricardo
Poet, Curator

Ricardo Pau-Llosa is a poet and specialist in Latin American art. His love of visual art informs his poetry, and he continues to work in both fields.

Early life

Pau-Llosa was born in Havana, Cuba, in 1954. Following the Cuban Revolution of 1959, and President Fidel Castro's conversion to communism the following year, Pau-Llosa's family, like many Cubans, moved to the United States. The family settled in Florida, and after high school Pau-Llosa attended a number of colleges in the Miami area.

In 1973, while still at college, Pau-Llosa paid to publish his first collection of poetry, *Veinticinco Poemas* (Twenty-Five Poems). He graduated from Miami's Florida International University in 1974 and then attended Florida Atlantic University at Boca Raton, where he received a master of arts degree in 1976.

Professional career

After completing his second degree, Pau-Llosa worked as an English language teacher. In 1979 a second piece of his writing, a nonfiction essay in Spanish and English, was published by Editorial Playor.

In 1980 Pau-Llosa joined his old school, Florida International University, as an adjunct professor of Latin American art history. In 1983, while teaching at Florida International, Pau-Llosa won the first Anhinga Poetry Prize, a national poetry prize awarded by Florida State University for his collection of poems, *Sorting Metaphors*. The Anhinga Press published the poems the same year.

KEY DATES

1954 Born in Havana, Cuba, on May 17.

1960 Moves to the United States.

1973 Publishes first poetry collection.

1983 Wins Anhinga Poetry Prize from Florida State University.

1988 Cocurates *Mira! The Canadian Club Hispanic Art Tour III.*

1993 Nominated for Pulitzer Prize for *Cuba.*

2003 Publishes poetry collection, *The Mastery Impulse.*

▲ **Ricardo Pau-Llosa is a Latino poet who writes exclusively in English.**

After the success of *Sorting Metaphors*, Pau-Llosa published no further collections of poetry until 1992, when the *Bread of the Imagined* appeared. *Cuba*, published the following year, was nominated for the Pulitzer Prize.

Pau-Llosa continued to teach until the mid-1980s, when he became more involved in the art world. He was the cocurator of two major exhibits of Hispanic American artists in the late 1980s. The first show, *Outside Cuba/Fuera de Cuba*, featured the work of 48 Cuban artists living outside Cuba. The second, *Mira! The Canadian Club Hispanic Art Tour III*, included works by Chicanos, Cuban Americans, Puerto Ricans, and other Hispanic Americans. In 1997 and 1999 Pau-Llosa was a guest curator at the Lima Biennials in Peru.

Since the late 1990s, Pau-Llosa has published more poetry books. *Vereda Tropical* appeared in 1999 and *The Mastery Impulse* in 2003. Another book, *Parable Hunter*, will be published in 2008.

Further reading: Pau-Llosa, Ricardo. *The Mastery Impulse*. Pittsburgh, PA: Carnegie Mellon University Press, 2003. www.pau-llosa.com (Pau-Llosa's Web site).

PELLI, Cesar
Architect

Cesar Pelli is one of the most renowned living architects. He has designed some of the largest buildings in the world and has been a leading figure advocating the use of office complexes as a means of urban regeneration.

High-rising architect

Pelli was born in Tucumán, Argentina, in 1926, graduating in architecture from the Universidad de Tucumán in 1948. In 1952 he went to the United States to study for a master's degree at the University of Illinois, at Champaign.

Graduating in 1954, Pelli decided to stay in the United States. He started his professional career in the office of Eero Saarinen, working on such landmark buildings as the TWA Terminal at John F. Kennedy International Airport in New York City. After ten years with Saarinen, Pelli moved to Los Angeles, California, to work at the firm of Daniel, Mann, Johnson, & Mendenhall from 1964 to 1968 and at Gruen Associates from 1968 to 1977.

In 1977 Pelli was appointed dean of the School of Architecture at Yale University in Connecticut. He held the position until 1984, when he established his own firm, Cesar Pelli Associates, with the architects Diana Balmori and Fred W. Clarke in New Haven, Connecticut. The firm has since grown to an 80-strong operation with offices in New Haven and New York City. It designs large buildings for mainly corporate and government clients in the United States and abroad.

Great buildings

Pelli's buildings are prominent examples of U.S. postmodern architecture, in which sophisticated construction and environmental technologies are used. Among his firm's main buildings are the Residential Tower of the Museum of Modern Art, New York (1984), the World Financial Center, New York (1987), Herring Hall at Rice University, Houston,

▲ *Cesar Pelli's architectural practice has designed some of the world's tallest buildings, including the Petronas Towers in Kuala Lumpur, Malaysia.*

Texas (1984), Mattatuck Museum, Waterbury, Connecticut (1984), Canary Wharf Tower, London, England (1986), the Carnegie Hall Tower, New York (1990), and the NTT Headquarters, Tokyo, Japan (1990). Its most celebrated building is the Petronas Towers in Kuala Lumpur, Malaysia (1998), which was the world's tallest building until 2004. It consists of two 88-story towers linked by a bridge. Pelli's son Rafael joined the firm in 1993, and it has since been renamed Pelli Clarke Pelli Associates.

Award winners

Pelli's architectural practice has received several awards, including the Firm Award from the American Institute of Architects (AIA) in 1989. Pelli was selected one of the 10 most influential living U.S. architects and received the AIA Gold Medal in 1995. His projects were the subject of a retrospective exhibition that was shown at the National Building Museum, Washington, D.C., in 2000.

Further reading: Pelli, Cesar. *Observations for Young Architects.* New York, NY: Monacelli Press, 1999. http://www.pcparch.com (Pelli Clarke Pelli Web site).

KEY DATES	
1926	Born in Tucumán, Argentina, on October 12.
1954	Earns master's degree from University of Illinois.
1977	Founds Cesar Pelli Associates.
1995	Awarded Gold Medal from the American Institute of Architects.

PEÑA, Albert A., Jr.
Lawyer, Judge

Lawyer, activist, and judge Albert A. Peña, Jr., was the first Mexican American to serve as County Commissioner in Bexar County (San Antonio), Texas. He was also presiding judge of all San Antonio courts.

Early life
Born on December 15, 1917, Peña was the son of Albert Peña, a lawyer, and Dolores Lopez Peña. Known as "Peanut" because of his small frame, Peña grew into a tough young man while fighting off bullies in the San Antonio barrios. After the attack on Pearl Harbor in December 1941, Peña and his two brothers, Ricardo and Antonio, joined the U.S. Navy. Following an honorable discharge, Peña went to college. Although he wanted to be a politician, his father encouraged him to be a lawyer, and he graduated from the South Texas School of Law in 1950.

Civil rights attorney and organizer
In 1951 Peña passed the Texas state bar and began practicing law in San Antonio. He joined the League of United Latin American Citizens (LULAC) and later the American GI Forum, an organization of Mexican American veterans. As a member of these organizations, Peña embarked on a career of civil rights advocacy and litigation. Asked by Héctor P. García, head of the American GI Forum, to investigate school segregation, he unilaterally challenged and desegregated various school districts in the surrounding areas of San Antonio.

In 1952 Democratic nominee Adlai Stevenson campaigned in Texas. Peña organized the Loyal American Democrats and pressured the state party to allow a Chicano political rally on the West Side of San Antonio. Peña also advocated for a civil rights agenda in the Democratic Platform in 1960, and became the lone

▲ *Albert A. Peña, Jr., became a judge in the Municipal Courts in San Antonio in 1977, before becoming presiding judge in 1982.*

Chicano delegate from Texas to the national convention. Together with other Chicanos across the Southwest, Peña helped form the Viva Kennedy Clubs that contributed to the election of John F. Kennedy as president in 1960.

Six years later, when President Lyndon Johnson pushed for national meetings with Chicano leaders, Peña led a series of protests and walkouts in Albuquerque and in El Paso over empty promises and failed commitments. On the home front, Peña joined with younger activists of the Mexican American Youth Organization (MAYO) to form a local community development organization and regional network of these groups, which became known as the National Council of La Raza. With other civil rights lawyers he cofounded MALDEF, the Mexican American Legal Defense and Education Fund, in the Southwest.

In 1977 Peña was appointed judge of the Municipal Courts in San Antonio; he rose to become the presiding judge in 1982. He also helped form the Advocates, a loose federation of community groups that seek to hold elected officials accountable for their actions.

See also: García, Héctor P.; National Organizations

Further reading: http://libraries.uta.edu/tejanovoices/interview.asp?CMASNo=015 (brief biography and interview).

KEY DATES	
1917	Born in December 15.
1950	Graduates from the South Texas School of Law; works for the American GI Forum in desegregating schools.
1960	Appointed Bexar County Commissioner, until 1974.
1977	Appointed municipal judge.
1982	Appointed presiding judge of the municipal courts.

PEÑA, Amado
Artist

Amado Peña is a Mexican American painter whose life and work have had a key influence on the course and development of the Chicano art movement.

Early life

Of mixed Mexican and Indian descent, Amado Maurilio Peña was born in 1943 in Laredo, Texas. His father was a fireman, and his mother was a housewife. Peña always wanted to draw; it fascinated him to create figures and images. His parents, however, wanted him to pursue a conventional career in a less precarious line of work. As a compromise, he agreed to become an art teacher. He took a degree at Texas A&I University (now Texas A&M–Kingsville), where his classmates included Carmen Lomas Garza and César Martínez, both of whom were also destined to become famous artists. While studying, Peña entered a competition to create a mascot for the university; his winning design, an image of a javelina (wild boar), is still used today.

On graduating in 1965, Peña kept his word to his parents and taught in a high school in Laredo. In 1970, however, he returned to Kingsville as a graduate student,

▼ **Amado Peña is a Chicano artist whose paintings are critically acclaimed and command high prices in the market.**

KEY DATES

1943	Born in Laredo, Texas.
1965	Receives BA degree from Texas A&I University; takes teaching job in Laredo.
1970	Returns to college.
1971	Receives MA in art and education; resumes teaching.
1980	Quits teaching to become a full-time painter.

and received an MA in art and education in 1971. Meanwhile, he became a major influence in the Chicano art movement. After teaching in Crystal City and Austin, Peña quit in 1980 to become a full-time artist.

Artistic development

Much of Peña's early work was executed in black ink on paper, and often featured figures with one huge eye. He then experimented with watercolors, producing beautiful images using a mix of earth tones and pastels. He tackled a wide range of subjects in a variety of media—silkscreen prints and etchings, as well as conventional oil paint on canvas—but his abiding themes were life and landscape in the U.S. Southwest. His mature paintings, which typically featured stylized images of mestizos, became enormously popular. Peña made a fortune through the sale of original work, limited-edition prints, and reproduction posters. Among the most famous private collectors of Peña's paintings are Lloyd Bentsen, a U.S. senator and 1988 Democratic vice presidential candidate, Tom Brokaw, a writer and former broadcast journalist, and Lou Diamond Phillips, the movie actor.

Many U.S. art galleries have major works by Peña. Outstanding examples can be viewed at the National Museum of American Art in Washington, D.C., the Whitney Museum in New York City, the Heard Museum in Phoenix, Arizona, and the New Mexico Fine Art Museum in Santa Fe.

See also: Lomas Garza, Carmen; Martínez, César

Further reading: Peña, Amado Maurilio. *Peña on Peña.* Waco, TX: WRS Publishing, 1995.
http://www.penaofficial.com (official Web site).

PEÑA, Elizabeth
Actor

Known for her adventurous spirit, Elizabeth Peña has transcended stereotypically ethnic roles to become one of the leading Latina actresses working in Hollywood today.

Early life
Elizabeth Peña was born in Elizabeth, New Jersey, in 1961. Shortly after her birth, her parents moved the family to Cuba, where Elizabeth lived until the age of nine. In 1970 the Peña family returned to the United States.

Peña's father, Mario, a renowned Cuban American theatrical director, actor, and novelist, founded the off-Broadway Latin American Theater Ensemble. Elizabeth had known that she wanted to be an actress from the age of eight. At the age of 10, she began acting professionally. While attending New York's famed High School of the Performing Arts, Peña performed in repertory theater productions and also appeared in a handful of television commercials. After graduating, she went on to appear in more than 20 off-Broadway shows and toured with a theater troupe for two years as Shakespeare's Juliet.

Feature films
In 1979 Peña played the role of a rebellious teen in her debut feature film, the award-winning independent movie *El Super*. After three more low-budget films, she moved west to pursue an acting career in Hollywood.

Determined to break into the mainstream film industry, Peña asked a studio security guard to deliver her demo tape to the studio's casting director. Forty-five minutes later Peña received a phone call inviting her to an audition. She was cast in the role of a sultry maid named Carmen in *Down and Out in Beverly Hills*. The film turned out to be a hit comedy that showed her talents well. Following her big break, Peña appeared in other films like *La Bamba*, *Blue Steel*, and *Batteries Not Included*.

▲ **Elizabeth Peña (left) with her Tortilla Soup costars, Jacqueline Obradors and Tamara Mello. Peña won an award for her performance in this 2001 film.**

In 1990 Peña starred opposite Tim Robbins in her first feature film lead as the tempestuous Jezebel in Adrian Lyne's *Jacob's Ladder*. This complicated role—requiring her to switch rapidly from being loving to being malicious and back again—was a difficult one, but Peña put in a fine performance. Peña has said that she got the role against stiff opposition, including Susan Sarandon, Robbins's longtime companion, and international superstar Madonna.

Mainstream actress
In the years since, Peña has worked steadily in both film and television, continuing to deliver high-caliber performances. In 1996 she won an Independent Spirit Award for her role in the acclaimed film *Lone Star*, and in 2001 she won an American Latino Media Arts Award for *Tortilla Soup*. She has also appeared in the Emmy Award-winning television film *Drug Wars: The Camarena Story* and has starred in popular television series such as *LA Law* and *Resurrection Blvd*.

Further reading: http://www.acidlogic.com/elizabeth_pena.htm (interview).

KEY DATES	
1961	Born in Elizabeth, New Jersey, on September 23.
1979	Appears in *El Super*, her debut film performance.
1990	Has her first lead role as Jezebel in *Jacob's Ladder*.
2005	Appears in *Transamerica*.

PEÑA, Federico
Politician

Federico Peña had a successful career as a politician, first as mayor of Denver, Colorado, and then working in the administration of President Bill Clinton. A highway linking Denver's airport to the interstate is named for him.

Early life
Federico Fabián Peña was born in Laredo, Texas, in 1947. His parents had moved there from Brownsville, Texas, in search of better work opportunities. Peña was a bright student in high school, and went on to attend the University of Texas at Austin. He arrived there during the height of the Chicano movement, in which Hispanic Americans celebrated their identity and fought for civil rights. Peña embraced the counterculture, growing a ponytail that he kept into his first job as a legal-aid attorney in El Paso, Texas.

The promise of Denver
The Mexican American Legal Defense and Education Fund offered Peña a job in Denver. Within a matter of years he was in contact with the city's political players. He ran for the state legislature, winning easily. His colleagues in the Democratic Party selected him as their minority leader.

Peña then ran for mayor. He beat a 14-year incumbent to become Denver's first Hispanic American mayor, at the age of just 36. As mayor, Peña initiated some ambitious building projects. He built a new international airport, attracted a major league baseball team, and constructed a city convention center and central library. He was easily reelected to a second term. When Clinton, then governor of Arkansas, sought the U.S. presidency, Peña signed on as a campaign adviser on transportation issues.

▲ *Federico Peña answers questions as President Bill Clinton's secretary of transportation in 1993. In Clinton's second term, Peña was secretary of energy.*

The cabinet positions
Once elected president, Clinton appointed Peña as secretary of transportation in 1993. The secretary regulates all transportation in the country. Peña supervised 60,000 employees and administered a multibillion dollar budget.

With Clinton's reelection in 1996, Peña was asked to serve as a secretary of energy. Peña was given oversight of power production and transmission. However, Peña had promised his family that they would return to Denver, so he served in the role for only a year before returning home.

Investment banker
Peña had begun an investment banking firm during his last years as mayor of Denver. He returned to that business once he left the Clinton administration. He was later also offered a partnership with Vestar Capital Partners, a major New York-based investment firm.

Further reading: http://www.insc.ru/main/people/pena.html (biography).

KEY DATES

1947 Born in Laredo, Texas, on March 15.

1979 Elected to the Colorado House of Representatives.

1983 Elected as mayor of Denver, Colorado.

1993 Takes up post of secretary of transportation for President Bill Clinton.

1997 Becomes secretary of energy.

1998 Senior adviser and partner at Vestar Capital Partners.

PÉREZ, Jorge
Entrepreneur

Crowned the "Condo King of the Tropics" and often compared to Donald Trump, Jorge Pérez is Florida's leading luxury housing developer. Despite his financial success—Pérez was ranked the 645th richest man in the world by *Forbes* magazine in 2005—he says that he is more driven by the need to create and redefine spaces that inspire him.

From Argentina to the United States

Born in 1950 in Argentina, Pérez was raised in Colombia by Cuban parents. At the age of 18, he gave up a place in his family's pharmaceutical business to study urban planning in the United States. After completing his master's degree at the University of Michigan, Pérez briefly thought about a career in academia. He began working as an urban planner for the city of Miami instead. A chance meeting with New York developer Steven Ross led to a life long partnership. The two men founded the Related Group of Florida in

▼ *Jorge Pérez believes that each time a person acts, "not only are you defining yourself, but you're defining the world around you."*

KEY DATES	
1950	Born in Argentina.
1968	Leaves Colombia to study urban planning in the United States.
1979	With Steven Ross founds the Related Group of Florida.
2004	Company's folio is valued at more than $10 billion.
2005	Ranked the 645th richest person in the world by *Forbes* magazine.

1979. Pérez commented: "The time was just right to create a company and do something I knew how to do. I never saw myself as a businessman; it was more about my desire to do things on my own—and to create."

Using the expertise he garnered working for the city, Pérez specialized in building low-income housing projects for the next 10 years. When he began to feel restricted by the rigid parameters of government projects in the late 1980s, Pérez steered the company toward suburban homes and apartments. Fifteen years later he shifted his interest to the condo market, building high-rise towers and transforming drab neighborhoods into prime real estate.

In the early 21st century, with more than 50,000 housing units in South Florida and a further 10,000 under construction, Pérez's company was the driving force behind South Florida's rapid development. The largest Hispanic-owned business in the United States, in 2004 the Related Group of Florida boasted a portfolio valued in excess of $10 billion.

Pérez is a keen art lover with a personal collection that includes works by Latin American artists such as Frida Kahlo and Diego Rivera. Pérez knows that art and culture can infuse an environment with vitality. He acknowledges the role that style and culture play in the life of a flourishing city. Preoccupied at the start of the 21st century with the revitalization of downtown Miami, Pérez aimed to transform it into a great international city in which business and culture could happily merge.

Further reading: http://www.webspawner.com/users/petergottschall/jorgePérezceoch.html (biography of Jorge Pérez on the Related Group of Florida's site).

PÉREZ, Loida Maritza
Writer

Dominican-born Loida Maritza Pérez burst onto the U.S. literary scene in 1999 with the publication of her novel, *Geographies of Home*. She is featured regularly on lists of promising young Hispanic writers, along with notable contemporaries such as Junot Díaz.

Early life

Pérez was born in the Dominican Republic in 1963. At the time the Dominican Republic was in turmoil following the assassination of the dictator Rafael Trujillo. An elected government was then overthrown by the Dominican military. In 1965 a civil war broke out as military factions fought for control.

Pérez escaped from the chaos when her family moved to the United States when she was three years old. She grew up in Brooklyn, New York. While at junior high, Pérez, who has African ancestry, read *For Colored Girls Who Have Considered Suicide, When the Rainbow Is Enuf* by novelist Ntozake Shange (1948–). The novel helped Pérez decide to study English at college, rather than medicine or law as her parents had hoped. Pérez majored in English at Cornell University in Ithaca, New York, and began *Geographies of Home* while an undergraduate in an autobiographical writing course taught by the African American literary scholar Henry Louis Gates (1950–).

Grants and scholarships

While working on her novel, Pérez won fellowships that allowed her to concentrate on writing. In 1992 she was awarded a New York Foundation for the Arts grant for writing. Two years later, in 1994, she won the Ragdale Foundation's U.S.-Africa Writers Project, and in 1996 the Djerassi's Pauline and Henry Louis Gates, Sr., Fellowship.

Novel

Geographies of Home, which originated as a short story, tells the story of a family at a moment of crisis in its life. At the center of the novel is Illiana, who is forced by family circumstances to drop out of college and return to her parents and 13 siblings who live in a crumbling townhouse in a Hispanic Brooklyn barrio. The story of how this situation came to pass is told in a series of flashbacks that draw together the family's experiences of being immigrants in Brooklyn with their former lives in the Dominican Republic.

KEY DATES	
1963	Born in the Dominican Republic.
1966	Moves to the United States.
1987	Graduates from Cornell University.
1992	Awarded New York Foundation for Arts grant to support her writing.
1994	Wins Ragdale Foundation U.S.–Africa Writers Project.
1999	Her novel *Geographies of Home* is published.

In the book, Pérez explores issues of cultural dislocation, family duty, alienation, and sexual abuse. At the heart of her novel is the realization that for this family the American dream has failed. Pérez writes as a member of a generation that has been brought up in the United States but for whom the land of their parents is a very real presence. The cultural heritage of immigrant families is reflected in her dissection of how the family's father and mother have failed in many ways to adapt to their adopted country. They consider returning to the Dominican Republic but realize that their grown-up children, whose home is Brooklyn, still need them around.

Reflecting on her novel, Pérez comments: "There is no typical experience either for Dominicans living in this country or for those in the Dominican Republic, just as there is none for Americans who have lived in the United States since their ancestors arrived on the *Mayflower*."

Other work

Pérez has had a number of short stories published in different magazines. She revealed that her second novel would be called *Lamentations* and be set during the time of the Trujillo dictatorship in the Dominican Republic. Pérez currently teaches creative writing at the University of New Mexico at Albuquerque.

See also: Díaz, Junot

Further reading: Pérez, Loida Maritza. *Geographies of Home: A Novel*. New York, NY: Viking, 1999.
http://voices.cla.umn.edu/vg/Bios/entries/perez_loida_maritza.html (biography).

PEREZ, Rosie
Actor

Her skills as a dancer helped Rosie Perez get a role in a feature film in 1989. Since then she has flourished as an actress, appearing in a wide range of movies, from mainstream comedies to cult art-house dramas.

Brooklyn born and bred

Born in 1964 into a large Puerto Rican family, Perez was brought up by her aunt in New York's borough of Brooklyn, where she still lives. Her childhood was difficult at times. Perez was unhappy at a predominantly white school where she felt singled out and mistreated.

Despite studying marine biology at college in Los Angeles, California, Perez pursued a career in entertainment and began to work as a dancer on *Soul Train,* a long-running African American music television show. Perez progressed to become a choreographer on music videos for stars such as LL Cool J and Bobby Brown. She also earned three Emmy nominations choreographing routines for the television sketch series *In Living Color.* In this capacity she helped the Latina star Jennifer Lopez get her career off the ground.

Acclaimed director Spike Lee admired Perez's dancing abilities and hired her for his landmark independent movie *Do the Right Thing* (1989), filmed on the streets of Brooklyn. Perez played Tina, the girlfriend of Lee's own character. She performs an eye-catching dance during the film's title sequence.

Perez proceeded to give feisty comic performances in *White Men Can't Jump* (1992), *Untamed Heart* (1993), and *It Could Happen to You* (1994). She also revealed a greater depth with her Oscar-nominated turn as a grieving mother in the 1993 film *Fearless.* Although the character Perez played in the original novel was an Italian American, the movie's director, Peter Weir, chose to make her Latina so Perez could take the role.

▲ *Actress Rosie Perez arrives at New York's Tribeca Film Festival in 2005.*

Star turns and social concerns

Perez has played mainly supporting roles. Her leading performances include the tempestuous title role of *Perdita Durango* (1997), a femme fatale created by cult author Barry Gifford. She took another strong, but very different, lead role as a businesswoman embarking on motherhood in *The 24 Hour Woman* (1999), which probed the difficulties of parental and professional responsibilities.

For many years Perez has worked hard to raise awareness of AIDS. In 2005 she appeared in a UNICEF-backed short film, directed by Spike Lee, about a young girl who is HIV positive.

Perez has also turned her hand to directing with a documentary called *I'm Boricua, Just So You Know!* Boricua is the Native American name for Puerto Rico, and the film explores the rich history of Puerto Rico.

See also: Lopez, Jennifer

Further reading: http://www.hispaniconline.com/magazine/2003/march/CoverStory/ (interview with Perez).

KEY DATES

1964 Born in Bushwick, Brooklyn, on September 6.

1989 Makes feature film debut in *Do the Right Thing.*

1994 Nominated for an Oscar for her performance in *Fearless.*

2005 Directs documentary *I'm Boricua, Just So You Know!*

PÉREZ, Tony
Baseball Player

Tony Pérez was the clubhouse leader of one the greatest baseball teams in history, the Cincinnati Reds' "Big Red Machine," which dominated the National League in the early 1970s. A seven-time All-Star, Pérez had 1,652 runs batted in (RBIs), recorded 2,732 hits, and helped Cincinnati win the 1975 and 1976 World Series.

Early life

Atanasio "Tony" Pérez Rigal was born in 1942 in Ciego de Avila, Cuba. As a child, he and his father huddled around the radio, listening to Cuban baseball star Minnie Minoso playing baseball in the United States.

Like his father, Pérez worked on the nearby sugar plantation, and played baseball in the streets after work. The sugar-cane company learned of Pérez's baseball skills, and asked him to play on the company team. Soon scouts in Havana heard how Pérez dominated the company league and signed him to a U.S. major league contract at just 17.

▼ *Tony Pérez at a training camp in Tampa Bay, Florida, in 1971.*

KEY DATES

1942   Born in Ciego de Avila, Cuba, on May 14.

1960   Signs with the Cincinnati Reds.

1975   Hits a home run in game seven of the World Series to lead the Big Red Machine to the first of two consecutive titles.

2000   Is the first Cuban player voted into the National Baseball Hall of Fame.

Playing career

Just as Pérez left to play in the United States, Fidel Castro took power in Cuba. This meant that Pérez could no longer go home to see his family. He arrived in the U.S. knowing only two words of English, "yes" and "no." Despite the cultural adjustment, Pérez dominated on the baseball field.

Pérez debuted with the Cincinnati Reds in 1964. He established himself as a skillful first baseman and one of the best clutch hitters in the game. Pérez appeared in his first of seven All-Star Games in 1967, in which he ended the 15-innings nail biter with a game-winning home run for the National League. Statistically, Pérez had his best season in 1970, when he hit .317, with 40 home runs, 129 RBIs, and a .401 on base percentage. All these figures were career highs.

In 1975 Pérez cemented his legacy by leading the "Big Red Machine" to the first of two World Series championships. In game seven of the 1975 World Series against the Boston Red Sox, Pérez hit a two-run home run to help the Reds win the game and the series. A year later, the Reds team president, Bob Howsam, traded Pérez to the Montreal Expos, a move he later regretted. Pérez played three seasons with the Expos, three with the Red Sox, and one with the Philadelphia Phillies, before finishing his career in 1986 back with the Reds.

Pérez remained close to baseball and was manager of the Reds in 1993 and the Florida Marlins in 2001. In 2000 Pérez was inducted into the National Baseball Hall of Fame.

See also: Minoso, Minnie

Further reading: http://www.baseballhalloffame.org/ hofers_and_honorees/hofer_bios/Perez_Tony.htm (Pérez's Baseball Hall of Fame entry).

PÉREZ FIRMAT, Gustavo
Academic, Writer

Cuban American Gustavo Pérez Firmat is a leading critic of modern Spanish and Latin American literature as well as an acclaimed poet and novelist. He is best known for his studies of the Cuban American experience, which he has famously defined as "life on the hyphen," a reference to the hyphen sometimes included in Cuban American. "Having two cultures," he writes, "you belong wholly to neither one. You are both, you are neither." Pérez Firmat is today the David Feinson Professor of Humanities at Columbia University, New York City.

A one-and-a-halfer

Gustavo Pérez Firmat was born in Havana, Cuba, in 1950. He was the son of a prosperous food wholesaler. In October 1960, the Pérez Firmat family fled their homeland after their business was confiscated by the communist regime of Fidel Castro. Like tens of thousands of other Cuban exiles, the family settled in Miami, Florida, where Pérez Firmat was raised and educated. In his work, Pérez Firmat has described the generation of Cubans who left their homeland as children as "one-and-a-halfers"—people who feel they are not quite Cuban like their parents yet not quite American like their own children.

After high school, Pérez Firmat studied at the University of Miami, where he earned first a bachelor's degree in English and then a master's degree in Spanish. In 1978 he completed a PhD in comparative literature at the University of Michigan at Ann Arbor.

The Cuban condition

Pérez Firmat subsequently began a career in academia. For over 20 years, he taught Hispanic American literature at Duke University in Durham, North Carolina. He began teaching at Columbia University in 1999, although he has continued to live in North Carolina.

KEY DATES

1950	Born in Havana, Cuba.
1960	Goes into exile in the United States with his family.
1994	Publishes *Life on the Hyphen*—a study of Cuban American culture.
1999	Becomes a professor of humanities at Columbia University, New York City.

▲ *Gustavo Pérez Firmat, a Cuban American academic and poet, at his home in North Carolina.*

After publishing a series of academic studies of Spanish literature, Pérez Firmat won a national reputation for two witty and sometimes controversial dissections of Cuban American life—*The Cuban Condition* (1989) and *Life on the Hyphen* (1994). He examined these ideas from a personal perspective in *Next Year in Cuba* (2005), in which he gave a moving and brutally honest account of his own and his family's struggles with exile in the United States. Pérez Firmat's bilingual collections of poetry, including *Carolina Cuban* (1987) and *Scar Tissue* (2005), also express his feelings about his cultural identity.

Further reading: Pérez Firmat, Gustavo. *Next Year in Cuba: A Cubano's Coming-of-Age in America.* Houston, TX: Arte Público Press, 2005.

http://www.gustavoperezfirmat.com (Pérez-Firmat's Web site).

PICO, Andrés
Politician

▲ *Andrés Pico was a Californian leader before and after the state was transferred from Mexican rule to U.S. control.*

As a wealthy landowner and soldier, Andrés Pico was a leading figure in the struggle between Mexico and the United States for control of California during the Mexican War (1846–1848). He was a Californio (a Californian of Mexican heritage), and was the brother of California's last Mexican governor, Pío Pico. Pico led Mexican forces in battle against the United States, and it was he who surrendered California to U.S. forces in 1847. A few years after California became part of the United States, Pico had become a successful politician.

Born in Mexico
Pico was born in San Diego in 1810. Today it is one of the largest cities in California. At that time, however, it was part of Mexico. Pico had a life of privilege and owned large areas of land with his brother. As Pico was growing up, the United States was looking to expand to the west and was in competition with Britain to claim territory along the West Coast, north of Mexican California. At the same time, the United States was disputing the border between Mexico and Texas.

In 1846 the United States attacked Mexico, and the two countries were soon fighting in several parts of the Southwest, including California. Pico led a group of lancers against the troops of Colonel Stephen Watts Kearny at San Pascual, near San Diego. The Californio troops defeated the U.S. soldiers, and Kearny lost an arm in the battle. However, the following year Kearny returned and defeated Pico's defenders. Pico surrendered and signed the Treaty of Cahuenga on January 13, 1847, in a house in what is now North Hollywood. While the war continued for another year in other places, the treaty essentially broke California away from the rest of Mexico and passed the territory to the United States.

U.S. rule
Pico and other Californio landowners eventually lost much of their land to U.S. settlers. As an elite Californio, however, Pico often sided with Anglo Americans. For example when the bandit Juan Flores led a small insurrection in Los Angeles in 1857, Pico rode with Anglo-American vigilantes against Flores's force. For this loyalty Pico was made a brigadier in the California militia. Pico also served in the California State Assembly and was a state senator. During the Civil War (1861-1865), Pico was offered the rank of general in the Union Army, in charge of a California cavalry unit. However, he declined the post owing to ill health.

Late in his life Andrés Pico lived in a large two-story convent building at San Fernando Mission. He died in 1876, and in that same year the city of Los Angeles bought one of his adobe homes. Pico Adobe was built in 1832 and is the second-oldest surviving house in Los Angeles. It is now the home of the San Fernando Valley Historical Society.

See also: Flores, Juan; Pico, Pío

Further reading: http://www.sfvhs.com/AndresPicoAdobe.htm (Pico Adobe Web site).

KEY DATES

1810   Born in San Diego, then in northern Mexico.

1847   Surrenders to Colonel Kearny and signs Treaty of Cahuenga, which ends the fighting in California.

1852   Elected to California State Assembly and serves as presidential elector.

1876   Dies in Los Angeles, California.

PICO, Pío
Governor

Pío Pico was the last governor of Mexican California. He was also a soldier and wealthy landowner in southern California. He lived under three nations claiming control of California. It was part of the Spanish colony of Mexico until 1821, then the most northerly province of an independent Mexico between 1821 and 1848, and finally a U.S. state after 1848. Pico's ability to maneuver into positions of power in these changing times testifies to his skill as a politician.

Early life
Pío de Jesús Pico was born at San Gabriel Mission, California, in 1801. His father was a corporal at the mission. His parents had came to California from Mexico with the explorer Juan Bautista de Anza in the 1770s.

▼ *Pío Pico pictured in 1870. Despite great success in business and politics as a young man during a turbulent period in California's history, Pico's later life was one of failure and poverty.*

Pico was the eldest child in a large Californio (Mexican Californian) family of three boys and seven girls. His brother Andrés was also a well-known figure during California's transfer from Mexico to the United States. Pico's father, José María, had been a proponent of Mexican independence from Spain and was jailed briefly in 1811. José María died in 1818, leaving the family destitute. They moved in with their mother's family. Pico's mother and sisters worked as seamstresses to support the family.

Rise to prominence
After Mexico became independent in 1821, Pico joined the Mexican army. In 1828 he became a member of California's territorial assembly, known as the Diputación. In 1829 he received a land grant from the Mexican government. It was Rancho Jamul, almost 35 square miles (90 sq. km) located near San Diego. (Since Pico could not read English he would later sign away this and other lands in deeds he thought were mortgages.)

In 1831 Pico led a revolt in support of the ousted Californio governor, who had been replaced by one appointed from central Mexico. After the coup, Pico, who was senior speaker of the Diputación, became governor for the first time, but for only 20 days.

Pico then became the administrator of Mission San Luis Rey. In 1834 he married María Ignacia Alvarado, a member of a prominent Californio family from Los Angeles. She died young and they had no children. Instead Pico had several children with his housekeeper.

Taking charge again
In 1841 Pico and his brother Andrés shared another huge land grant: Rancho Santa Margarita, near present-day Camp Pendleton, California. In 1844 Pico formed a citizen's

LEGACY

Pico is a name known throughout southern California. However, stories about him are of dubious reliability. Some who remembered Pico said he was fond of children and always had candy for those who visited his houses. They claim he was influential in southern California history and respected until his death. Others claimed that Pico was a man of mixed ethnic ancestry and of humble origins who presented himself as a pure-blood Spaniard and acted in a superior way to other Mexicans, particularly after the U.S. succession. Pico was also a gambling man who borrowed money to bet on horse racing. When he did not win, the result was often financial ruin. He was also swindled out of several properties, making him a tragic victim of American imperialism in the eyes of some observers.

Late in life Pico gave Hubert Howe Bancroft an oral history and introduced him to other living Californios for the same purpose. However, Bancroft's aide, Thomas Savage, thought Pico was an inveterate liar and found his memoirs to be almost useless.

militia to maintain public order. He did so again in 1853, as a Los Angeles City councilman, when he gave 100 broken (trained) horses to the Anglo vigilante group Captain Hope's Rangers. He demonstrated a desire to maintain law and order and protect his interests and those of other wealthy landowners, regardless of which nation ruled California.

California was a Mexican territory until 1836 and then a department. A central question for those living in California was whether officials would be locally elected or appointed from Mexico City. In 1845 Pico led a coup against the appointed governor. The short battle took place near the current location of Universal Studios.

As the senior member of the Diputación, Pico was soon recognized by Mexico City as the governor of California. He was immediately beset by a dispute between factions over where the capital of California would be located. Northern and southern California had been governed separately on occasions in the past, and Pico entered a power struggle with southern politician José Castro. He moved the capital from Monterey to Los Angeles, making Castro treasurer. As a southerner himself, Pico appointed many of his southern friends to important positions and rewarded their loyalty with property seized from church missions. In 1846 Pico called for an end to disputes among Californios when U.S. forces began to attack Mexico across the Southwest.

Joining the United States

In 1846 Pico and his generals met in Santa Barbara, California, and planned defensive strategies. They considered contacting the French and British for assistance. In August Pico went to Mexico for safety and to appeal to the Mexican government for more troops. He was ordered to remain in Hermosillo, Mexico, and later in Guaymas, to await support that never came. Pico returned to California the following year after his brother Andrés

had signed the Cahuenga Treaty that surrendered California to the United States. On his return, Pico was jailed briefly but later released after convincing the authorities that he did not threaten U.S. interests.

After the U.S occupation, Pico printed dozens of bogus land grants and gave them to friends in an effort to maintain power and keep land out of the incomers' hands. Because he was the legitimate governor of California at the time the grants were written, the U.S. courts struggled to overturn them. The grants were valid even if they were poorly drawn and overlapped. Anglo squatters, however, claimed they were fraudulent.

Pico and his brother went into the mortgage business. This was an unsuccessful move and cost them most of their land. Pico also lost money gambling, particularly on horse racing. In 1852 Pico personally raced José Sepulveda and lost badly. He paid the winner $1,600 and 300 head of cattle. After that Pico's racing career was mainly to show off his horses because he had no money left to bet with.

With the coming of the Civil War, Pico was asked to demonstrate his loyalty to the United States yet again. In June 1861, Pico swore his allegiance to President Lincoln and the Union Army, as did others in his family.

In 1870 Pico sold his last land grant in the San Fernando Valley to finance the construction of the Pico House hotel, the first three-story building in Los Angeles. He lost the hotel to creditors and was swindled out of his home. He died in poverty at his daughter's home in 1894.

See also: Bautista de Anza, Juan; Castro, José; Pico, Andrés

Further reading: Gómez-Quinones, Juan. *Roots of Chicano Politics, 1600–1940.* Albuquerque: University of New Mexico Press, 1994.
http://www.piopico.org/The_Life_of_Pio_Pico.htm (biography).

PIETRI, Pedro
Poet

Pedro Pietri was a Nuyorican poet. Nuyorican is a blend of the words New York and Puerto Rican. It is a word used to describe the people or culture of Puerto Ricans located in or around New York City. In the 1970s, Pietri helped establish the Nuyorican Poets Café on the Lower East Side of New York. Before his death in 2004, Pietri published more than 20 plays and books. He is best known for his nationalist poem "Puerto Rican Obituary."

Early life
Born in Ponce, Puerto Rico, on March 21, 1944, Pietri had three brothers and a sister. The Pietri family moved to Spanish Harlem, New York, in 1947, eventually settling in the Grant Houses, a housing project on Amsterdam Avenue. Pietri's aunt, Irene Rodríguez, nurtured her nephew's love of poetry. He first began to write and perform his poems while attending Haaren High School.

After graduation Pietri was drafted into the U.S Army, where he served as part of a light infantry brigade in the Vietnam War. He returned home disillusioned by his experiences. He said that they had shown him not only the absolute horror of war but also the dreadful discrimination that nonwhite U.S. soldiers often suffered.

Nuyorican poet
Following his return to New York, Pietri began to concentrate on writing and performing poetry. He became increasingly interested in Puerto Rican activism, and joined the group the Young Lords. In 1969 he wrote and performed the poem "Puerto Rican Obituary" (not published until 1973), which was about five Puerto Ricans and their unfulfilled dreams.

Pietri was influenced by Jorge Brandon (1902–1995), one of several writers who met to discuss writing at Miguel Algarín's Sixth Street apartment. Jesús "Tato" Laviera and Miguel Piñero also met there often to read

▲ **Pedro Pietri, photographed at his Nuyorican Poets Cafe in 2003.**

the first drafts of their work. Pietri later said that this was the "original Nuyorican Poets Café." In the 1970s Pietri opened the Nuyorican Poets Café with Piñero and Algarín. It quickly became a meeting place for Puerto Rican artists and intellectuals.

Through his work Pietri became known as an activist, campaigning on nationalist issues and for AIDS awareness. Performances of his play *El Puerto Rican Embassy* were popular with audiences. During the play, audiences were given Puerto Rican passports filled with poetry and art and the Spanglish National Anthem was sung.

After Pietri was diagnosed with terminal stomach cancer, he decided to seek holistic treatment for the disease in Mexico. His fans raised more than $30,000 toward his treatment. He died in March 2004.

See also: Algarín, Miguel; Laviera, Jesús; Piñero, Miguel

Further reading: Pietri, Pedro. *The Masses Are Asses.* New York, NY: Green Integer Press, 2003.
http://www.tribes.org/cgi-bin/form.pl? karticle=647 (interview).

KEY DATES	
1944	Born in Ponce, Puerto Rico, on March 21.
1947	Pietri family moves to New York City.
1969	Reads "Puerto Rican Obituary."
2004	Dies of cancer on March 10.

PIÑERO, Jesús T.
Politician

From 1946 to 1948 Jesús T. Piñero served as the first native governor of Puerto Rico. He was also the last governor to be appointed by the U.S. president. From 1948 the governors of Puerto Rico have been elected directly by the citizens of the island.

Piñero was a founding member of the Partido Popular Democrático de Puerto Rico (PPD; Popular Democratic Party of Puerto Rico) and a close political ally of the party leader, Luis Muñoz Marín. Like Muñoz Marín, Piñero was an important figure in the transitional period that led up to the declaration of Puerto Rico's Commonwealth status in 1952, after more than 55 years of direct rule from Washington, D.C.

The young intellectual

The son of wealthy middle-class criollo (Puerto Rican of Spanish descent) parents, Jesús Toribio Piñero Jiménez was born in 1897, in Carolina, in northwest Puerto Rico. Like many of the criollo elite on the island, Piñero was educated for a time on the U.S. mainland. He attended the Colegio Janer, a Spanish-language high school in Baltimore, Maryland, and then returned to Puerto Rico to study at the University of Puerto Rico at Río Piedras, where he graduated in 1914. Back in the United States, he studied engineering at the University of Pennsylvania, Philadelphia, where he obtained a bachelor's degree.

By 1920 Piñero had returned to his hometown, Carolina, where he became an entrepreneur in the sugar industry. Like many other young Puerto Rican intellectuals at this time, Piñero grew increasingly dissatisfied with the state of affairs in his homeland and was impatient for change. After more than two decades of U.S. rule, Puerto Rico remained economically and socially backward. The vast majority of the population lived in poverty, and almost three-quarters of the population were unable to read or write. In overcrowded cities like the capital, San Juan, sanitation was so poor that outbreaks of deadly waterborne diseases like cholera were common.

Bread, land, and liberty

During the 1920s Piñero became increasingly active in the island's politics. As a liberal intellectual, he supported the cause of the Alianza (Alliance). This was a broad grouping of politicians who wanted Puerto Rico to have greater political autonomy (independence) from the United

▲ *Jesús T. Piñero was a leading Puerto Rican politician in an era in which Puerto Ricans were eventually given full democratic rights.*

States. In 1928 Piñero was elected to a seat in the municipal assembly of Carolina and for a while served as the assembly's president. In 1932, along with Muñoz Marín, he joined the newly formed Partido Liberal (Liberal Party), led by Antonio R. Barceló (1868–1938), and from 1935 worked for the Puerto Rico Reconstruction Administration (PRRA), which was attempting to reform the island's economy under the aegis of President Franklin D. Roosevelt's New Deal.

During the mid-1930s, the Partido Liberal was increasingly split by disagreements. In 1937 Luis Muñoz Marín was expelled from the party and went on to found, along with Piñero and other political allies, the Partido

| INFLUENCES AND INSPIRATION |

Piñero's career as a politician and his contribution at a crucial period in Puerto Rico's history have been largely overshadowed by those of the charismatic leader Luis Muñoz Marín. If Piñero is remembered at all, it is simply as Puerto Rico's first Puerto Rican governor, a designation that does scant justice to the scope, depth, and influence of his achievements.

Even at the time, however, Piñero was often viewed merely as Muñoz Marín's principal ally and follower rather than as an independent politician in his own right. In this light, Piñero's appointment as governor was easily interpreted as an almost transparent front for the de facto governorship of Muñoz Marín himself.

This interpretation of the situation seemed to be confirmed little more than two years later when Muñoz Marín succeeded Piñero as governor. Piñero, however, seems to have resented this view of his period as governor, as it effectively undervalued the key role he had played as resident commissioner in Washington, D.C., where he had worked hard for the PPD's political goals and securing greater independence for Puerto Rico. Viewed in this light, his appointment as Puerto Rico's first Puerto Rican governor was a fitting and honorable climax to a lifetime of service to his homeland and its people.

Popular Democrático (PPD). While the PPD wanted independence for the island, its more immediate concern was with addressing Puerto Rico's pressing economic and social problems. In 1940, under the revolutionary slogan "Bread, Land, and Liberty," Muñoz Marín took his party to victory in the island's elections and was chosen president of the island's senate. Piñero, meanwhile, won a seat in the Puerto Rican House of Representatives.

The first Puerto Rican governor

During the next four years, the PPD was able to begin to carry through its promised reforms, in collaboration with the new forward-looking American governor, Rexford Guy Tugwell (1891–1979). In 1944 the party was returned to power, winning overwhelming majorities in both the Senate and House of Representatives. This outright victory enabled Muñoz Marín to appoint his close ally Piñero as resident commissioner and replace the conservative

incumbent Bolívar Pagán (1897–1961). As commissioner, Piñero became Puerto Rico's sole representative in the U.S. House of Representatives and thus a key player in handling the Puerto Rican government's delicate yet crucial relations with the United States.

Piñero served as resident commissioner in Washington, D.C., for the next four years, sitting on a number of committees as well as working to further the cause of Puerto Rican democracy. His tactful diplomacy won him respect across the political divide, and in 1946 President Harry S. Truman appointed Piñero as the new governor of Puerto Rico. It was a milestone in the island's history. Piñero's appointment as the first native governor amounted to a tacit recognition by the U.S. administration that Puerto Rico did indeed have a right to govern itself.

Such an interpretation was confirmed the following year, when the Elective Governor Act of 1947 amended the 1917 Jones Act to allow the governor to be elected by the Puerto Rican people. Puerto Rico's first gubernatorial elections were held the following year, resulting in a landslide victory for the PPD candidate, Muñoz Marín. Four years later, on July 25, 1952, the Commonwealth of Puerto Rico was created, and the island was given authority over its internal affairs. Piñero died only a few months after, having played a key role in moving one step toward his political dream—Puerto Rican independence.

See also: Muñoz Marin, Luis

Further reading: Schultz, Jeffrey D. *Encyclopedia of Minorities in American Politics.* Phoenix, AZ: Oryx Press, 2000. www.loc.gov/rr/hispanic/congress/pinero.html (biography).

KEY DATES

1887   Born in Carolina, Puerto Rico, on April 16.

1944   Becomes Puerto Rico's resident commissioner at the U.S. House of Representatives.

1946   Appointed as governor of Puerto Rico, the first Puerto Rican to serve in that role.

1949   Luis Muñoz Marín becomes the first elected governor of Puerto Rico.

1952   The Commonwealth of Puerto Rico is creates on July 25; Piñero dies in Loíza, Puerto Rico, on November 19.

PIÑERO, Miguel
Writer

With little education or formal training in the theater, Miguel Piñero wrote some of the most exciting Hispanic American plays of the 1970s and 1980s. His writing established him as one of the leading Nuyorican (New York Puerto Rican) writers before his early death in 1988.

Troubled upbringing

Piñero was born in Gurabo, Puerto Rico, in 1946 but raised on New York's Lower East Side. His family had moved to the United States when Piñero was four years old. His father soon abandoned the family, leaving his wife and children without a home and on the streets until his pregnant mother found a job. Piñero started grade school but was soon skipping class. He dropped out of junior high school and his formal education ended until he was sent to prison, where he joined a prison workshop.

Arrested for the first time at the age of 13, Piñero's teenage years were spent in and out of juvenile detention centers. He began to use and supply drugs. At the age of 24, Piñero was sent to the New York State prison at Ossining, known as Sing Sing, for two years.

Prison playwright

While in prison Piñero joined a theater program, where he wrote the first draft of his most famous play, *Short Eyes: The Killing of a Sex Offender by the Inmates of the House of Detention Awaiting Trial*. *Short Eyes* was first performed in a New York church in 1974. It was a tough play, which dealt with guilt, prison violence, and the abuses of power. The production received good reviews and transferred to Broadway, where it won the New York Critics Circle Award for Best American Play of 1974 as well as Obie and Drama

▲ *Playwright Miguel Piñero (right) in New York City with film director Marvin Camillo in 1974.*

Desk awards. The play was made into a movie in 1977, for which Piñero wrote the screenplay as well as playing a small role.

From prison to Princeton

Piñero was amazed by his success. He was asked to lecture at Princeton and Rutgers, among other universities. In the 1970s, he cofounded the Nuyorican Poets Café as a platform for Puerto Rican writers to perform their work.

Piñero published a collection of poems in 1980, *La Bodega Sold Dreams*. In 1982 he was awarded a Guggenheim Fellowship. Two years later a collection of three plays—*The Sun Always Shines for the Cool, Midnight Moon at the Greasy Spoon,* and *Eulogy for a Small-Time Thief*—were published. In 1986 another collection, *Outrageous One-Act Plays*, appeared. In addition, Piñero wrote for several television series, such as *Miami Vice* and *Kojak*, and had small walk-on roles in *Miami Vice* and movies such as *The Godfather*.

Piñero died from cirrhosis of the liver in 1988, after years of drinking and drug taking, at the age of just 41. In 2001 Piñero's life was made into a Hollywood movie, *Piñero*, starring Benjamin Bratt.

Further reading: Piñero, Miguel. *Outrageous: One Act Plays*. Houston, TX: Arte Público Press, 1986.
www.donshewey.com/arts_articles/pinero.html (biography).

KEY DATES

1946 Born in Gurabo, Puerto Rico, on December 19.

1971 Sent to Sing Sing prison in New York for armed robbery.

1974 *Short Eyes* wins New York Critics Circle Award for best play.

1988 Dies in New York City on June 16 of cirrhosis of the liver.

PLUNKETT, Jim
Football Player

Jim Plunkett is a Hispanic American who emerged from a severely underprivileged background to become a star of the National Football League (NFL) in the 1970s and 1980s.

Early life

Born in 1947 in Santa Clara, California, Jim was the third child of Mexican Americans William Plunkett and Carmen Blea. Both his parents were visually handicapped, and had met while they were pupils at a school for the blind in Albuquerque, New Mexico. During World War II (1939–1945), they moved to San Jose, California, where William opened a newsstand.

After graduating from public high school, Jim Plunkett enrolled in 1967 at Stanford University, where he made the football team in his freshman year. He earned the starting quarterback job his sophomore year. As a junior, he threw for 2,673 yards and 20 touchdowns, and was named to the Associated Press's All-America third team. The next year he led Stanford to a 27–17 win over heavily favored Ohio State in the Rose Bowl in Pasadena, and won the Heisman Trophy, an award presented annually to the United States's top collegiate player.

Professional career

The New England Patriots made Plunkett a first-round draft pick in 1971. The team had high hopes for him, but he suffered numerous injuries over the next five seasons and was traded to the San Francisco 49ers. He failed to make an impact there, and was released after two seasons.

▲ *Raised by blind parents and injured for much of his NFL career, Jim Plunkett overcame adversity to become one of the leading professional football players of his generation.*

Next, the Oakland Raiders took a chance, and signed Plunkett during the 1978 season. When he did not play at all that season, and threw only 15 passes in 1979, his career looked finished. However, when injuries to other players brought him a recall to the team, he entered the finest period of his career. He led the Raiders to a Super Bowl victory over the Philadelphia Eagles in 1981, and was named NFL Comeback Player of the Year.

A thumb injury forced Plunkett to miss most of the 1981 season. In 1982—the year the Raiders moved to Los Angeles—the team failed to reach the Super Bowl. During the 1983 season, Plunkett was benched, but when his replacement was injured, he returned to the starting lineup and led the Raiders to a crushing 38–9 Super Bowl win over the Washington Redskins. Plunkett retired in 1986.

Further reading: Plunkett, Jim, and Dave Newhouse. *The Jim Plunkett Story: The Saga of a Man Who Came Back.* New York, NY: Arbor House, 1981.

http://www.superbowl.com/history/mvps/game/sbxv (Super Bowl Web site).

KEY DATES

1947 Born in Santa Clara, California, on December 5.

1970 Wins the Heisman Trophy in his senior year at Stanford University.

1971 Drafted by the New England Patriots and named NFL Rookie of the Year.

1981 Helps the Oakland Raiders to a 27–10 victory over the Philadelphia Eagles in Super Bowl XV.

1984 Leads the same team, now the LA Raiders, to a 38–9 win over the Washington Redskins in Super Bowl XVIII.

1986 Retires at end of NFL season.

POLITICAL MOVEMENTS

The U.S. Latino population, which in 2004 comprised 14 percent of the nation's total population, is made up of people from different countries and cultures. While these groups share certain common aims, including the attainment of equal rights and bilingual education, they also have many different and often competing political interests and agendas.

In the last 150 years or so Latinos have exercised their political power in a number of ways, including through the ballot box. Political organizations such as the American GI Forum (AGIF) and movements such as the Chicano civil rights movement have formed an important part of Latinos' history and their relationship to mainstream U.S. society; indeed, many have shaped and influenced the U.S. political landscape.

Mexicans in the United States

From the mid-19th century, when about 55 percent of Mexico and 100,000 Mexicans became part of the United States at the end of the Mexican War (1846–1848), Mexicans and Mexican Americans began to experience an erosion of their rights. Encountering racism, segregation in schools, bans on the use of Spanish in school and in the workplace, loss of land rights,

César Chávez (seated center) applauds John Giumarra (right), a California table grape grower and representative of 26 growers, who signed a contract with the Farm Workers' Union in July 1970.

WHAT'S IN A NAME

For Mexican Americans and Latinos in general, the name of El Movimiento Estudantil Chicano de Aztlán (MEChA) is steeped in symbolic significance. The word *Aztlán* comes from Nahuatl, the ancient language of the Aztecs who ruled Mexico before it was conquered by the Spanish in the 16th century. *Aztlán* literally means either "white place" or "the northlands," but figuratively in modern times it has come to represent the political aspirations of Chicanos and Chicanas who regard themselves as the heirs or descendants of the pre-Columbian inhabitants of North and Central America.

The acronym MEChA may seem contrived, but it, too, has a deeper meaning: *Mecha* is the Spanish for "fuse," and the underlying idea is that, once lit, it will spark a fire of change.

The motto of MEChA is *La unión hace la fuerza* (Unity makes Strength). One of its best-known slogans is "*Por la Raza todo, fuera de la Raza nada,*" which literally means "for the race, everything; outside the race, nothing." It has been denounced as racist by political opponents, but liberal supporters render it as the Spanish equivalent of "United we stand, divided we fall."

and harassment by law enforcement agencies, among other things, many Mexicans began to object to these injustices. Some joined together with other like-minded people to form political organizations, believing that there was greater strength in numbers and that they might have a more effective political voice.

During the last 100 years, several Chicano political movements have arisen. Some promote Mexican nationalism in the United States, such as through the Partido Liberal Mexicana (PLM; Mexican Liberal Party), while others focus on assimilation to mainstream America, through organizations such as the League of United Latin American Citizens (LULAC), which promotes loyalty to the United States and to the members' Mexican heritage. Still others promote Mexican American nationalism and pride in Chicano cultural heritage.

The Chicano movement
The most significant Mexican political initiative was the Chicano movement, which had its roots in the earlier activist groups of the 20th century. Mexican American veterans paved the way for the Chicano civil rights movement by forming such organizations as the AGIF. The AGIF campaigned for equal rights for Latinos who had fought in World War II (1939–1945) in defense of the United States but who were still treated as second-class citizens.

The Chicano movement promoted a unique Chicano national identity as separate from that of the rest of the United States, emphasizing the importance of Chicano history, language, and culture.

Several events combined to make the 1960s the right moment for such a political force to arise. One was the growth of the civil rights movement, which involved many Latino activists. Also significant were the election and assassination of President John F. Kennedy, who was a fierce advocate of civil rights. Another factor in the political climate change was growing opposition to the Vietnam War: Latinos were highly critical of the conflict.

Meanwhile, the Great Society and the War on Poverty programs began, and the U.S. government ended the Bracero Program, which had brought cheap short-term Mexican labor into the United States and undermined Mexican labor rights and unions in general. Also during the 1960s there was a Chicano Renaissance among artists, musicians, and writers, and increased pride in Mexican heritage. Hispanic college students wanted to study subjects that were relevant to their culture.

Many important political organizations came out of this broader umbrella movement. In the early 1960s César Chávez led the United Farm Workers of America. He organized several successful boycotts of table grape and agriculture workers in California in order to help them win greater rights. Chávez's actions inspired several other Chicano activists, especially those involved in the student protests of the second half of the 1960s.

Reies López Tijerina headed the Alianza Federal de Mercedes (Federal Alliance of Land Grants),

which represented the heirs of Mexican landowners who had been dispossessed after the Treaty of Guadalupe Hidalgo (1848).

MEChA

One of the most enduring Chicano political organizations is the Movimiento Estudiantíl Chicano de Aztlán (MEChA; the Chicano Student Movement of Aztlán) (*see box on page 125*). A legacy of the nationalist Chicano student movement of the late 1960s, MEChA is a political and educational organization promoting the goals of Chicano self-determination, empowerment, and pride. MEChA chapters are found in U.S. high schools, colleges, and universities, particularly in the Southwest and Midwest.

In March 1969 students from across the Southwest and Midwest assembled in Denver, Colorado, for the First National Chicano Youth Liberation Conference. The Conference was convened by Rodolfo "Corky" Gonzales. At the conference, participants adopted El Plan Espiritual de Aztlán (the Spiritual Plan of Aztlán), a nationalist manifesto for the formation of a Chicano identity.

The Chicano Council on Higher Education (CCHE), a collective of students, faculty, staff, and community leaders, met at the University of California at Santa Barbara later that year. They drew up a comprehensive blueprint for implementing ideas from the plan, through higher education and political action.

El Plan de Santa Barbara (the Santa Barbara Plan) established MEChA as an organization that sought to address the educational

Rodolfo "Corky" Gonzales is flanked by guards at Colorado State Penitentiary during a Chicano Conference in September 1971.

inequality and discrimination that Chicano youth faced in the U.S. educational system.

Education had long been regarded by the Mexican American community as a primary avenue to personal enrichment and community advancement. Mexicans had vehemently fought segregation, as witnessed in the 1930s in the Lemon Grove incident, in which Mexican parents challenged a school board's decision to build a separate school for their children. The 1940s' legal challenge to segregation, *Mendez v. Westminster,* was cited as a precedent in the landmark case *Brown v. Board of Education,* viewed by many as ending segregation in public education in the United States.

Chicanos realized that educational opportunities would have to be created from within the community. MEChA therefore called on those in higher education to provide leadership and schemes such as mentoring to help increase the accessibility and success of others in the community and to increase the number of educated and active Chicanos.

El Plan de Santa Barbara also created a new schema for a dedicated Chicano curriculum. Supporters believed that it was necessary to change the content of higher education courses to reflect the diverse histories and life experiences of various ethnic American groups, including Mexican Americans.

MEChA chapters across the country helped create Chicano studies programs and departments in high schools and colleges. Students in MEChA also actively promoted the hiring of Chicano faculty members and staff for the classroom and support services.

The organization went beyond higher education, addressing leadership in the communities or barrios. It tied Chicano leadership to the schools, and made the universities work for Latinos, not the other way around. Students in MEChA served as bridges between organizations, creating networks of Chicanos.

Political awareness and participation were also goals articulated in El Plan de Santa Barbara, eventually leading to the formation of La Raza Unida Party (RUP; the United Race), which recorded important electoral victories in the early 1970s. MEChA achieved these goals through walk-outs, sit-ins, self-education, community meetings, voter registration, and many other tactics used during the black civil rights movement.

MEChA trained many young people in organization and leadership, and helped them graduate from college and contribute in important ways to their communities and society as a whole. MEChA lost influence in the 1970s and 1980s, but made a comeback in the 1990s, when Chicanos began to refamiliarize themselves with the goals of the 1960s' movement.

These young people were vital in forming the National Chicano Moratorium in Los Angeles in 1970. The largest anti-Vietnam War rally to that point, the Moratorium attracted more than 30,000 people. The police forcefully dispersed the crowd, and several people were killed, including *Los Angeles Times* reporter Rubén Salázar.

The Chicano movement also saw the emergence of more militant-style groups. The Brown Berets, established in the 1960s, arose in the barrios of the Southwest. The group was frequently compared to the militant African American organization the Black Panthers and also to the Puerto Rican Young Lords.

Puerto Rican nationalism

Like their Mexican and Chicano equivalents, Puerto Rican political movements have shifted focus over time, but most are essentially concerned with the legal status of their island. The central political question throughout the 20th and into the 21st century has remained that of whether the island should become the United States's 51st state, remain a commonwealth, or become an independent nation. These questions are often dealt with in Puerto Rican nationalist literature and music.

In the early 20th century, Puerto Ricans were focused on national self-defense and cultural preservation, much like some of the Mexican organizations of the time. Demonstrations supporting Puerto Rican independence were held in New York, home to the largest Puerto Rican community outside the island.

By the 1950s and 1960s, however, organizations were less focused on nationalism and more

---

KEY DATES

1929   League of United Latin American Citizens (LULAC) founded.

1969   Puerto Rican Young Lords formed in New York City; Movimiento Estudiantíl Chicano de Aztlán (MEChA) established during Chicano movement.

1970   La Raza Unida candidates sweep City Council election in Crystal City, Texas.

1981   Cuban American National Foundation (CANF) founded.

1985   Radio Martí broadcasts for the first time.

2006   Latino community members in California, Texas, Arizona, and other U.S. states march against proposed immigration reform.

concerned with socio-cultural issues. It was during this time that the famous Puerto Rican Day Parade was established in New York City.

By the late 1960s and early 1970s, many Puerto Rican activists, like their Chicano counterparts, took a more radical and nationalist turn in favor of independence. They also worked diligently to add more Puerto Ricans to electoral processes. Three of the most influential organizations at this time were the Young Lords Party, the Puerto Rican Socialist Party, and El Comité-Movimiento de Izquierda Nacional Puertoriqueno (MINP; the Action Committee of the National Puerto Rican Left).

The Puerto Rican Young Lords Party emerged from a 1950s' street gang of the same name in Chicago, Illinois. The Young Lords were most active and militant in New York, where they protested the neglect of urban communities. However, they were also pro-independence, supporting Puerto Rico's right to break away from its commonwealth status under the United States.

The Young Lords had a 13-point program and published *Palante*, a newspaper whose name literally meant "go forward," but with overtones of leaving some place or thing behind. They fought against urban renewal or gentrification programs, which often led to the displacement of ethnic minority groups from their own communities in order that wealthier, white residents could move into the area.

The Young Lords also led protests over public health issues, such as lack of medical clinics and inadequate public sanitation. They

formed their own breakfast programs, daycare, and health clinics, similar to the programs established during the Chicano civil rights movement by the Alianza Federal de Mercedes (Federal Land Grant Alliance) and the Crusade for Justice. In 1977, five years after the party's demise, former members took over the Statue of Liberty and hung the Puerto Rican flag over the crown as a symbol of independence for the island.

The Puerto Rican Socialist Party originated on the island itself. By 1964 a branch had been established in New York City. The Puerto Rican Socialist Party was pro-independence and helped organize migrant farmworkers.

El Comité (The Committee) was set up in the early 1970s. It dealt with some of the same issues as the Young Lords Party: gentrification and urban neglect of the barrio. El Comité supported bilingual education and other social programs. It became

Reies López Tijerina was a leading member of the Chicano movement and the head of Alianza Federal de Mercedes, whose members were the heirs of displaced landowners.

radicalized and moved in a more leftist direction, as did the Puerto Rican Socialist Party.

Just as many of the Chicano political organizations failed, so did their Puerto Rican counterparts. By the late 1970s all three organizations had dissolved, but they left lasting legacies. These movements demonstrated a desire not only to promote culture and political autonomy, but also to address some of the more pressing social problems of the day, including illiteracy and poverty.

Puerto Ricans on the mainland and the island have often banded together to fight injustices. In 1971 the U.S. Navy began using the island of Vieques, Puerto Rico, for live-ammunition exercises. In 1999, several residents were killed

RADIO AND TV MARTÍ

Radio Martí first broadcast from Florida on May 20, 1985, Cuban Independence Day. Radio Martí was created through the lobbying efforts of the Cuban American National Foundation and named for the 19th century Cuban writer José Martí.

Originally suggested by President Ronald Reagan in 1981, who wanted to set up a Radio Free Cuba station, Radio Martí came into being after the Radio Broadcasting to Cuba Act was passed on October 4, 1983. Although Fidel Castro and many liberal Americans complained about the establishment of such a station, Radio Martí first broadcast in 1985. Shortly afterward, Castro broke an immigration agreement with the United States.

Some critics claim that Radio Martí violates the sovereignty of another nation, but supporters argue that it provides balanced coverage of issues to Cubans.

The station broadcasts news, literature, music, and soap operas, and includes messages to families in Cuba. The programs are broadcast on shortwave AM radio frequencies and the Cuban government tries to jam transmissions. TV Martí later opened, broadcasting shows such as *Kate and Ally*, as a means of cultural infusion.

during a military operation. Mainland and island Puerto Ricans mobilized to protest, engaging not only in political lobbying but also in acts of civil disobedience reminiscent of the radical political movements of the 1960s and 1970s. By 2003, the U.S. government had bowed to mounting political pressure and pulled out of Vieques.

Cubans

Much like Chicanos and Puerto Ricans, Cuban Americans have made use of their regional concentration in Florida to influence electoral politics and public policy. Cuban immigration increased greatly after Fidel Castro's 1960 political coup and the adoption of a communist system by the island. Many Cuban immigrants joined together in the United States to fight for Castro's overthrow.

By the 1970s, it was clear that the 1959 Cuban Revolution was not fleeting. Some Cuban exiles decided that they needed to become actively involved in the U.S. political process.

In 1972, Mario Vizcaino formed the Cuban American National Council (CNC). The CNC conducted research, published policy analyses, and worked with other Latino organizations such as the National Council of La Raza (NCLR). Since its inception the CNC has expanded to provide a range of social services to low-income Latinos, particularly in southern Florida, where Dominicans, Haitians, and other Hispanic groups have joined Cuban exile communities.

In 1981, the nonprofit Cuban American National Foundation (CANF) was founded in Florida. Its objectives were to end Castro's government and to install democracy and a market-based economic system in Cuba. CANF has successfully lobbied the federal government to tighten the U.S. embargo against Cuba. CANF also helped establish Radio Martí, which broadcasts anti-Castro programs to the island.

The greater community

Other Hispanic groups are equally political, forming organizations such as the Central American Resource Center (CARECEN) and the Coalition for Human Immigrant Rights of Los Angeles (CHIRLA) to fight for equality of opportunity.

In March 2006, Latinos demonstrated their collective power against proposed immigration reforms targeting undocumented workers. Hundreds of thousands of people marched in the streets of major cities around the United States. That event showed the potential strength of organized Latino political mobilization.

See also: Chávez, César; Civil Rights; Gonzales, Rodolfo "Corky"; Hispanic Identity and Culture; Martí, José; Salázar, Rubén; Tijerina, Reies López

---

Further reading: Geron, Kim. *Latino Political Power.* Boulder, CO: Lynne Rienner Publishers, 2005.
http://www.brown.edu/Research/Coachella/introduction.html (activism and education).
http://www.washingtonpost.com/wp-dyn/content/article/2006/04/09/AR2006040900515.html (article on the Hispanic civil rights movement).

POLITICAL REPRESENTATION

Latinos are underrepresented politically in the United States. There are several reasons for their lack of involvement in the democratic process. One is that two-thirds of those Latinos entitled to vote in elections are not registered to do so. As a result, the U.S. Census consistently undercounts the Latino population, and political policy does not adequately reflect the people's needs and aspirations.

The youth of the Latino population also counts against it: In 2000, approximately one in every three Latinos was under the age of 18, and hence ineligible to vote. Another important consideration is the large number of Latinos above age 18 who are not U.S. citizens. Together, under-18s and non-U.S. citizens comprise approximately 60 percent of the Latino population.

Historical background

The current situation has developed from a long history of Latino disenfranchisement. In 1848, about 100,000 Mexicans became Mexican Americans when the United States took over half of Mexico's former territory. Almost immediately, various ploys were introduced to deprive them of the voting rights that they were guaranteed by the Treaty of Guadalupe Hidalgo. One was the imposition of poll taxes, charges that were a precondition of the right to vote. Although such measures were proscribed in 1870 by the Fifteenth Amendment, which extended to all races the

right to vote, many southern states introduced so-called "grandfather clauses." Such measures exempted citizens whose ancestors had previously voted without having to pay for the privilege, but levied the charge on more recent immigrants. Since most of the people thus affected—particularly Mexican Americans and African Americans—were too poor to pay the tax, they were effectively excluded from the electoral process.

Among the other barriers to Latino participation in the democratic system were literacy tests, which disqualified non-English speakers from voting, and gerrymandering, the corrupt

During elections held in November 2004, a Latina voter at César Chávez Elementary School in the Mission District, San Francisco, California, walks from the polling booth to deposit her ballot.

practice of redrawing electoral boundaries in favor of one particular candidate. Such abuses persisted until the 1950s.

Nonvoting participation

Despite efforts to exclude them, Latinos demonstrated that political influence can be exerted in other ways than at the voting station. Their power gradually increased through a whole range of actions and initiatives that established them firmly in the fabric of U.S. society. Although at various times they have worked outside the law—some of the earliest Latino protesters against injustice were bandits, and there have been more recent instances of armed resistance—they have made their greatest impact through *mutualistas* (mutual aid societies), and labor unions, which began in the late 1800s and became powerful in the 20th century. They have also lobbied and protested through civil rights organizations, church groups, veterans' organizations, and litigation. Another important catalyst for the growth of Latino influence has been intermarriage between Hispanic Americans and Anglo-Americans: The children of such unions blurred ethnic boundaries, and made it harder to discriminate on racial lines.

Bloc voting

In an effort to ensure fair and adequate representation of their interests, Latinos have often tended to vote in blocs. As a result, most of the Latinos who have been elected to local, state, and federal offices have been voted in by predominantly Latino communities. The largest such populations are concentrated in Arizona, California, Colorado, Florida, Illinois, New Jersey, New Mexico, New York, and Texas.

Exceptional cases

Although Mexican Americans faced discrimination in the late-19th century, and were never fully enfranchised, from time to time some exceptional individuals won election as local officials and state congressmen. By the 1890s, however, few Mexican names could be found anywhere in U.S. politics. In the early 1900s, Mexican Americans began to regain a few seats. Women also became involved. One notable Chicana was Concha Ortiz y Pino, who was elected to the New Mexico state legislature in 1936.

Puerto Ricans

The second-largest Latino group in the United States is of Puerto Rican heritage. The history of Puerto Rican political representation contrasts sharply with that of Mexican Americans, mainly because of the different circumstances of the islanders' assimilation into the United States. After the Spanish-American War of 1898, the Constitution of the Commonwealth of Puerto Rico made all Puerto Ricans U.S. citizens, thus eliminating the questions of nationality that always hung over Mexican Americans. Puerto Ricans soon formed effective political organizations, and in 1937 Oscar Garcia Rivera became their first elected representative when he won election to the New York state legislature.

Cubans

The third-largest group of Latinos came to the United States from Cuba. Although not present in large numbers until the mid-20th century, Cubans have always exercised considerable political power. Their influence is well illustrated by their success in lobbying for the Teller Amendment (1898), passed on the eve of the war with Spain, which affirmed that the United States had no territorial designs on the Caribbean island.

LATINO NATIONAL POLITICAL SURVEY

Carried out in 1988, the Latino National Political Survey (LNPS) was an important measure of Hispanic American attitudes. Its findings heavily influenced the conduct of politicians in the late 20th and early 21st centuries.

The one-off survey took random representative samples of the three largest Latino groups (Mexican, Puerto Rican, and Cuban) in an attempt to increase understanding of people's attitudes and voting behavior.

In the absence of established national research agencies willing to undertake a project about Latinos, the LNPS was created from scratch by dedicated social scientists, with support from a number of private organizations, including the Ford Foundation and Rockefeller Foundation.

The LNPS was controversial, the main criticism being that it was conducted only in English, but it shaped the political landscape. It proved that there are specific Latino issues, and that there is also a "Latino vote." Once the latter had been identified, politicians courted it at every opportunity, especially in areas with significant numbers of Latino voters.

POLITICAL REPRESENTATION

The first half of the 20th century saw a steady stream of immigrants from Cuba to the United States, with periodic waves of refugees during political and economic crises on the island. Newly arrived Cubans and established Cuban Americans became increasingly involved in U.S. politics. Unlike Mexicans and Puerto Ricans, who tended to vote with the Democratic Party, most Cubans supported the Republicans.

Unelected officials

Latinos have historically had less influence on U.S. politics than would normally be expected, given their statistical significance as a percentage of the population. Nevertheless, several individuals have achieved prominence in U.S. life, even if they did not always attain elected national office. Among the Latinos who have held important cabinet positions and judicial appointments outside the electoral process are Vicente Ximenes, who was appointed to the Equal Employment Opportunity Commission by President Lyndon B. Johnson in 1967, and Alfredo Gonzalez, the first Latino U.S. attorney general, who was appointed in 2005 by President George W. Bush.

Political organizations

The number of political organizations representing Latinos proliferated after World War II (1939–1945). In 1960, many Latinos rallied behind the presidential candidacy of John F. Kennedy. "Viva Kennedy" clubs were formed across the United States. It was the first time Latinos had participated in large numbers in a presidential election. It was through the network of clubs that the Political Association of Spanish-speaking Organizations (PASO; later PASSO) was formed later that year. Despite its ambitious objective of becoming a national Latino political body, PASSO was successful only in Texas.

Unlike earlier organizations, such as the League of United Latin American Citizens (LULAC) or the GI Forum, PASSO was an overtly electoral entity, which aimed to teach Latinos about the political process, register them, and get them out to vote. PASSO's greatest success came in the 1963 council election in Crystal City, Texas. Five Mexican Americans were elected to the city council. Known as "*Los Cinco*" (the five), they comprised the first all-Mexican American U.S. city council. PASSO demonstrated the power of Mexican Americans to organize politically, and paved the way for organizations such as the Mexican American Youth Organization (MAYO) and the Raza Unida Party (RUP).

The CSO, the NALEO, and the CHC

In 1949, Edward R. Roybal became the first Chicano since 1881 to be elected to the Los Angeles city council. His campaign was backed by several Mexican American groups, particularly the Community Service Organization (CSO). Roybal was keenly aware of how few other Latinos and Latinas were in office around him. In 1975, he founded the National Association of Latino Elected Officials (NALEO) to increase the number of Latino elected officials. NALEO's goals were to educate and register voters, create legislation that was supportive of Latinos, lobby Congress, and get Latinos out to vote. Like the Mexican American Legal Defense and Education Fund (MALDEF) and other organizations spawned by the Chicano civil rights movement, NALEO is still active in the 21st century. Every year, it sponsors a summer institute and internship program to train future leaders in the Latino community. NALEO also conducts research into Latino politics. It identified 28 percent of U.S. congressional districts with a Latino electorate that is higher than the national average. It is in those districts that the organization has concentrated its efforts to mobilize support. NALEO has been an important reason for the increasing number of Latinos at all levels of government.

The aims of the Congressional Hispanic Caucus (CHC) are similar to those of NALEO. The CHC was formed in 1976 to increase the number of Latinos and Latinas in

---

KEY DATES

1929 Founding of LULAC in Corpus Christi, Texas.

1960 Viva Kennedy clubs support election of first Catholic U.S. president.

1968 National Council of La Raza (NCLR) founded as Southwest Council of La Raza.

1975 Founding of National Association of Latino Elected Officials (NALEO).

1976 Founding of the Congressional Hispanic Caucus.

1988 Latino National Political Survey (LNPS).

In May 2005, supporters of Antonio Villaraigosa celebrate his election as the first Latino mayor of Los Angeles for 133 years.

national elected office. Just as MALDEF and the Puerto Rican Legal Defense and Education Fund (PRLDEF) were modeled after the legal defense and education fund of the National Association for the Advancement of Colored People (NAACP), the CHC took as its model the Congressional Black Caucus.

In 1978, the CHC formed the Congressional Hispanic Caucus Institute to provide financial assistance and a contact network for Latino political hopefuls.

The CHC currently has 19 members. It has been heavily, and sometimes exclusively, Democratic. In response, the Republican Party formed the Congressional Hispanic

Conference, which typically has fewer than 10 members.

The idea of the CHC has spread to the state level, as well. For example, the Latino Caucus of the California state legislature is a progressive organization that has formulated groundbreaking policies on education, immigration, employment, and health care. It has installed a Latino lieutenant governor in the state, Cruz Bustamante, and a Latino head of the assembly, Fabian Nuñez. Its power also helped usher in Antonio Villaraigosa, the first Mexican American mayor of Los Angeles in more than 100 years.

Conclusion

Latinos have played an increasingly important role in the U.S. political system since their assimilation into the nation, either by conquest or

through immigration. Although there have been attempts to exclude them, they have increased their participation at nearly all levels. One of their most significant modifications to the political process since the mid-19th century has been their success in securing the use of Spanish-language ballots and voting materials, and introducing Spanish-language debates into a political discourse that was previously conducted almost exclusively in English.

See also: Bustamente, Cruz; Guadalupe Hidalgo, Treaty of; Roybal, Edward R.; Villaraigosa, Antonio; Ximenes, Vicente

Further reading Vasquez, Francisco, and Rodolfo Torres (eds.). *Latino/a Thought: Culture, Politics, and Society.* Lanham, MD: Rowman and Littlefield, 2003.

PONCE, Mary Helen
Writer

Mary Helen Ponce celebrates the Hispanic culture of her childhood in her novels. A prolific writer of books, articles, and short stories, her work centers on the life of Hispanic Americans in 1940s and 1950s California.

Learning and writing

Ponce was born María Elena Ponce in Pacoima in the San Fernando Valley, California, in 1938. Her schoolteachers anglicized her name to Mary Helen. Ponce was the youngest in a Chicano family of seven daughters and three brothers, and cites her sisters as a major influence in her life. She and her siblings grew up in the 1940s among Mexican Americans whose families had recently moved to southern California in the previous few decades.

After she graduated from high school, Ponce married, and then stayed at home to raise her four children. When her youngest child began kindergarten, Ponce returned to school to start a college education. She graduated from California State University at Northridge with a bachelor of arts degree in 1978. She earned a master's degree in Mexican American studies two years later, and a second master's in history from the University of California at Los Angeles (UCLA) in 1984.

While studying, Ponce started to write about her life and the three most important elements in it: the church, her family, and schooling. She also taught Chicano studies

between 1982 and 1987 at UCLA. She completed her academic studies with a PhD from the University of New Mexico, Albuquerque, in 1988. Ponce then started teaching at the University of New Mexico, where she served in the women's studies program until 1992.

Published writer

In 1981 Ponce had been invited to read her work at the Mexican American National Women's Association meeting in Washington, D.C. The invitation, and the recognition she received at the meeting, showed Ponce that her peers considered her a writer, and encouraged her to pursue a career as an author. She published *Recuerdo: Short Stories of the Barrio* in 1983, and followed it with another collection of short stories, *Taking Control*, in 1987. *Taking Control* was well received. Two years later, Ponce published her first novel, the popular *The Wedding*.

Although Ponce admitted that the fictional town of Taconos resembled her home of Pacoima in many ways, she maintains that *The Wedding* is not autobiographical. The novel, set in the 1950s, tells the story of the wedding day of Blanca and her fiancé, Sammy-the-Cricket, a gang leader. Blanca, who wants her wedding to be the best in the barrio, must overcome several obstacles. While Ponce argues her novel is really a love story, some Hispanic American critics criticized the book for enforcing stereotypes about the Mexican American community.

Exploring identity

In 1993 Ponce published *Hoyt Street: An Autobiography*. The book was an attempt to capture the cultural uniqueness of growing up in a loving Chicano family in Pacoima in the 1940s.

Ponce writes in English and uses her work to explore the themes of bilingualism, biculturalism, and integration. As a schoolgirl, she was prohibited from speaking Spanish at school. She claims she had forgotten how to speak Spanish by first grade and she had to teach herself her mother tongue in later life.

KEY DATES	
1938	Born in Pacoima, California, on January 24.
1978	Graduates with a bachelor's degree from California State University at Northridge.
1980	Earns first master's degree in Mexican American studies.
1983	Publishes *Recuerdo: Short Stories of the Barrio*.
1984	Graduates with second master's from the University of California, Los Angeles (UCLA), this time in history.
1987	Publishes more short stories in *Taking Control*.
1988	Awarded a PhD from the University of New Mexico, Albuquerque.
1989	Publishes *The Wedding*.
1993	Publishes *Hoyt Street: An Autobiography*.

Further reading: Ponce, Mary Helen. *Hoyt Street: An Autobiography*. Albuquerque, NM: University of New Mexico Press, 1993.
http://www.lasmujeres.com/maryhelenponce/poncebio.shtml (biography).

SET INDEX

Set Index

Set Index

Set Index

Set Index

Picture Credits

c = center, t = top, b = bottom.

Cover: Corbis: Bettmann t, c; **Courtesy Indiana University:** b; **TopFoto.co.uk:** Revolution Studios/Phillip V. Caruso, SMPSP cb; **West Carolina University:** ct.

Courtesy Anaheim Public Library: 117; **Photo of Luis Pales Matos is reprinted with permission from the publisher (Houston: Arte Público Press-University of Houston © 2005) from AAP Files:** 96; **Courtesy of The Bancroft Library, University of California:** 34, 116; **Courtesy Dr. Hector P. Garcia Papers, Special Collections, Bell Library, Texas A&M University, Corpus Christi:** 42; **Photo by Tino Mauricio courtesy of the Benson Latin American Collection, University of Texas Libraries, University of Texas at Austin:** 103; **Photograph by Adolfo Gonzalez, Ramsey Muniz Papers (Box 1 Folder 20), courtesy of the Benson Latin American Collection, University of Texas at Austin:** 26; **William J. Clinton Presidential Library:** 67; **Corbis:** 27, Bettmann 38, 123, 124, 126, 128, 98, Louie Psihoyos 106, Reuters/Lou Dematteis 130, Reuters/Robert Galbraith 133, Reuters/Gary I.Rothstein 97, Sygma 47; **Empics:** AP 73, 114, 120, AP/ Danny Johnston 45, AP/Andres Leighton 94, AP/Jerry T. Mosey 122, AP/LM Otero 41, AP/Chad Rachman 40, AP/Stuart Ramson 113, AP/Stephan Savoia 16, AP/Christian Seeling 104, AP/Charles Tasnadi 86, AP/Nik Ut 20, AP/Yesikka Vivancos 111, AP/ Susan Walsh 44, PA/Toby Melville 13; **Getty Images:** 18, 30, 64, Lawrence Lucier 119, Steve Snowden 108; **The University of Georgia/photo by Sartino:** 90; **Courtesy Houston Metropolitan Research Center, Houston Public Library:** 15; **Lebrecht Collection:** 102; **Library of Congress:** repro no. LC-UZ62-115387 4, repro no. LC-UZ62-113060 7, repro no. LC-UZ62-105832 61, repro no. LC-DIG-cwpbh-04448 95; **Delilah Montoya:** 5; **Cherrie Moraga:** 10; **Gabriel Morales:** 105; **Edward Morin:** 24; **Elias Miguel Munoz:** 28; **Luis Munoz:** 29; **NASA:** 60, 71, 78; **Nogales Investors Management, LLC:** 57; **Operational Technologies Corporation:** 50; **Victor Orozco Ochoa:** 75; **Oviatt Library, Special Collections and Archives, California State University Northridge:** 48; **Courtesy Palace of the Governors (MNM/DCA) neg.no.87663 8; neg.no. 152218 91, neg. no. 89756 93; Gustavo Perez-Firmat:** 115; **Photos12.com:** Madrid National Library 79; **The Antonia Pantoja Papers, Archives of the Puerto Rican Diaspora, Centro de Estudios Puertorriqueños, Hunter College, CUNY:** 101; **Redferns:** Andrew Lepley 77; **Rex Features:** David Allocca 69, Everett Collection 22, SNAP 80; **Retna:** G. Binuya 82; **San Antonio Conservation Society Foundation:** 59; **San Antonio Light Collection, Institute of Texan Cultures at UTSA:** Courtesy Hearst Corporation photo no. 072-1796 61; **Victor Ochoa Papers, Archives Center, National Museum of American History, Behring Center, Smithsonian Institution:** 76; **South Texas Archives, Texas A&M University-Kingsville:** 88; **Tempest Entertainment:** 99; **Texas State Library and Archives Commission:** 49; **TopFoto.co.uk:** 85, 89, 100, 110, The Image Works 62, The Image Works/ Bob Daemmrich 35, MGM Cinema 25, New Line Cinema 14, Samuel Goldwyn Films 109; **U.S. Navy:** 51; **Walter P. Reuther Library, Wayne State University:** 84; **Photo used with permission from Wells Fargo Bank, N.A:** 72; **Western Carolina University:** 55.

The Brown Reference Group has made every effort to trace copyright holders of the pictures used in this book. Anyone having claims to ownership not identified above is invited to contact the Brown Reference Group.

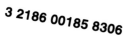

3 2186 00185 8306